The Handbook for Aspiring Higher Education Leaders

A volume in
Research, Theory, and Practice Within Academic Affairs
Antione D. Tomlin and Sherella Cupid, *Series Editors*

Research, Theory, and Practice Within Academic Affairs

Antione D. Tomlin and Sherella Cupid, *Series Editors*

Voices of the Field: DEIA Champions in Higher Education (2023)
    Antione D. Tomlin and Sherella Cupid

Black Faculty Do It All: A Moment in The Life of a Blackademic (2023)
    Antione D. Tomlin

Don't Forget About the Adjuncts! (2023)
    Antione D. Tomlin

The Handbook for Aspiring Higher Education Leaders

edited by

Antione D. Tomlin
Anne Arundel Community College

INFORMATION AGE PUBLISHING, INC.
Charlotte, NC • www.infoagepub.com

Library of Congress Cataloging-in-Publication Data

A CIP record for this book is available from the Library of Congress
http://www.loc.gov

ISBN: 979-8-88730-625-4 (Paperback)
       979-8-88730-626-1 (Hardcover)
       979-8-88730-627-8 (E-Book)

Copyright © 2024 Information Age Publishing Inc.

All rights reserved. No part of this publication may be reproduced, stored in a retrieval system, or transmitted, in any form or by any means, electronic, mechanical, photocopying, microfilming, recording or otherwise, without written permission from the publisher.

Printed in the United States of America

CONTENTS

Introduction ix
Darian Senn-Carter

SECTION I
JOURNEY TO LEADERSHIP

1 Who's Got Your Back? Mentorship as Sponsorship 3
  Juan M. Hernandez

2 Graduate Students Need Support Too 11
  Shauntisha Pilgrim

3 Reflective Journeys of Two Black Faculty Administering a
  Minority-Specific Academic Program in the Post-Racial
  Reckoning Educational Landscape 19
  James Calvin and Susan Swayze

4 *Siempre el único* (Always the Only One): Reflections From a
  Latino Senior Student Affairs Administrator 27
  Juan R. Guardia

5 Take the Lateral 35
  Becki Tankson-Artis

6 Career Advancement and Trajectory in Higher Education 43
  Felix Quayson

v

SECTION II
PREPARATIONS FOR LEADERSHIP

7   Testimonios From Those Who Have Successfully Navigated the Doctoral Pipeline While Working Professionally in the Field of Student Affairs 55
    Jennifer Alanis and Tony Jimenez

8   Being Prepared: How to Navigate the Course When Embarking on the Academic Leadership Journey 65
    Karen Marie Wagner-Clarke

9   White People Explain Things to Me: Experiences and Recommendations on Surviving "Know-Your-Place Aggression" 77
    Amir Asim Gilmore

10 Strive to Serve 87
    Jacob Ashby

11 Unpack, Unlearn, Unleash 95
    Tasha Wilson

SECTION III
LEADERSHIP TRANSITIONING

12 Understanding Organizational Structures, Leadership Theories, and Identity Matters for Effective Higher Education Leadership 103
    Heather D. Maldonado

13 From Staff to Faculty: Navigating the Transition and Thriving in a New Role 115
    Nadia Ibrahim-Taney

14 From University Administrator Back to Full-Time Faculty: Transitioning and Mentoring the Next Generation of Leaders 125
    Mark Gillen

15 Waiting to Excel 133
    Alea Cross

16 Practicing from a Place of Authenticity 149
    Dawn Shafer

SECTION IV
LEADERSHIP IN ACTION

17 What You Really Need: Empathy 157
   D'Shaun Vance

18 Psychological Safety: Setting the Tone for Team Effectiveness 167
   LaToya Jordan

19 Academic Leadership at a Small Liberal Arts College 175
   Bradley Fuster

20 Creating a Ripple Effect through Small Leadership Strategies 187
   Lauren Harris

21 Leadership in Student Affairs 193
   Merab Mushfiq

22 Navigating Title IX Obligations and Student Support: Lessons
   From Faculty Experiences in and out of the Classroom 201
   Jaclyn Stone

23 Between Academic and Student Affairs: Advice for New
   Student Services Leaders in Academic Units 213
   Zayd Abukar

24 My Journey Into Higher Education Leadership as a Black
   Immigrant 221
   Neijma Celestine-Donnor

About the Editor 227
About the Contributors 229

INTRODUCTION

Today's leaders, regardless of the industry, face a multitude of challenges and opportunities. Higher Education in particular, is in quite an unusual era of transformative change. Changes brought on by a myriad of factors, to include: recovery from a global pandemic, Diversity, Equity, Inclusion, Anti-racism, and Accessibility (DEIAA), technological advances, population and demographic shifts, economic pressures, and vacillating societal views on the role and value of education. Higher education literature is replete with theories, studies, and approaches to support student success in higher education (Kuh, 2006). While leadership is important, and holding leadership roles can certainly be impactful we acknowledge that sometimes, leadership picks us instead of us choosing it (Tomlin, 2022, 2023). Morevoer, there is generally no agreed upon definition of leadership, or what it means to be an effective leader. Furthermore, there is certainly no clear path, journey, or guide to obtain leadership roles within higher education.

PURPOSE OF THIS BOOK

The aim of this book is to allow past and present higher education leaders to offer wisdom and advice for new and potential leaders. Each chapter shares experiences, strategies, and recommendations for both academic and student affairs leaders across divisions and departments to help new and aspiring leaders on their journey to success. While there is no one true

The Handbook for Aspiring Higher Education Leaders, pages ix–xii
Copyright © 2024 by Information Age Publishing
www.infoagepub.com
All rights of reproduction in any form reserved.

definition of leadership, we are hopeful that this text will add to the conversation about impactful and effective leadership.

Each chapter is rich in knowledge and perspective that support the current and next generation of leaders. We approach this book as a handbook, where chapter authors reflect upon their journeys to glean insight and wisdom. Each chapter is formatted in a similar way. Each author details their unique journeys into their respective fields, and trajectory to leadership, and experiences that helped to shape their leadership approaches. Then, authors look back to discern advice that they would share with themselves as new higher education leaders, and what (if anything) they would do differently. Lastly, authors share rich tips, strategies, and recommendations for new and potential higher education leaders on how to achieve success in the field. We are confident that there will be a notion or practice within these chapters to support all who read. Chapter authors are from a variety of disciplines.

We see this book as a volume that can be used by practitioners and aspiring practitioners across the nation as inspiration to higher education leaders on how to navigate careers in higher education, and how to be an effective leader. Throughout the book, we offer four themes that provide more insight into tips, strategies, and recommendations for new and potential higher education leaders on how to achieve success in the field. While each chapter in this book follows the structure mentioned above, the themes illuminate the experiences of higher education leaders, and their individual and collective journeys. Below, you will find a brief description of the chapters that contribute to each of the themes throughout the book.

JOURNEY TO LEADERSHIP

The Journey to Leadership is complex and in this theme we explore the role of mentorship, leadership development while in graduate school, faculty minority leadership, student affairs minority leadership, advancement through lateral positions, and career advancement in higher education. Chapters within the Journey to Leadership theme include:

- Who's Got Your Back? Mentorship as Sponsorship by Dr. Juan Hernandez
- Graduate Students Need Support Too by Dr. Shauntisha Pilgrim
- Reflective Journeys of Two Black Faculty Administering a Minority-Specific Academic Program in the Post-Racial Reckoning Educational Landscape by Dr. James Calvin and Dr. Susan Swayze
- Siempre el único (Always the only one): Reflections from a Latino Senior Student Affairs Administrator by Dr. Juan Guardia

- Take the Lateral by Becki Tankson-Artis
- Career Advancement and Trajectory in Higher Education by Dr. Felix Quayson

PREPARATIONS FOR LEADERSHIP

Within the theme Preparations for Leadership we examine the doctoral pipeline while working in higher education, preparations to navigate the leadership journey, experiences and recommendations to thrive as a minority leader, the aggression paradox, and unleashing your greatest potential as a leader in higher education. The following chapters examine Preparations for Leadership:

- Testimonios from those who have successfully navigated the doctoral pipeline while working professionally in the field of student affairs by Dr. Jennifer Alanis and Dr. Tony Jimenez
- Being Prepared: How to navigate the course when embarking on the academic leadership journey by Dr. Karen Marie Wagner-Clarke
- White People Explain Things to Me: Experiences and Recommendations on Surviving
- "Know-Your-Place Aggression by Dr. Amir Gilmore
- Strive to Serve by Dr. Jacob Ashby
- Unpack, Unlearn, Unleash by Tasha M. Wilson

LEADERSHIP TRANSITIONING

Leadership Transitioning is vital for aspiring and current higher education leaders. This theme looks into organization structures and leadership identity, transitioning from staff to faculty, transitioning from administrator back to faculty, creating momentum to excel, and leading with authenticity. Chapters within the Leadership Transitioning theme are as follows:

- Understanding Organizational Structures, Leadership Theories, and Identity Matters by Dr. Heather Maldonado
- From Staff to Faculty: Navigating the Transition and Thriving in a New Role by Nadia Ibrahim-Taney
- From University Administrator Back to Full-Time Faculty: Transitioning and Mentoring the Next Generation of Leaders by Dr. Mark Gillen
- Waiting to Excel by Alea Cross
- Practicing from a Place of Authenticity by Dr. Dawn Shafer

LEADERSHIP IN ACTION

Within our last theme, chapters delve into Leadership in Action. This theme addresses setting the tone for team effectiveness, academic leadership at a small institution, creating transformative change through the ripple effect, leadership in student affair, Title IX and student support, and new student service and academic leaders. Chapters within Leadership in Action theme include:

- What You Really Need: Empathy by Dr. D'Shaun Vance
- Psychological Safety: Setting the Tone for Team Effectiveness by Dr. LaToya Jordan
- Academic Leadership at a Small Liberal Arts College by Dr. Bradley Fuster
- Creating a Ripple Effect Through Small Leadership Strategies by Lauren Harris
- Leadership in Student Affairs by Merab Mushfiq
- Navigating Title IX Obligations and Student Support: Lessons from Faculty Experiences in and out of the Classroom by Dr. Jacki Stone
- Between Academic and Student Affairs: Advice for New Student Services Leaders in Academic Units by Dr. Zayd Abukar
- My Journey into Higher Education Leadership as a Black Immigrant by Neijma Celestine-Donnor

—**Darian Senn-Carter**

REFERENCES

Commissioned Report for the National Symposium on Postsecondary Student Success: Spearheading a Dialog on Student Success George D. Kuh Jillian Kinzie Jennifer A. Buckley Indiana University Bloomington Brian K. Bridges American Council on Education John C. Hayek Kentucky Council on Postsecondary Education July 2006

Tomlin, A. D. (2022). I'm a Black PhD, and I still have to fight! We're not OK. *Black Faculty Experiences and Higher Education Strategies, 58*.

Tomlin, A. D. (2023). The Black department chair: Black experiences in White space. In J. A. Kuykendall, D. J. Smith, and J. M. Jackson (Eds.), *The future of Black leadership in higher education: Firsthand experiences and global impact* (pp. 129–135). IGI Global.

SECTION I

JOURNEY TO LEADERSHIP

CHAPTER 1

WHO'S GOT YOUR BACK?

Mentorship as Sponsorship

Juan M. Hernandez

ABSTRACT

Mentorship and sponsorship are vital markers for success. This is true for all but is especially true for aspiring higher education leaders. Mentorship, formal or informal, allows the individual to lean on others who have been in their shoes before. Just as important, mentorship provides the individual with an ally who can provide sponsorship as career opportunities present themselves. Climbing the ladders in academia is not an easy task. Combatting institutional and societal factors alone is heavy burden. In this chapter, the reader will learn of my own journey and trajectory to leadership. The reader will also be introduced to the concept of mentorship as sponsorship for aspiring higher education leaders as a tool in their tool belt. This chapter will conclude with a series of recommendations as to how aspiring education leaders can find a mentor.

I grew up in Chicago, Illinois before moving to the State of Connecticut for college. I graduated in 2013 with a bachelor's degree in history and political science from Trinity College in Hartford. While working at Trinity

College as a Graduate Assistant in the Office of Multicultural Affairs, I was able to complete my master's degree in public policy with a concentration in education policy in May of 2015. After a year and a half of policy work for the City of Hartford, in 2016, I transitioned to the University of New Haven as the Director of the Myatt Center for Diversity and Inclusion which reported through Student Affairs. About a year into my journey at New Haven in 2017, I began my studies at the University of Hartford as a member of the Fall cohort in their Doctoral program in Educational Leadership (EdD). In September of 2020, in the middle of the COVID-19 pandemic, I transitioned to Goucher College in Baltimore, Maryland, as the Associate Dean of Students for Diversity, Equity, Inclusion, and Title IX. I completed my doctoral work in December of 2021 and was then promoted to Assistant Vice President for Diversity, Equity, Inclusion, and Title IX in July of 2022.

MY JOURNEY IN ACADEMIA

My journey in higher education officially began as an undergraduate student. I quickly became engaged on campus in some of the identity based cultural organizations that were created to support students of color on a predominantly White campus. I remember investing my time into organizations around men of color and their experiences, the Latinx organization on campus, Student Government, and I committed myself to supporting the work of my peers. Professionally, however, my journey in higher education began because of racial trauma. On a normal night in the middle of my sophomore year, I was dropping off a friend at her residence hall. It was late and a Thursday, which was a big party night on campus. As I began driving back to my residence hall, what I would eventually identify to be a beer can crashes into my front windshield. When I stopped my car to see what had happened, I noticed a tall, White man and two White women running away from my car. As he ran, the White man yells, "Get off my campus, you n****r." He repeats it multiple times. My first reaction was to chase him, but I remembered that my 1994 Honda Accord was parked in the middle of the street with my keys still in the ignition. I decided, instead, to report the incident to Campus Safety, which I did. When I got back to my room, I immediately wrote an email to the entire administration explaining what had just happened and that I expected results. This led to me spending a significant amount of time in the Office of Multicultural Affairs which quickly began feeling like another home away from home. Of course, we were able to get that student expelled from the institution.

The decision to get more involved in the Office led to other doors opening. I remember attending conferences planned by the Consortium on High Achievement and Success, CHAS for short. Their Men of Color conferences were amazing and allowed me to connect with other men of color on other small, private, liberal arts campuses. It also introduced me to higher education professionals at other institutions. Some of those men are mentors today. In addition to CHAS, being in the Office everyday allowed me to witness our Dean of Multicultural Affairs do her job every day. I witnessed her struggle, and I witnessed her succeed. She was honest and plainspoken. She supported us with no questions asked. Her leadership is the guiding light I follow today.

After two years in Multicultural Affairs at my alma mater, I took a short break from higher education to focus on the policy side of my passion. At a protest on campus in response to the racial incident during my sophomore year, I met a member of the Board of Trustees. He was running for City Council and would eventually be elected as the Council President. When I graduated with my Master's degree in 2015, he hired me as his Executive Aide. I was able to use the next year and half from early 2015 to late 2016 to focus on developing my leadership and political skills. These are skills that I continue to use today.

During my year and a half doing policy work, I consistently kept my ears to the ground for opportunities locally that could lead to my return in higher education. A position opened up at a local University and they were looking for a Director for their new diversity center. I was eventually hired and began working at the institution in September of 2016. I was running a brand new diversity center as a one-person office for the vast majority of my four years there. Eventually, towards the end of my tenure, the Student Government Association decided to support the Center by hiring a full-time Coordinator-level position that would serve the Center half time and Student Engagement half-time. Overall, I felt very supported by the students. I had somewhat supportive divisional leadership. But leadership at the top of the institution severely lacked. Right before the pandemic started, the President decided it was time to hire a VP-level Cabinet member whose priority would be diversity, equity, and access. As that process unfolded, we were all being sent home because of the pandemic. Due to budgetary restraints, I was furloughed. This continued until the Fall semester. By this time, I was already a finalist for my current position, which I began in September of 2020.

In September of 2020, I began working as an Associate Dean of Students. I was attracted to the position due to the responsibilities I would own but I would also be reporting to two Black women with significant leadership experience. In this role, I have failed many times. In this role, I have succeeded many times. But I have always felt supported and confident in my own skills.

To summarize, there were three main experiences throughout my journey that have shaped me as a leader:

1. The incident my sophomore year of college showed me what diversity centers and offices do for students of color every day. The servant leadership that I witnessed and the mentorship that I received really showed me who I wanted to be and who really had my back.
2. I understood that my institution was not financially stable enough to survive the pandemic without making some difficult staffing decisions. Being furloughed during the COVID-19 pandemic "made sense" as someone who worked primarily with students. But being furloughed and having both Breonna Taylor and George Floyd murdered during that time led to leadership at the institution calling on me while furloughed. I was supporting students every day while furloughed. When we arrived back in person in the fall, that work was never acknowledged. It reminded me that as loyal as we tend to be to institutions, they are never loyal to you.
3. When the University decided to hire a Vice President for Diversity, Equity, and Inclusion, a group of Black and Brown faculty and staff as well as a leadership group amongst the students advised the President. While this advice wasn't sought out, it was given nonetheless. Not only did the President ignore every single recommendation, his internal hire attended every single one of our meetings without ever telling us he was planning on being a candidate, or the only candidate the President would consider. We felt betrayed. To make matters worse, in his announcement email to the campus, it was shared to the entire campus the Diversity Center that I managed would be moving under this new Vice President. In that moment, it felt as if the work I had done the previous four years earned me zero respect. I believed I had earned a "heads up" from the institution that these changes were being considered and nothing ever came. Again, this showed me the kind of leader I wanted to be and the kind of leader I never wanted to be.

LOOKING BACKWARDS TO MOVE FORWARD

Looking back, there were several pieces of advice I wish someone gave me. First, I wish someone would have recommended that I consider the PhD and that I start it much earlier instead of waiting as long as I did before beginning my terminal degree. I do not regret pursuing my EdD. In fact, the specific program I chose was perfect for me. However, I remember falling in love with the History major during my years as an undergrad and I wish I gave myself the space to pursue that before deciding on the EdD program. I appreciated that the EdD program was cohort-based and that our faculty provided us with the opportunity to see ourselves as colleagues.

Additionally, my program required no comprehensive exams or any standardized tests. Not only do I struggle with standardized testing, I also believe that they fail to be an accurate measure of how successful a student will be in a program.

Next, I wish I would have gotten more involved in the professional associations associated with my field. I began attending NASPA conferences and especially enjoyed attending the Latinx/a/o Knowledge Community but did not continue doing so after I left my graduate assistantship in 2015. I have never attended an ACPA conference or NCORE. Instead, I participated in CHAS conferences as an undergraduate student and attended the NASPA Escaleras Institute. I see immense value today in getting more involved regionally with organizations like NASPA and ACPA. I also see value in connecting with colleagues doing similar work at nearby institutions.

Another piece of advice that I wish someone had imparted in me is to write as much as possible. Writing itself is not an issue but writing with the goal of publishing work is not something I considered until I was halfway through my doctoral journey. I should have used my time more effectively and I would already have published work. Writing is a priority because it helps get your name out there past your own network and inner circle. Writing, like presenting at conferences, is a quick way to expand your network and to begin building a profile. Additionally, it shows the rest of academia that student affairs folks are also scholars and can contribute to the literature around their field.

Finally, I should have looked for and requested formal coaching opportunities. When you are hired for Director-level or Dean-level opportunities, you are expected to arrive on day one being able to do that job well. This is the case even if you have never held a similar role before. Coaching can always be negotiated when negotiating and I wish someone had shared with me before I applied for my current role.

MY RECOMMENDATIONS: MENTORSHIP AND SPONSORSHIP AS VITAL MARKERS OF SUCCESS

The following are a series of recommendations, tips, and strategies for new and potential higher education leaders on how to achieve success in the field. These are based on my own personal experiences and what I have heard has worked from others who have made it to Cabinet level positions. Overall, I have centered these recommendations around the concept of mentoring and sponsorship being vital markers of success for those of us in higher education.

1. Identify mentorship that works for you. A mentor can provide you with the everyday advice that you may need for success. You could

also lean on that person or have someone else that mentors and guides you on career opportunities. Not only can that person serve as a reference, they may also serve as a sponsor by recommending you for opportunities or putting in a good word when opportunities present themselves. While you do the work and you earn your opportunities, mentors are very important and can accelerate your climb up the higher education ladders of success.
2. Once you have your chosen field, begin identifying and participating in professional organizations that align with your chosen field. By attending these conferences, you will meet others who are in a similar position as yourself. You can also begin introducing yourself to leaders at institutions that you may one day like to call home. I have made connections at these conferences that have proven to be very beneficial for all parties.
3. Remember where you come from. When you meet a young professional and you have already achieved the role of Director, or Dean, or Vice President, remember that someone else may have provided you with mentorship that aided your journey. If you felt that you did not receive mentoring that you felt you needed, remember that feeling as well.

Mentoring can be an important part of a person's personal and professional development, their learning, and their experiences. It can be either a formal or informal relationship between someone with more familiarity and experience and someone who is interested in adding to their knowledge.

The academy is known to suffer from an abundance of silos across a campus and they must be broken down so that we may truly thrive (Blockett et al., 2016; Campbell, 2018). Faculty and staff of color, especially those who are newer to the academy, are typically left outside of the conversation. Campbell (2018) explains that administrators of color, especially those who are settled in the field, have a responsibility to mentor and advise others. The literature shows that mentoring makes a difference, especially for administrators of color who once likely considered themselves to be mentees and might now consider themselves to be mentors (Blockett et al., 2016; Campbell, 2018).

As I have tried to explain throughout this chapter, the mentor-mentee relationship should be a mutually beneficial relationship built on trust (Crisp & Cruz, 2009; Merriweather & Morgan, 2013; Tillman, 2018). To successfully progress in higher education, you must accept all of the support possible. It may be rare to find a mentor that holds similar identities or life experiences, but we cannot discount the value that mentoring provides. Mentors tend to be individuals who are willing to provide advice, connect you to resources, and who may look to push you in the right direction when you may feel lost. That may lead to opportunities you would have never considered. As future leaders in higher education consider what their futures may hold, they should always consider that there are successful individuals out there who are more than willing to provide their time, energy, and resources to help them succeed.

REFERENCES

Blockett, R. A., Felder, P. P., Parrish III, W, & Collier, J. (2016). Pathways to the professoriate: Exploring Black doctoral student socialization and the pipeline to the academic profession. *The Western Journal of Black Studies, 40*(2), 95–110.

Campbell, C. D. (2018). Leadership from the middle pays it forward: An academic administrator of color's career development narrative in postsecondary education. *The Qualitative Report, 23*(7), 1702–1716.

Crisp, G., & Cruz, I. (2009). Mentoring college students: A critical review of the literature between 1990 and 2007. *Research in Higher Education, 50*(6), 525–545.

Merriweather, L. R., & Morgan, A. J. (2013) Two cultures collide: Bridging the generation gap in a non-traditional mentorship. *The Qualitative Report, 18*(6), 1–16.

Tillman, L. C. (2018). Achieving racial equity in higher education: The case for mentoring faculty of color. *Teachers College Record, 120,* 1–18.

CHAPTER 2

GRADUATE STUDENTS NEED SUPPORT TOO

Shauntisha Pilgrim

ABSTRACT

There is a need for graduate students to be engaged and receive support from student affairs. However, this practice is not widespread. As a student affairs professional that supports students in a professional graduate program, my background, journey into leadership, advice, and recommendations for new and aspiring leaders are discussed.

BACKGROUND

For many years, I was a parent striving to show my children that it's possible to persevere despite obstacles. Some of the ways I demonstrated my perseverance was by accomplishing my academic and professional goals. After earning my master's degree in social work, I worked with young adults to help them overcome some of the challenges they experienced in life. Although rewarding, I wanted to work in higher education. This desire led me to become a Field Liaison and an Adjunct Professor, where I taught aspiring social workers in a graduate-level program. Now, I work to support graduate students full-time as the Director of Student Affairs and Admissions in a School of Social Work. In my role, I recruit and admit students into the university. Then, once admitted, I engage and support students to help them graduate. The intersectionality of being an African American, teen mother, non-traditional, and three-time first-generation student (Bachelor, Master, and Doctorate degrees) from an urban area made achieving my goals challenging, but it has influenced my passion for advocating and shaped my worldview; all of which has impacted my leadership style.

JOURNEY INTO LEADERSHIP

My collegiate journey began immediately out of high school; however, due to the difficulties of balancing motherhood, coursework, and being a part-time employee, I withdrew from college after two years. I never gave up pursuing my post-secondary education because I knew the importance of earning a degree. I returned to school in my mid-twenties and eventually earned my BSW degree. One year later, I became a first-generation graduate student when I earned my MSW degree. This accomplishment was not only significant for my parents, but it was the example I wanted to set for my children.

I worked in the social work profession for one year and then applied to a doctoral program that focused on leadership in higher education. While enrolled in my doctoral program and working as a social worker, I began working as a Field Liaison in the same program I earned my undergraduate and master graduate degrees. I was excited about the opportunity to help develop aspiring graduate-level social workers while they began their internship experience. After two years of being a Field Liaison, I shifted to being an adjunct professor in the MSW program. I was zealous about teaching new graduate students and helping them develop their social work identity.

My experiences of being a college student, an adjunct professor, and background of being a social worker influenced my career aspirations. When I applied to my doctoral program, I knew I wanted to focus on supporting students. In my courses, I learned more about leadership, student affairs, and the impact on the development of students in higher education. I believed that I could marry my education and passion for helping others. As a student who was parenting, I always had challenges balancing my responsibilities. There was little support from the colleges and universities I attended to help me work through everything. Today, there are more programs and recognition for supporting student parents, first-generation and non-traditional students. However, the establishment of support is not widespread for graduate students. Historically, academic departments or graduate schools were responsible for providing support and addressing the needs of graduate students (Nesheim et al., 2006). But the unique challenges that some graduate students face are not always addressed by academic departments (Lehnen, 2021).

There is an expectation that graduate students will be ready for the demands of graduate school, understand the hidden curriculum, have a work-life balance, and be able to recognize and address their academic and personal needs (Nguyen and Yao, 2022). But this is simply not realistic. Institutions recognize that everyone comes from different backgrounds and experiences, and student affairs professionals take the necessary steps to help students develop at the undergraduate level. Still, all students will not be at the same level when entering a graduate-level program. As a field liaison and adjunct professor, I realized that many of the graduate students in my classes needed support outside of the academic realm. So, at the beginning of every class, I began to use the time to discuss personal, professional, or academic challenges, stressors, and any other concerns that may have been impacting their success. From my experience, providing emotional support, encouragement, and a safe space for students was the norm for many professors. However, since the faculty's central role is in instruction, many challenges could not be addressed in the classroom. Those moments at the beginning of the classes revealed a need for student affairs professionals to support graduate students.

My students were diverse and had many challenges as they strived to develop their professional identities. Most of the students I taught were African Americans, but they ranged in age, professional experience, maturity, and socioeconomic status. My experiences as a student and in the classroom with students shaped me as a leader. I wanted to be sure that I created an environment that encouraged students to feel comfortable seeking assistance. When I was a student, I did not always feel like there was someone with whom I could go to discuss some of the challenges I was experiencing. I knew, as a leader, that so many of the students shared some of the same identities as me while also dealing with various issues that could impact their success. I needed to provide a safe and supportive space for students to help them be successful.

While I was a doctoral candidate, I was hired as the Director of Student Affairs and Admissions in the School of Social Work. This position was in the program I was an alumna of and where I had been an adjunct professor for several years. The expectation was to focus on growing the program and developing student affairs in the school. The position was not new in the School of Social Work, but the student affairs aspect was not developed. I knew it would be challenging when I accepted the position, but I was eager to engage and support more graduate students than those enrolled in my courses. Nyugen and Yao (2022) asserted that the how graduate students are supported can impact their experiences as a student and their degree completion. I envisioned that I would have a team dedicated to supporting student's academic and professional development.

ADVICE FOR A NEW LEADER IN HIGHER EDUCATION

Looking back, the advice I would share with myself as a new higher education leader is that you should trust yourself and seek out groups where you can get support along your journey. Student affairs in a graduate or professional program are different than what students, faculty, and staff may be used to, and there must be some level of buy-in that I never considered would be a challenge. Although faculty may believe a graduate student can benefit from support, some believe it is not their job, and they should not handhold graduate-level students. Early in my career, an executive-level administrator expressed concern that graduate students should not need significant support. There needs to be an investment in graduate students institutionally-wide, and I believe the effort to achieve that will be ongoing.

As mentioned, working with graduate students or in a professional program as a student affairs professional will look different than working in student affairs geared toward undergraduate students. This is important to remember, even if you have studied student affairs. In my program, there are not many whom I can talk to about my work. Getting involved with organizations or finding a mentor to support you as you navigate supporting graduate students while being a higher education leader is critical. After a year, I became involved in a national student affairs organization with groups or communities focused on African Americans in Student Affairs, Women in Student Affairs, and Supporting Graduate and Professional Student Success. These communities were beneficial in my development as a leader in higher education because getting involved provided me with insight into how student affairs professionals supported their students on campuses across the country.

My desire to support students was rooted in my own experiences, deepened once I had the opportunity to work in higher education, and developed further as I acquired the knowledge and skills while matriculating in my doctoral program. Looking back, one of the most important things I would have shared with myself is that it is important to trust yourself. I was prepared to do the work, but the resistance from faculty and staff influenced my doubt. So, trust yourself, and use the resources available to help you make the best decisions for your students.

RECOMMENDATIONS

Success is measured differently by everyone, especially in higher education. I succeed when I help students have a good experience, engage them, and provide support as they adjust to expectations and develop while achieving their academic goals of earning a graduate degree. What you deem successful may look different depending on the institution and population you serve. However, no matter your personal perspective, it will be influenced by how the professional program or university views success. I will offer some recommendations for new and aspiring higher education leaders.

As a leader supporting graduate students, it is critical to understand the population you will serve. This is vital whether you are working in a professional program or in graduate school at your institution. Understanding the population will impact what support you will offer and how you will approach engaging students. In my space, our student body consists of predominantly African American women who are first-generation graduate students and grew up in urban communities. Considering the significant number of first-generation graduate students in our program, socialization in graduate school goes beyond orientation. It includes frequent programming to ensure students understand what they can access and how to utilize those services. It also includes ways students can become involved on campus. According to Gansemer-Topf et al. (2006), knowledge acquisition, investment, and involvement influence socialization in graduate school. In addition, we uncover the hidden curriculum early in the program. The hidden curriculum is a set of implied and hidden messages, assumptions, beliefs, values, and attitudes within academia (Lyles, et al., 2022). It includes how students should engage with faculty, understand excellent writing, and the norms of professional conferences. The hidden curriculum is uncovered early into the first semester for our new graduate students. Ensuring students are aware of expectations can assist in the student's success.

Graduate students are diverse and come with a multitude of responsibilities therefore, one must be creative to engage them. In addition, the support master-level students need may differ significantly from a doctorate-level graduate student. As a leader in higher education, understanding the population is critical, but it is also important to recognize students' needs and satisfaction. Satisfaction is related to being connected to campus activities and experiences and increases students' overall engagement. As a new or aspiring leader, I recommend conducting frequent needs assessments and evaluations. To help students succeed, it is critical to understand students' expectations, and institutions should utilize the information to address the needs of students (Kuh et al., 2006). From my experience, engagement activities related to research agendas, dissecting the dissertation, mental health, career seminars, writing support, mentoring, student organizations, and the opportunity to chat with the Dean or other leaders have been the most engaging and satisfying for students. Even with great interest in those activities, there is a need to be creative so that our graduate students can be supported.

The need to be creative does not end with engagement that can meet the needs of our graduate students, but it also includes being financially resourceful. Given my role, there is a recognition of the need to support graduate students. As mentioned, there does not appear to be a full investment, and buy-in from some faculty, staff, and administrators is lacking. This is most visible when it comes to funding allocations. Therefore, as a leader in higher education, you will be forced to do a lot with limited funding. Besides being resourceful, I also recommend that you be patient. Use the needs assessments and evaluations to advocate for more funding and support. Change within a culture is not always immediate.

CONCLUSION

Graduate-level student affairs professionals are needed to support and help in the development of students. The support has primarily focused on undergraduate students. While this support is significant for undergraduates, it is also important for graduate students. Support for graduate students can be beneficial for all students, especially those who are first-generation graduate students. The recommendations can help new and or aspiring higher education leaders engage and support graduate students in a professional or university program.

REFERENCES

Gansemer-Topf, A. M., Ross, L. E., & Johnson, R. M. (2006). Graduate and professional student development and student affairs. *New Directions for Student Services, 2006*(115), 19–30.

Kuh, G. D., Kinzie, J., Buckley, J. A., Bridges, B. K., & Hayek, J. C. (2006). *In what matters to student success: A review of the literature. Commissioned report for national symposium on postsecondary student success: Spearheading a dialogue on student success.* https://nces.ed.gov/npec/pdf/Kuh_Team_Report.pdf

Lehnen, C. A. (2021). Skills, support networks, and socialization: Needs of dissertating graduate students. *The Journal of Academic Librarianship, 47*(5), 102430.

Lyles, C. H., Huggins, N., & Robbins, C. K. (2022). Unveiling the hidden curriculum within graduate education. In D. Nguyen & C. W. Yao (Eds.), *A handbook for supporting today's graduate students* (pp. 86–102). Stylus Publishing, LLC.

Nesheim, B. E., Guentzel, M. J., Gansemer-Topf, A. M., Ross, L. E., & Turrentine, C. G. (2006). If you want to know, ask: Assessing the needs and experiences of graduate students. *New Directions for Student Services, 2006*(115), 5–17.

Nyugen, D. J., Yao, C. W., & Austin, A. E. (Eds.). (2022). *A handbook for supporting today's graduate students.* Stylus Publishing, LLC.

CHAPTER 3

REFLECTIVE JOURNEYS OF TWO BLACK FACULTY ADMINISTERING A MINORITY-SPECIFIC ACADEMIC PROGRAM IN THE POST-RACIAL RECKONING EDUCATIONAL LANDSCAPE

James Calvin
Susan Swayze

ABSTRACT

In this chapter we highlight selective formative personal perspectives about key challenges and opportunities we have faced as scholars working independently and in collaboration in higher education. The current situational reality is that one must be a resilient academic in the post-racial reckoning academic landscape given persistent challenges to the inclusion and education of Black, Brown, and Native American students. We offer for consideration why we think that the academic journey matters as preparation for higher education leadership. We make a case to be cognizant of the need to build early career resilience in the rapidly changing field of higher education.

AUTHORS OVERVIEW OF WHO WE ARE

My name is James Calvin, PhD. I am currently a professor of management and organization practice at the JHU Carey Business School professor, Center for Africana Studies at the JHU Krieger School of Arts and Sciences, and faculty, Bunting Neighborhood Leadership Program, Urban Health Institute. I am also faculty academic program director of the Leadership Development Program at the Carey Business School. Prior to my current academic roles, I have held several positions in education beginning with associate director, Office of Research and Development. Subsequently, I was director, National Education and Social Policy Fellowship Program at The Institute for Educational Leadership as well as the academic director, MS in organization development/strategic human resources and academic program director MBA in organization development and the interim director, Center for Africana Studies.

My name is Susan Swayze, PhD, MBA. For the past 15 years I have held a faculty role in educational research in the Graduate School of Education and Human Development at The George Washington University. I brought 15 years of experience in research, evaluation, and assessment to my academic role that includes teaching research, and dissertation committee service. As part of my research agenda related to diversity and inclusion in the academy, I collaborate with Dr. Calvin on research related to the Leadership Development Program at the JHU Carey Business School.

INTRODUCTION

Journey and Trajectory to Leadership—James Calvin

My journey as James Calvin, PhD, has been to transition from one administrative career path to an academic career where I have advanced to the rank of tenured professor. My research and practice in the fields of leadership, management and organization, and human and community development started when I was a management trainee who became a manager in a retail organization. In that role, I began to learn that communication was fundamental and a critical key to presenting a clear vision to meet a goal. As a manager I learned to listen and elicit feedback to guide my team to meet and work together to fulfill goals set by the leadership of the larger organization.

Two Black men, the Brown brothers, inspired me because they had risen from the lowest level in a retail business to the rank of Corporate Vice President.. Their story and trajectory inspired me to envision myself ascending to their level. In my second year in the manager role, I was invited to be a guest lecturer at Malcolm-King Harlem College Extension, a community college in Harlem, New York. The experience of teaching was exhilarating and a rush that changed the direction of my life. After I delivered the guest lecture, I was invited to develop a full semester business communication course which was a pivotal and energizing experience for me. Within six months of teaching the business communication course, I decided to leave the full-time management position. At the time, I was enrolled in an interdisciplinary PhD program in arts and humanities with a focus on phenomenology, culture, and communication. I obtained a half-time teaching position at a four-year college because of excellent teaching evaluations and a strong recommendation from the dean for my teaching at a community college. I was also not shy in the interview when I stated my desire for feedback, to seek clarity when communicating with students, and to value different opinions. At the four-year college I was able to add to my teaching ability and supervision of undergraduate student projects. As a doctoral student, I also began to take on new assignments that added new skills and understanding when I was appointed an assistant research scientist, and administrator and evaluator for a PhD level scientist-in-training program at for a PhD level scientist-in-training program at Brookhaven National Laboratory. I recognized early that it was important to ask questions, and in doing so I gained several new insights about how doctoral research differs if it is theoretical, experimental, or is social sciences-based inquiry (or a hybrid). The three-year experience with doctoral students in a science research degree provided me with additional insights about the differences in PhD program foci, guidance, and dissertation requirements. My role as a research scientist further expanded into a new learning opportunity for me when I was next detailed as a research coordinator with the citywide New York City Partnership that involved the business community, public education principals and leadership, and civic leaders and community leaders. The opportunity was a very different on the ground experience. There I learned to deal with and manage attitudinal biases that shaped decision-making impacting the future educational outcomes of young Black and Brown students attending public schools. The data and interviews that were collected were put together as one snapshot at a time as a standard of proof. I could compare and contrast and evaluate a science experiment and outcome that meets a standard as a proof that can be replicated over and over again in both condition and outcome.

After receiving my PhD, I accepted a new administrative role as assistant director of the office of sponsored research where I learned about research and training grants as well as grants administration. At the university I was hired initially as assistant director and then promoted to associate director during my three-year tenure because of successful grant awards received as a team leader. Through research administration I collaborated with faculty and post docs, the assistant dean for development, and the dean of the school. I received continuous feedback from faculty members in building relationships that allowed for the exchange of ideas, the understanding of research interests, and the overall grantmaking process. My grants team and I wrote, packaged, presented, and negotiated very competitive grant applications that were funded at a higher rate than prior to my arrival in the position. The constant interaction and pressure boosted my academic confidence and was clear point of growth for me until I began to feel some burnout. When my appointment as an administrator was negotiated, it was structured upfront so that I would also teach as an adjunct assistant professor in a department. This was important leverage because I wanted to avoid early career trepidation of being trapped in administration as an early career Black scholar. It was during my time in role in sponsored research that I was extended an offer to take on a new roll of assistant dean of students (which I declined). Soon thereafter, I agreed to another opportunity presented by my dean which was to administer a statewide leadership development and public/social policy program for advancing leaders working in K–12 and broadly in higher education. Subsequently, I was appointed a director at a national institute in Washington, DC. The institute experience was an encompassing journey where I led, managed, co-developed, and delivered leadership development programs nationally for leaders from a wide variety of fields. There was also some opportunity to pursue international leadership development work.

My co-author and I met at the institute in Washington, DC and we were able to come together to collaborate as faculty and as evaluators to administer, manage, and sustain the Leadership Development Program for Minority Managers (LDP) — an academic program at a major private university. At its inception in 1990, the LDP was established as a pathway for academic achievement to foster economic participation by racialized minorities seeking to advance as early to mid-career minority managers and professionals. The LDP is in its second iteration and my co-author and I are collaborating again to provide research insights to be utilized by business leaders, educators, and policymakers because there is scant academic research related to Black, Brown, and Native American mid-career professionals. As we administer the LDP, it is imperative to remain mindful of the persistent challenges to the inclusion and education of graduate students from racialized backgrounds in a predominantly White institution. To some, inside and outside of the academy, the concept of equity in the form of a race-specific academic program is an attack on the majority.

Journey and Trajectory to Leadership—Susan Swayze

My journey as Susan Swayze, PhD, can be described as a research-based inquiry into undergraduate and graduate student experiences in, with, and after higher education. I have worked applying research, evaluation, and assessment principles to university decision-making since earning a PhD in 1995. My first position was in a department of institutional research and assessment at a research university. In that role I had responsibilities for internal and external quantitative studies that directly impacted on university administrative and academic decision-making. Next, I held a position in teaching, learning, and assessment at an institution that was an early adopter of online instruction. In this role my focus was to identify the appropriate variables with which to compare student satisfaction and success across modes of instruction and then develop instruments to measure the student experience. These prior experiences contribute to current work with a leadership development program focused on minority managers in which I examine the nuanced ways in which the business curriculum and business-focused student programming contribute to end of program and subsequent success. Additionally, as a faculty member who teaches quantitative research, statistics, and qualitative research courses as well as contributes extensive dissertation committee service, I direct research skill development among doctoral students culminating in the completion of their doctoral dissertations.

My quest began in college when I realized that my educational experiences were quite different from those of other students. I switched my major to one that focused on society so that I could work toward answering the questions, "What are the college experiences of Black students? Why are they different from those of White students?" After earning my undergraduate degree, I enrolled in research-based master's and doctoral degree programs culminating in a PhD at the age of 26. My dissertation, titled "UCLA undergraduate college involvement and outcomes: Does race or gender matter?" quantitatively examined differences among undergraduate students based on their demographic characteristics. Powering through graduate education after completing my undergraduate education as a first-generation college student was the first experience that shaped my leadership journey. The need to advocate for myself, chart my own path, pump myself up, and push myself when others were not invested in my success set the stage for my subsequent roles in higher education. One pivotal experience in my early career taught me that my mere presence had the potential to inspire others. One semester I participated in a community leadership program and my group of five decided to design a leadership program for a class of seniors from an under-resourced school. The program included lectures focused on college-going and culminated in a graduation ceremony after a brief residency at a local college. At the graduation ceremony a mother approached me and thanked me for inspiring her daughter and her daughter's best friend to attend college. I thanked her and asked whether she meant me particularly or the program itself because I had not spent specific time with the two young ladies. The mother remarked that the young ladies said something to the effect—"We are going to college because we want to be Dr. Swayze." This experience demonstrated that one's presence can inspire others. The other early career experience that shaped my leadership journey occurred while I was a doctoral student in 1992. I was asked to speak at a teaching assistant conference on the topic of diversity and inclusion in the classroom. More than 30 years later I am still speaking and conducting research on the topic of diversity and inclusion. The 1992 presentation was a harbinger of the work ahead. Looking back, I should have journaled about my experiences as a college student, graduate student, and newly minted PhD. The content could have contributed to a book or maybe an essay on being a Black woman in the academy. Others might have learned from my experiences, and I would have learned more about myself and my growth as a leader.

I would make three recommendations to early-stage higher education leaders—journal, pause, and reflect. The first six months to one year in the higher education field is fast-paced and rife with a myriad of personalities, diverse practices, and in some cases a hidden curriculum. To make sense of it all, it is important to write down your experiences, advice that is given to you, and any information or practices that seem contrary to expectations. It is impossible to make sense of experiences as they occur. By writing them down, you provide an opportunity for reflection and understanding at a later date. Additionally, it is important to embrace the power of the pause. With a new position comes a considerable amount of new information from numerous people. It is critical to allow yourself time to process information before making decisions about people (their intentions—aka, friend, or foe) and projects (is the proposed project in my job description—think unpaid work). In some ways we are conditioned to be agreeable and say "yes" to requests. But what we do early in a position becomes the expectation, so pause before making decisions so that you have time to process possible intentions and outcomes. Lastly, make time to reflect. After you have been in your new role for a month or two, set aside time to reflect on how you feel about the position and the place. Ask yourself: Do you like the people that you work with? Do you like the higher education institution? Do you feel that you are in the right place at the correct time? Do you see your career growing here? When you create and implement a plan that includes journaling, pausing, and reflecting, you establish a framework that centers you in your career progression.

LOOKING BACK: WHAT ADVICE WOULD I SHARE WITH MYSELF?

Reflecting on our past experiences we feel that there are two fundamental lessons to share that are instructive and potentially useful for future consideration. First, it is critically important to continuously gather, understand, and accurately interpret changing information and to do thorough research on the concerns of multiple constituencies, interests, and voices. Second, it is important to continuously scan the environment because policies and procedures especially at Federal and State levels can become hindrances in fast changing conditions regarding who can be admitted and served in an education program that serves specific groups. We also draw from cumulative experience that we have been able to remain open to the reality that multiple influences are always active and exerting pressure on the academic program. Remain fully prepared with sound data, information, and idea and reason to make the case for the academic program you champion. In doing so, ask for and seek input that challenges your assumptions and thinking. Further, seek, establish, and sustain effective and strong communicative connections with all of the parties who are involved at your school and university, and this also applies to external agencies, interest groups and parties. Lastly, actively listen to inquiries and statements, comments and even disagreements so that you achieve discernment and understanding to further progress, adjudicate, and deliver an academic program.

CHAPTER 4

SIEMPRE EL ÚNICO (ALWAYS THE ONLY ONE)

Reflections From a Latino Senior Student Affairs Administrator

Juan R. Guardia

ABSTRACT

Many student affairs administrators have heard the common adage "*You'll need to move around in order to move up in the field.*" In my experience, this adage could not be truer. After more than two decades in the student affairs profession, I have lived in five states in order to advance professionally in the field. I encourage others to embrace these moves, yet, depending on where those moves may take you, you may, as I have been, the only Latino-identified student affairs administrator. As a first-generation, Cuban American from South Florida, I have not had the privilege of living near my family for over 20 years, yet every opportunity and space I have had the privilege to work and live in has provided me a wealth of experiences and knowledge I have greatly benefited from. In this chapter I share my career trajectory, reflections, and describe how such opportunities are life changing, personally and professionally.

CÓMO TODO EMPEZÓ (HOW IT ALL BEGAN)

My journey begins in the Southeast United States. My parents are Cuban immigrants who fled Cuba in the 1960's from the communist regime. My younger brother and I were born and raised in Miami Dade County, in a heavily Latino and multiethnic community. Our first language was Spanish, and we learned English in Miami-Dade County Public Schools. My father learned English and always worked a variety of jobs, including shoe salesman, factory worker, and delivery man. My mother, who only speaks Spanish, was our homemaker and cleaned others' homes for a living.

The importance of education was always stressed from my family. In 1992, I was the first in my family to complete high school graduating from Homestead Senior High School. I attended Miami-Dade Community College (renamed Miami Dade College in 2003) and earned my associate in arts degree in Broadcasting and then transferred to Florida State University where I earned my Bachelor of Science degree in Communication and a Master of Science degree in Higher Education. Later I enrolled at Iowa State University of Science and Technology where I earned my Doctor of Philosophy in Educational Leadership/Higher Education and a graduate certificate in community college teaching. To date, my niece and I are the only college graduates in our immediate family.

I have been in the higher education and student affairs field for over two decades and in that time, I have worked at a variety of institutions in several roles, including:

- Kids to College Coordinator, Tallahassee Community College
- Assistant Director for Diversity Programs and Services, George Mason University
- Director, Center for Multicultural Affairs, Florida State University
- Assistant Vice President for Student Affairs, Northeastern Illinois University
- Assistant Vice President for Student Affairs and Dean of Students, University of Cincinnati
- Vice President for Student Affairs, Texas A&M University–San Antonio

In the following section, I will discuss my experiences and how I moved up in my career pathways in these aforementioned roles.

MI CAMINO (MY PATHWAY) IN HIGHER EDUCATION

My leadership trajectory in higher education and student affairs consists of two avenues: professional and personal development opportunities. My first professional position after completing my master of science degree was at George Mason University (GMU) in Northern Virginia in the Office of Diversity Programs and Services. As Assistant Director, I was responsible for leading, coordinating, and executing support programs and services for Hispanic/Latina/o/x and Indigenous/Native American identified students. In this position I was the only Latino administrator in the unit. I left GMU to pursue my doctoral degree at Iowa State University as a full-time student where I was the only Latino in my cohort. After earning my doctoral degree, I returned to my alma mater, Florida State University (FSU), where I served as Director of the Center for Multicultural Affairs where I managed and provided leadership for co-curricular educational activities, programs, and trainings designed to enhance student, faculty, and staff awareness around diversity, equity, inclusion and belonging (DEIB). I was also the only Latino director within the division of student affairs. During my time at FSU, I was also adjunct faculty in the higher education master of science program and taught several courses including student development theories, diversity in higher education, and the American college student.

After experiencing cold Iowa winters, I did not think my professional path would bring me back to the Midwest. Alas, my next professional administrative role was at Northeastern Illinois University (NEIU) as Assistant Vice President for Student Affairs. I served as the chief administrator for the Angelina Pedroso Center for Diversity and Intercultural Affairs overseeing five identity-based spaces: the African/African-American, Asian/Global, Latina/o/x, LGBTQA, and Women's resource centers. In addition, I supervised new student and family programs, the student affairs communications team, and served as interim supervisor to student health and counseling services and student rights and responsibilities. NEIU was the first time I worked with a fellow Latino student affair administrator at the senior level. This experience also provided me additional leadership responsibilities above and beyond my DEIB subject matter expertise and understanding of additional areas in my professional toolbox which influence students' holistic development. I also had the privilege of serving as adjunct faculty at Loyola University Chicago, a private, Jesuit and Catholic institution, in the higher education master of education program where I taught the student affairs profession and American college student courses. Although I thrived in my time in Chicago, due to state of Illinois and NEIU budget cuts, my position was eliminated.

My next and most recent leadership role was also in the Midwest: I served as the Assistant Vice President for Student Affairs and Dean of Students at the University of Cincinnati (UC). I was the first Latino identified administrator to serve in this role and the only Latino, male, and gay identified administrator on the student affairs leadership team. In that role I supervised five areas: bearcat bands, dean of student's office, marketing and communications/parent and family programs, resident education and development, and student conduct and community standards. My decision to make a lateral move was prompted by the units in my portfolio; it allowed me to add new functional areas and strengthened my toolbox. At UC, I was the only male, gay Latino on the student affairs leadership team for the division. I was also adjunct faculty in the higher education program at the UC College of Education, Criminal Justice, and Human Services teaching various courses, including student development theory, introduction to student affairs administration, and organization and administration in higher education.

Personal professional development opportunities have also expanded my leadership skills and training. I have been actively involved in various leadership roles with the American College Personnel Association (ACPA) and the National Association of Student Personnel Administrators (NASPA) including ACPA Latinx/a/o Network Co-Chair & NASPA Latinx/a/o Knowledge Community Co-Chair. I was also Co-Director of the NASPA Escaleras Institute for Latina/o/x student affairs professionals, director of the NASPA Institute for new AVPs, and served on the AVP steering committee and the editorial board for the NASPA *Journal of Student Affairs Research and Practice.*

I am a lifetime member of Phi Iota Alpha Fraternity, Inc. and my fraternity has provided me with a variety of avenues for involvement and leadership. Some of those experiences include serving as Southeast provincial governor, Peru community service co-trip leader, and on the board of trustees. Phi Iota Alpha Fraternity is a member of the National Association of Latino Fraternal Organizations (NALFO), an umbrella organization representing 16 Latina/o/x fraternities and sororities. I volunteered in a variety of leadership roles within NALFO, including director of public relations, vice-chair, and national chair. Those experiences allowed me to network and connect with fraternity and sorority leaders and professionals, on and off campus. Moreover, I am also a member of the Association of Fraternity/Sorority Advisors and serve on the editorial board for the association's *Journal of Sorority and Fraternity Life Research and Practice* as well as the national elections committee.

My career trajectory has been informed via professional and personal development involvement. With the exception of NEIU, I have always been the first Latino administrator in each position. Although that has been a privilege, it is also remarkably lonely. It is challenging not living near family or close friends. Personally, I sought professional counseling, which assisted me greatly during my career transitions. It was also important for me to seek out colleagues I can connect with authentically; I do not trust easily so making deep connections is very important to me. In the past, I have been burnt by colleagues whom I trusted and as such, I am very careful with who I share personal and professional matters with. In order for me to genuinely trust someone, I take the time to authentically get to know them, which allows me to open, share, and reciprocate aspects of myself in time. In addition, the students I served constantly told me how important it was for them to see a Latino in my role. I have always known that representation matters yet hearing the same message from students on multiple campuses confirmed why I needed to be there at that time and in those moments.

The professional development opportunities have allowed me to flourish and network with colleagues from across the country. Some of those experiences, whether in higher education association and fraternal spaces have contributed greatly to my professional and personal development. Moreover, the networking opportunities have opened doors to serve as an external consultant for functional areas, programs, and services on various campuses across the nation. These opportunities are important for higher education leaders as it allows for idea exploration and development of best practices that can be applied on their respective campuses and in the greater higher education and student affairs profession.

MI CONSEJO (MY ADVICE)

My higher education journey has taught me to be open to all opportunities and possibilities. Looking back, I do not have any regrets. Had you asked me over 20 years ago if I would be open to the moving around the country, I would have absolutely said no. Truth be told, I believed attending FSU was far enough. Little did I know how life would open my eyes to new places, people, and unforgettable opportunities. As such, I am thankful for the experiences that have informed my professional and personal development and the wonderful people I have met along the way.

My journey has also taught me about resiliency. As the only Latino-identified administrator at various institutions, I have learned and understood the importance of representation not just for students, but for other student affairs and faculty colleagues. I am also aware how that impacts me personally, such as when I accepted my previous role at the University of Cincinnati; it was the first time moving to a city where I did not know anyone. As I shared earlier, I am thankful for the mental health resources provided to me as it has made me a better professional in my role. As such, my resiliency has taught me I can accomplish and be successful anywhere I choose to go.

The following are some strategies and personal recommendations to achieve success in your role.

Remain Steadfast in Your Authentic Identity

My most important salient identity is my *Latinidad*. I am a PROUD Cuban American and the resiliency my family has taught me carries me everywhere I go. As such, although I may not be near my family physically, they are with me in spirit. My latinidad is not up for discussion; it is an important part of who I am. I do not have the privilege to "pass" (and do not want to) as my ethnicity is very noticeable based on my accent and features. Moreover, my latinidad is also an important part of how I lead, and I utilize Elliott et al. (2021) Identity-Conscious Supervision model with my team and it has provided a space where we respect and value our authentic identities, creating a stronger sense of self, and fostering morale, professionally and personally.

Ethics, Morals, and Values Will Always Guide Your Work

My morals and values are an important part of who I am and how I represent myself, personally and professionally. I am ethical to a fault, and will not bend my ethics for anyone, regardless of an individual or employer. I recall an incident where a colleague asked to borrow my syllabus for a graduate course I previously taught to gather ideas as they would be teaching the same course, only to find out a month later she used my syllabus without giving me any credit for my work. I had a conversation with her and told her I did not appreciate my trust being violated, being lied to, and ultimately, their demonstration of unethical behavior. As such, I am steadfast in my belief it is important to demonstrate and remain grounded in one's morals and values.

Become Involved in Professional Development Opportunities

Association and professional development volunteer work provide invaluable experiences. As I shared earlier, such opportunities have opened doors to leadership positions that have provided transferable skills, professionally and personally. In addition, networking with colleagues from across the nation has also been fruitful as it has allowed for collaboration on program presentation at national and regional conferences and co-authoring publication opportunities. Research available volunteer opportunities via your association and organizations to get the most out of your membership.

Be Open to Opportunities Outside Your Home State/City

When I was younger, I believed I would complete my undergraduate degree at Florida State University and immediately move back to Miami. I did and yet after a few years, I returned to grad school outside of Miami and never looked back. My graduate school experience opened doors and opportunities for me to stretch myself and live in parts of the country I had not previously thought of. Since 2001, I have lived in six states: Florida, Virginia, Iowa, Illinois, Ohio, and currently Texas. I am thankful for each of the opportunities to experience working with different people, students, faculty, and staff alike. I have learned from them immensely and I would challenge others to do the same. Neale Donald Walsch said it best: "Life begins at the end of your comfort zone."

REFERENCE

Elliott, C., Desai, S., & Brown, R. (2021). Identity-conscious supervision: A model for equity. *New Directions for Student Services, 2021*, 53–62. https://doi.org/10.1002/ss.20396

CHAPTER 5

TAKE THE LATERAL

Becki Tankson-Artis

ABSTRACT

Working in student affairs can sometimes feel like chasing the next role. Leaders work hard and do what it takes to get to the next step on the ladder. Staying in entry-level roles for longer than a few years can be looked down upon. However, sometimes taking a lateral role is what is most beneficial. This chapter will explore how taking a lateral position is sometimes the best move for a student affairs professional. Not all student affairs professionals have the same trajectory for professional growth. This chapter will provide encouragement to for up-and-coming professionals to grow at their own pace, because success can still be in their future.

My name is Becki Tankson-Artis. I currently serve as a Residence Life Coordinator at the University of North Florida. I am a tattoo enthusiast, book lover, baker, and wife. I am also a professional that would consider myself to be in residence life for life. I aspire to be a director of a housing department one day, and my journey through leadership has taken some turns I was not anticipating.

I started working in higher education the same way many professionals do: I worked some jobs on campus while working on my bachelor's degree in sociology that sparked my love for working with college students. I spent a few semesters working as a student assistant in the President's Office on campus. I was a Resident Assistant for two years, both years in a first-year residence hall. I also served as an Orientation Leader for two summers, as I loved being at school and despised being in my small hometown. As graduation approached, I had no clue what I wanted to do. I knew I loved working on a university campus, and I did not see any careers at the career fair that allowed me to work with college students while utilizing my knowledge in sociology. I then had an epiphany many others do—my direct supervisor worked with college students on a university campus for a living. My supervisor was a graduate student earning a degree in College Student Affairs so she could work with college students professionally. My supervisor was doing something professionally that I did not quite understand existed until that moment. My supervisor's professional path was the direction I was wanting to go in. After speaking with my supervisor about how she got to where she is, she informed me that a master's degree would be helpful for me to continue working with college students professionally; that is exactly what she was doing. My supervisor pointed me in the direction of going to graduate school to earn a degree in higher education administration. This degree would allow me to work in many areas of higher education, but it would be incredibly helpful for working in the area I loved most: housing and residence life.

I attended graduate school and served as an Assistant Residence Life Coordinator as my assistantship. I held an internship during the summer of graduate school that focused on residential curriculum. I earned my Master of Science in Higher Education Administration with a concentration in Student Affairs. Since earning my master's degree, I have served as a Hall Coordinator at one institution, Residence Life Coordinator at another institution, and have found myself still serving as a Residence Life Coordinator at the institution where I earned my master's degree. My unofficial professional expertise is in taking lateral roles. I am in my third entry level position since 2019. These positions have taught me an incredible amount about how to be a leader. I have been a leader to many different types of teams and have supervised many different types of students. I learned that it is important to be the supervisor the students need to best help them be the most successful. I have learned to be an excellent listener and have learned when students want a listening ear versus wanting actual advice. I have learned that leading from an entry level position is possible and an important part of my professional journey because it had lead me to realize what steps I need to take next to reach my goal of being a director of residence life.

JOURNEY INTO THE FIELD

This is not where I thought I would find myself at this time in my life. Surely, I was going to be an Assistant Director by now. This would mean I am progressing in my career in a timely manner and my strong skills have carried me far in a short amount of time. That is what success looked like to me while growing up, and that is a perception that has changed in the past few years. While my trajectory into leadership has not been what I have expected, it has provided me with many experiences and lessons that have shaped me into the professional I am.

My first job after graduate school as a Hall Coordinator brought me the most challenges. I oversaw apartments for nontraditional students. On my very first day of work as a Hall Coordinator, a vehicle drove through one of the apartments. I had not been fully trained yet and was forced to think on my feet. I met a lot of important university players that day and had to make a good impression. I somehow figured it out, and I knew that I would be in for a wild ride at that job. From there, that community faced challenges with the internet not working properly after we implemented new routers to fix the previous issues, a group of squatters in a vacant apartment, and the students feeling like they were being brushed off due to the housing department announcing that the apartments would be permanently closing the following academic year. Through these challenges, I learned that I am a great problem solver and have excellent patience and customer service. I presented my first conference program during my time there and was invited to be a keynote speaker at a student leadership conference. However, even with all the growth and opportunities, the pandemic added to the top of the challenges was overwhelming, and I became worn out. During a duty call the summer of 2020, I had to call our leadership on-call for help moving a student into an isolation space and was refused help. That moment was when I realized I was giving this job more than what I was receiving from it. I missed being close to my family, and my partner was no longer enjoying our adventure in this new place. I no longer felt happy or satisfied. After a year and a half, it was time to look for something new.

My second job after graduate school as a Residence Life Coordinator was a lateral move I needed. It brought me closer to a familiar environment during some of the hardest years I have experienced and allowed me to hone my supervision skills by directly supervising graduate students. While this role was a lateral move, it still provided opportunities for growth. Learning how to directly support upcoming student affairs professionals was incredibly rewarding. It took some trial and error, but helping with questions about interviews, reviewing resumes and cover letters, and sharing my own experiences and truth about working in the profession provided upcoming student affairs professionals the support they needed to make educated decisions about entering the field. My graduate students trusted me and relied on my leadership; I could not disappoint them. I thought I would be staying in that position for three years, and then look for an Assistant Director role to depart from the university. I wanted to move *up and out*, not just out. The upward trajectory was something I wanted in order to show others that I was being successful.

At the beginning of a spring semester at this job, I was handed the most challenging supervisor I could have imagined. I believe this person was underqualified for the position and did not trust my leadership. This person withheld information from me that directly affected the work I did. This person frequently told lies and did not accept responsibility for their actions. This person made me miserable and made me dread going into work. It was bleeding into my personal life by sucking out all my energy, leaving me nothing to give to my personal happiness. I tried to give my supervisor some grace and I spoke with my supervisor about the challenges I was experiencing due to their leadership. I brought my concerns to my supervisor with respect, but I was met with disrespect and was brushed off. No matter what I did, I could not fix what was wrong. My supervisor never made an effort, even though I was making every effort, to improve our relationship. I could not work in an environment like that anymore. It took a few months, but when I finally realized my work environment was depleting my energy, I knew it was time to look for a new position.

This leads to my third and current lateral position, as another Residence Life Coordinator. Now, my supervisor is available when I am in need but leaves me to do my work on my own, which is something I greatly appreciate. I am tapped to assist with special department projects due to my skills and experiences. I am encouraged to seek new professional development experiences so I may continue to learn and grow. I am encouraged to speak about my passions that lay outside of student affairs. I am in a place where I am supported, I am trusted, and I am encouraged to soak up as much as I can. I can be my genuine self. I have taken all that I have learned from my previous positions to be the best coordinator I can be. I am patient, I am trusting, I am a problem solver, and I have strong crisis management skills. These are important aspects to do my job to its fullest potential. I assist my students effectively and efficiently daily; they trust me to assist in solving their problems, and I can do so. My colleagues, my peers, and those that I supervise know that I can work through any challenge that comes my way. My team can rely on me, and I always have their backs. To me, that makes me great leader.

I find myself comparing where I am in my leadership position to others that I graduated grad school with. One of them is a director of housing operations, and I am still a coordinator. I only feel that I am behind when I am comparing myself to others, though. I want to be successful in the eyes of others, not just my own eyes. I feel extra societal pressure to be outwardly successful because I am a young woman in this profession. I want to be taken seriously. However, if I measure my success by where I am compared to where I was, and the trajectory to where I want to be, I am delighted on how far I have come and the skills I have that will take me forward. Making comparisons to others may not be completely avoidable, but its impacts can be mitigated by reflecting on the journey thus far and remembering that success looks different for everyone. Focusing on the journey itself can also be a strategy to help find joy and contentment with the stage of success a new professional is in. There is no success without the journey to get there and focusing on the journey could help build and hone skills even more.

TAKING THE LATERAL

Throughout the years I have spent taking lateral positions and not moving upward in my career, I have learned a few lessons that I wish I would have known sooner. If I were able to give my past-self advice on my future career moves, the first thing I would say is to not be afraid of taking lateral positions; they are amazing! Just because a new position is on the same level as your old position, that does not mean it does not have anything to offer. I have learned and grown so much in my lateral positions. I have experienced many types of institutions and department sizes, as well as different types of student populations. I now know how to work in many different environments, and those skills will help me grow my career and my leadership. I have also experienced being a leader among my peers. While I am still in an entry-level position, I am not a brand-new professional. I have experiences and information that I have been able to share with my peers to help them become the best professionals in their roles as they can. I have been able to adjust to my new roles smoothly, as well, because I have not been starting from scratch when entering a new role. This has allowed me to learn even more skills and experience opportunities I may not have been able to, such as being selected to represent the coordinators during interviews for a new position in the department and being asked to serve as a peer mentor to a new coordinator.

 Taking lateral positions also allows time for new professionals to find where they want to have their forever place. For me, a forever place is where someone calls "home." It is the place someone wants to live forever; it is the place someone wants to put down roots. Lateral positions, especially in housing and residence life, allows professionals to experience different cities, and different parts of the country, without having to put roots down too deep. It offers the opportunity to get a feel for the surroundings and allows a chance to move on if a location is not providing what the professional needs and wants. Looking back, I wish I could tell my past-self that it is okay if it takes a bit longer than others find where my forever place is.

Something I wish I did more often in my past entry level positions is take more professional development risks. I used to think that big professional development opportunities were not meant for me because I was a new professional. That is not the case! During my first year as an entry level professional, I presented at a regional conference. It was an excellent experience that taught me how to present at a conference, and how to be an active conference attendee. After that presentation, I did not think there were any other professional development opportunities for me. I wish I would have explored presenting at a conference again, investigated attending different types of conferences, and researched other types of professional development opportunities. Just because an opportunity seems like it is meant for a more advanced professional does not mean it is not beneficial to an entry level professional.

One thing I would do differently is not get ugly when things get ugly. During the time I worked under a lackluster supervisor, I struggled to stay professional while working through the challenges I faced. Being overworked, I developed a short fuse and stopped caring as much as I used to about the work I was doing. I should have taken this as a sign to start looking for a new position sooner. Instead, I fought back and wore myself down even more. Being ugly when things got ugly ultimately did not help me; it took more energy from me and made going to work every day a challenge, when it used to be something I looked forward to. Instead of getting ugly, I wish I would have taken more time to notice the shift in department culture and care and used my energy to protect my peace. It was clear to me that I was too late to protect my peace because every experience related to that position was now tainted with negativity. I needed to find peace elsewhere. I searched for a new role, and at first, I wanted to pursue an assistant director role. However, I found a lateral coordinator position that was more aligned with the experiences I was searching for, and that would allow me more time to hone my skills before pursuing an assistant director role. I want to step into an assistant director role as the best version of myself. Losing my peace and energy did not leave me as the person I wanted to be while taking that next step into a higher leadership role.

FOR NEW LEADERS

The first piece of advice I have for new leaders is to keep an eye on what your options may be if you were to need a new position unexpectedly. I was not fully wanting or expecting to have to leave my last position, but because I had kept my eye on jobs being posted across the region I was interested in living and working in, I knew what was available when the time came. It is okay to check on positions that you are interested in, and a position that may be your dream position, so you know about how often it becomes available, and what materials may be needed to apply. Being able to relocate easily has also been an excellent way for me to hold the positions I have had. While moving is not fun for me, it has been an integral part in my career path thus far. Knowing what the options are for a lateral move may be the key in a new leader's next position, because if something were to happen and one must leave their current role, the leader is not starting a search completely from scratch. Additionally, that dream job may just become available when it is least expected.

The next piece of advice I have to offer is to always look for ways to grow. Growth exists in every position. Sometimes the growth is obvious, and sometimes the growth needs to be uncovered, but it is there. It could take a variety of forms: a new addition to the job description, an opportunity such as assisting with interviews for a new role in the department, leading training sessions for your peers, attending or presenting at a conference, learning about the roles of others within the department, or serving on a departmental, institutional, or regional committee. Finding ways to grow professionally and personally are important to finding success.

The final piece of advice I have is to not be afraid of lateral positions. Finding success in student affairs is not always about upward movement. Success can be measured by standards that each professional and leader sets for themselves. Sometimes, finding a new position is more about finding personal peace. Sometimes, finding a new position is more about being in an environment that makes the leader feel safe to grow. Sometimes, finding a new position is more about it being the best steppingstone to the end goal. Not all reasons for finding a new position are the same, but they are all valid. Lateral positions are sometimes the best move for a leader. They can offer time to continue learning and building skillsets. A professional's skillset will show for itself when it is time to move up, and lateral positions are wonderful opportunities to build that skillset. Not all student affairs professionals have the same trajectory for professional growth. Lateral positions can help leaders be the best version of themselves by allowing more time, more mentors, and more opportunities to assist with upward trajectory, and that will ultimately lead to the dream role.

Up-and-coming leaders should grow at their own pace, and it is my hope that new professionals feel comfortable and supported doing so. Lateral positions are an excellent opportunity for professionals to continue their journey. Take the lateral; it's worth it.

CHAPTER 6

CAREER ADVANCEMENT AND TRAJECTORY IN HIGHER EDUCATION

Felix Quayson

ABSTRACT

This chapter provides guidance for current and prospective leaders and professionals in higher education who aim to navigate the academic landscape while keeping career structure and development goals in mind. To achieve success in career advancement, individuals must consider the broader impact of their decisions, which may impede their professionalism and personality trajectory in higher education. The alliance of relationships in higher education is significant in facilitating career advancement and trajectory. Focusing on career structure leads to a deeper understanding of professional identity within the vocation. Misplaced thinking, gaslighting, and deficit thinking can negatively impact one's ability to recognize their self-worth. Thus, professionals must emphasize both personal and professional development. Ultimately, individuals must become their own strongest advocates while working in higher education.

BRIEF OVERVIEW OF MYSELF

I am an accomplished research scholar with specialization in Workforce Human Resource Development Education, Postsecondary Career & Technical Education, and Educational Leadership. With a passion for promoting career development and employment readiness, I have been recognized as a 22–23 national research fellow at North Carolina State University Belk Center, a prestigious national program sponsored by Educational Credit Management Corporation Foundation (ECMC). Through my extensive research in performance metrics, training, assessment, and evaluation, I am focused on improving outcomes for African American male students and adults in their transition to the workplace, labor relations, and training and development. I am a skilled researcher with expertise in various research methodologies, and my current projects utilize qualitative methodologies to address critical questions in educational studies. As an active member of the Association for Career and Technical Education Research (ACTER) and the American Educational Research Association (AERA—Career and Technical Education (CTE) Special Interest Group (SIG) / Postsecondary Division J), I am committed to advancing career development and promoting equitable opportunities for all. With my exceptional skills and extensive experience, I am a valuable asset to any organization seeking to improve outcomes in career development and workforce education. I have co-authored two books: *From Lecture Hall to Laptop* and *Journey to Financial Literacy and Freedom*. In addition, I have published in academic journals like Journal of Research Initiatives, and Interdisciplinary Journal of Advances in Research in Education. My scholarly work are cited at Google Scholar and ResearchGate. I served as Chair and Editor of research studies at Informing Science Institute where I was awarded the Gold Editor Award in 2019 and 2020. I established an academic journal and served as the founding Editor-in-Chief & Publisher, and co-founded an educational and business consulting firm in Texas, New Mind Media, LLC.

As an expert in my field, my research expertise focuses on several areas within the realm of education, including Workforce Human Resource Development Education, Postsecondary Career & Technical Education, and Educational Leadership. Specifically, my focus areas include College & Career Readiness, Academic Motivation & Achievement, African American Male Students, Workforce Development, Labor Market, Outcomes/Relations, Training & Development, E-Learning/EdTech, Industry Certification/Credentialing, Apprenticeship, and STEM Education.

In terms of my approach to research, I utilize a range of methodologies, including Research Methods & Design, Qualitative Research Designs, Descriptive Case Study, Policy Studies/Analyses, Phenomenology, and Data visualization. Through these approaches, I aim to gain a deep understanding of the complex issues surrounding education and workforce development, and to identify effective strategies for improving outcomes for students and employees alike.

My educational background has provided me with the foundational knowledge and skills necessary to excel in this field. I hold a Doctor of Philosophy (PhD) in Educational Studies in Workforce Development and Education, Career & Technical Education, a Doctor of Education (EdD) in Educational Leadership and Supervision, Higher Education, a Master of Arts (MA) in Educational Studies in Workforce Development and Education in Adult Education and Human Resource Development, and a Master of Science in Education (MSEd) in Educational Leadership and Policy Studies, Higher Education. Additionally, I have received a Harvard Graduate School of Education (CMTE) Certification in Media and Technology for Education and a Teaching English as Foreign/Second Language (TEFL/TESOL), Level 5 TQUK Teacher Certification. My Bachelor of Science (BSc) in Health Fitness Management, Public Health has also contributed to my expertise in this field. Overall, my research and educational background have prepared me to contribute valuable insights and findings to the field of education and workforce development.

DISCUSSING MY JOURNEY OF ESTABLISHING AN ACADEMIC JOURNAL

I have worked in diverse roles in higher education as a faculty member and a researcher, in project/program management roles at the state and local levels, and taught at the graduate, undergraduate, online, and internationally in the Kingdom of Saudi Arabia. One of the challenging tasks I ever embarked on was establishing an academic journal after graduating with my EdD degree. I called the project the labor of love. It was challenging for me because I didn't have anyone to ask for help or take advice from. I learned from reading over and over again online on how to establish an academic journal. I wanted the journal to be legitimate and gone through the right process with obtaining indexing numbers. I created an email account for the journal, paid several thousands of dollars to build a customized website for the journal, mobilized fellow doctoral peers to serve on the Editorial Board, and applied for ISSN number through the U.S. Library of Congress. Within a few weeks, I was approved for the ISSN number and I will never forget the joy and happiness that brought to my life. Establishing an academic journal is a task only few people in the academic world knows about or can even achieve. After establishing the academic journal (Interdisciplinary Journal of Advances in Research in Education), another task that I embarked on was making the journal reputable in the eyes of academics and researchers. I applied for the DOI indexing at Crossref and paid for the annual membership to assign a DOI number to published articles. By the end of 2023, I would apply for the Directory of Open Access Journal (DOAJ) indexing. The leadership trait in me helped me to complete the project of establishing an academic journal and making it reputable. Since establishing the journal in March of 2018, the journal is indexed in places like Australia National Library System, The Ohio State University, Crossref, U.S. Library of Congress, fatcat wiki, and soon to be indexed at DOAJ. With this in mind, I am certain that I can accomplish any task that is put in front of me. My experiences have impacted my leadership abilities in the following ways: (a) I do not wait for the right time, (b) I do not wait on anyone to help me, (c) I never stop learning on my own, (d) I don't hide the pain in my pride, and (e) I respect myself to give respect everyone.

Remember, that in higher education, you have to rely on your leadership abilities to make key and critical decisions regarding your interests and the projects that you would like to pursue. Do make friends and allies within your institutions, but always rely on your intuition and gut feelings to trust and respect your personal and professional decisions. My path to working in higher education was not a linear pathway. I would advise you to not expect a linear pathway for your career in higher education. However, if you do end up with a linear pathway, do your best to embrace your uniqueness and abilities as a capable person and professional willing to do great things. Each day make sure to take a step towards your goal, vision, and mission in life and in the work that you do. Working on your goals daily will improve your personal growth and mindset as an individual. Have the mentality to do great work. I will let you reflect on a quote that I heard from the late great NBA legend Kobe Bean Bryant, "Are you the same beast with the same mentality?"

TIPS/STRATEGIES/RECOMMENDATIONS FOR NEW/ POTENTIAL HIGHER EDUCATION LEADERS

The following advice are my tips, strategies, and recommendations for new and potential leaders to thrive in the higher education workplace:

Build Strong Relationships

Building strong relationships with faculty, staff, students, and other stakeholders is essential for success in higher education leadership. As a leader, it is critical to cultivate a culture of trust, collaboration, and respect, and to listen actively to the concerns and ideas of others. By building strong relationships, leaders can promote a sense of community and belonging,

TABLE 6.1	Advice for New Higher Education Leaders		
Advice	Description	Do's	Don'ts
Listen and learn	As a new higher education leader, it's important to take the time to listen and learn from your colleagues, staff, and students. Understanding their perspectives, experiences, and needs will help you build trust, establish credibility, and make informed decisions that benefit the institution.	Be quick to listen more than you are quick to speak on issues or voice your opinions. Be a valued friend without losing your morals, ethics, and identity.	Don't try to disrespect anyone because their position or salary grade might be lower than yours. Don't start rumors. Speak based on facts and evidence.
Building relationships.	Building strong relationships with faculty, staff, students, and other stakeholders is crucial for success in higher education leadership. Take the time to get to know people, ask questions, and show that you value their contributions. By building relationships based on trust, respect, and collaboration, you can create a positive and supportive culture that fosters excellence, innovation, and success.	Be active on professional networking platforms like LinkedIn. Send out messages to those in your field to ask for informational interviews or time to chat about your concern. Be prepared to know what you want and what you would like to get out of your networking. Write articles and post on LinkedIn about your interests and related topics within your field to get exposure.	Don't be a friend to everyone. Set your limits and boundaries. Don't say "Yes" to everything and anything. Exercise control to say "No" when it does not benefit your career or position.

(continued)

TABLE 6.1 Advice for New Higher Education Leaders (continued)

Advice	Description	Do's	Don'ts
Focus on priorities.	Higher education institutions often face competing demands and limited resources, so it's important to focus on the priorities that will have the greatest impact on the institution's mission and goals. As a new leader, take the time to understand the institution's strategic plan and priorities, and work with your team to align your efforts with those priorities. By focusing on what's most important, you can make a meaningful and lasting impact on the institution.	Spend the time to read and read and read over again on policies and handbooks. Prioritize your identity as a professional within your department because if you don't, you will suffer for it. Engage with your professional development strategies to learn and unlearn what makes you unique as an individual.	Don't engage in every opportunity presented to you because some are traps to make you forget who you are as an individual. Don't speak your mind about every issue or concern in the workplace. Learn to be quite and learn when to speak when your opinion is valued.
Be proactive.	As a higher education leader, you will face many challenges and opportunities, and it's important to be proactive in addressing them. Don't wait for problems to arise or opportunities to come to you—take the initiative to identify and address issues before they become major obstacles, and be open to new ideas and approaches that can help you achieve your goals. By being proactive and responsive, you can build a reputation as a dynamic and effective leader who is committed to the institution's success.	Be your own cheerleader. Celebrate your small wins and accomplishments. Always present yourself in a professional manner, including the way you speak. Pitch yourself to co-workers as problem-solver, not problem-creator. Make your ideas stand out as quality and valued.	Don't raise your voice. Improve your arguments with facts, data, and proof of evidence. Address yourself how you would like people to address you. Show respect, and respect will be given to you. Don't sell your reputation for a few dollars or promotion.

enhance communication and teamwork, and foster a supportive and inclusive environment.

Develop a Vision and Strategic Plan

To achieve success in higher education leadership, it is essential to have a clear vision of the institution's mission, values, and goals, and to develop a strategic plan to achieve them. A leader's vision and strategic plan should align with the institution's values and priorities, reflect the needs and aspirations of the community, and provide a roadmap for action and progress. Write your vision and strategic plan by utilizing the Strength, Weaknesses, Opportunities, and Threats (SWOT) analysis to inspire and motivate yourself to focus on efforts, resources, and the measuring of progress and success.

Embrace Innovation and Change

Higher education is undergoing rapid and profound changes, and leaders need to be adaptable, flexible, and open-minded to succeed in this dynamic environment. As a leader, it is essential to embrace innovation and change, and to foster a culture of creativity, experimentation, and risk-taking. Embrace innovation and change by being an open-minded individual to drive continuous improvement, promote excellence and innovation, and respond to emerging challenges and opportunities.

Invest in Professional Development

To achieve success in higher education leadership, it is essential to invest in professional development. As a leader, it is critical to stay informed of emerging trends, best practices, and research in the field, and to develop the skills and competencies needed to lead effectively. Invest in your professional development by attending conferences and workshops, pursuing advanced degrees or certifications, participating in mentoring or coaching programs, and seeking feedback and guidance from trusted colleagues and mentors. Professional development can enhance your knowledge and skills, build your networks, and help you stay current and relevant in your field (Mehra et al., 2006).

Embrace Technology and Digital Learning

Technology has transformed higher education, creating new opportunities for learning and collaboration (Quayson & Zirkle, 2022). Leaders and professionals should embrace the use of technology and digital learning tools to enhance student engagement, facilitate communication and collaboration, and promote accessibility and flexibility (Garrison, 2017). I will recommend creating a virtual database (self-organization toolkit) of digital learning and technology driven resources to help you be organized as a professional. The virtual database should have resources like your research interests and topics, leadership books and articles, management training and development, and policies/handbooks.

Understanding Academic Career Structures

Academic career structures can vary widely depending on the institution, field, and country in question. Generally, however, there are several common stages in the academic career path, including graduate school, postdoctoral positions, and tenure-track or tenured faculty positions (Bourne et al., 2017). Understanding these career structures and the expectations and requirements associated with each stage is critical for success in academia in the following ways: (a) it will help you not to overstep your role, (b) it will help you stay focus on improving yourself, (c) it will help you to approach the right people for opportunities and advice in your profession, and (d) it will help you to avoid unnecessary drama and backlash in the workplace.

Developing Strong Research Skills

Research is a central component of academic work, and developing strong research skills is essential for success in the field. This includes not only technical research skills, but also the ability to effectively communicate research findings to a wide audience, secure funding and grants, and collaborate with other researchers will deepen your leadership skills in higher education (Bourne et al., 2017).

Building a Professional Network

Networking is a crucial aspect of career development in academia. Building relationships with other researchers, faculty, and professionals in your field can provide opportunities for collaboration, mentorship, and career advancement. This can be done through attending conferences, joining professional organizations, and reaching out to colleagues and mentors for advice and guidance (Bourne et al., 2017).

Maintaining a Work–Life Balance

Academic work can be demanding, and it is important for aspiring academics/leaders to prioritize self-care and maintain a healthy work-life balance. This may involve setting boundaries around work hours, engaging in hobbies and leisure activities outside of work, and seeking out support and resources for mental health and wellness (Evans et al., 2018).

The Mentality Approach to Career Development

The mentality approach to career development is rooted in the idea that an individual's mindset can significantly impact their career success. This approach can be done by developing a growth mindset, which involves viewing challenges and setbacks as opportunities for learning and growth rather than fixed limitations (Dweck, 2006). Also, develop a growth mindset that cultivates self-awareness, setting ambitious yet realistic goals, and embracing a willingness to take risks and learn from failure (Seligman, 2018). You need to seek out and utilize feedback and mentorship to support your ongoing growth and development (Grant & Gino, 2010).

CONCLUSION

Building strong relationships, developing a vision and strategic plan, embracing innovation and change, and investing in professional development are essential strategies for new and potential higher education leaders to achieve success. By adopting these strategies, new leaders can inspire and motivate others, promote excellence and innovation, and drive progress and success within their institutions and communities. New and potential higher education leaders should listen and learn, build relationships, focus on priorities, and be proactive in addressing challenges and opportunities.

REFERENCES

Bourne, P. E., Polka, J. K., Vale, R. D., & Kiley, R. (2017). Ten simple rules to consider regarding preprint submission. *PLoS Computation Biology 13*(5): e1005473. https://doi.org/10.1371/journal.pcbi.1005473

Dweck, C. S. (2006). *Mindset: The new psychology of success.* Random House.

Evans, T. M., Bira, L., Gastelum, J. B., Weiss, T. L., & Vanderford, N. L. (2018). Evidence for a mental health crisis in graduate education. *Nature Biotechnology, 36,* 282–284. https://doi.org/10.1038/nbt.4089

Garrison, D. R. (2017). *E-learning in the 21st century.* Routledge.

Grant, A. M., & Gino, F. (2010). A little thanks goes a long way: Explaining why gratitude expressions motivate prosocial behavior. *Journal of Personality and Social Psychology, 98*(6), 946–955. https://doi.org/10.1037/a0017935

Mehra, A., Smith, B. R., Dixon, A. L., & Bruce, R. (2006). Distributed leadership in teams: The network of leadership perceptions and team performance. *The Leadership Quarterly, 17*(3), 232–245. https://doi.org/10.1016/j.leaqua.2006.02.003

Quayson, F., & Zirkle, C. (2022). Practical leadership in implementing online education programs. *Journal of Research Initiatives, 6*(3). https://digitalcommons.uncfsu.edu/jri/vol6/iss3/7/

Seligman, M. E. (2018). *The hope circuit: A psychologist's journey from helplessness to optimism.* PublicAffairs.

SECTION II

PREPARATIONS FOR LEADERSHIP

CHAPTER 7

TESTIMONIOS FROM THOSE WHO HAVE SUCCESSFULLY NAVIGATED THE DOCTORAL PIPELINE WHILE WORKING PROFESSIONALLY IN THE FIELD OF STUDENT AFFAIRS

Jennifer Alanis
Tony Jimenez

ABSTRACT

As we reflect on the process, we embarked on completing our educational journey towards our doctoral degrees while also being working practitioners. Our intersectionality of identities and our experiences with our Latinidad played a monumental role in our persistence toward terminal degrees. In the following pages, you will find the educational and professional testimonials of two individuals pushing toward obtaining their terminal degrees. Their perspectives and experiences based on their validation of their identities will be permanent through the pages, but the one constant was the validation of

---

The Handbook for Aspiring Higher Education Leaders, pages 55–63
Copyright © 2024 by Information Age Publishing
www.infoagepub.com
All rights of reproduction in any form reserved.

their Latinidad. You will hear the stories of being raised in the borderlands and experiences of being raised in the Midwest and a bronze star veteran's wife. Even though, as Latinos, these individuals may share a common identity or even a common language, geographic location, and gender identity added to the complexities of these groups.

Moreover, those educated at large public universities imposed on those that attended elite private universities can add to these complexities. As such, we feel these identities can add to the discourse on how the multiple forms of identities and resistance to the "norm" can lead to an emancipatory change in their respective community and increase representation in the field

As we reflect on the process, we embarked on completing our educational journey towards our doctoral degrees while also being working practitioners, what continued to be salient is the importance of validating our identity throughout our journey. Our intersectionality of identities and our experiences with our Latinidad played a monumental role in our persistence toward terminal degrees. In the following pages, you will find the educational and professional testimonials of two individuals pushing toward obtaining their terminal degrees. Their perspectives and experiences based on their validation of their identities will be permanent through the pages, but the one constant was the validation of their Latinidad. You will hear the stories of being raised in the borderlands and experiences of being raised in the midwest and a bronze star veteran's wife. Even though, as Latinos, we may share a common identity or even a common language, geographic location, and gender identity added to the complexities of these groups.

The diversity of perspectives from large public research universities to elite private universities has provided a unique lens to our professional experiences in student affairs. As such, we feel these identities can add to the discourse on how the multiple forms of identities and resistance to the "norm" can lead to an emancipatory change in their respective community and increase representation in the field.

JENNIFER ALANIS (MIDWEST FARMWORKERS GRANDDAUGHTER AND VETERANS SPOUSE)

As I reflect on the process of completing my educational journey toward my doctoral degree and dissertation, I am drawn back to where it all started. Growing up in a migrant working family in the midwest, I understood the importance of being an advocate and an ally for the students I worked with daily. As I continued to grow in my profession, I understood my place in academia and my power to enact positive change for the undocumented community. As I moved across the country while continuing my journey toward completing my dissertation, through the support I had from my family, my colleagues, and my students, I found the strength to persist to completion. My former students, current students, and those I will come into contact within the future propelled me to continue my research in the new state I called home. Individuals like the eight participants I had the pleasure of interviewing inspired me to tell their stories. They also allowed me to possibly enable some campuses in this region to begin educating themselves and continue supporting and advocating for the undocumented student population. This path towards a terminal degree also made me realize that reflecting on my privilege as a Latina woman administrator in higher education was vital. It also allowed me to understand that my place in academia is challenging to come by as a woman and a Latina. This reflection, along with the stories I can tell about a population who has lived in the shadows for most of their lives, is one I need to tell. Most importantly, it is a story that gives me the leverage to continue to advocate and create institutional procedures and opportunities for them to be successful on university campuses. According to Deluna (2017), One participant stated, "You push me to keep going, and when I want to give up, I know that if I come to talk to you, it will give me the strength to get a degree." (p. 103). Those words keep me fighting for this population of students across the country.

What has also been a constant in my life has been the struggle my husband has faced while obtaining his degree in higher education, and as a veteran's wife, his struggle also became my struggle. Enlisting in the military was my partner's choice at 18 years old. It was his choice, not because he wanted to serve his country out of pure love and because of family history. He enlisted to get his family ahead as, at 18, he had just learned he would be a father, and because he had not joined the military, he more than likely would have been a statistic. The military changed his perspective and life choices; it made him resilient. The military was his calling; when he was medically retired by the United States Army, he was lost; this was supposed to be his career.

The retirement also brought forth the difficulties of getting the support, benefits, and adequate medical care promised to my spouse upon enlistment. Veterans are forced to struggle through various red tape to get services. They are also asked to wait an extreme amount of time to get the appointments necessary for their health care; according to Urbi (2018), "Other veterans are facing wait times of months, or even years, to get an appointment at their VA care center (p. 1). The Department of Veterans Affairs is dealing with the need for more trust from those asked to serve. As my partner transitioned out of the military, he had first-hand experience dealing with the backlog of benefits, tired staff, and lack of support at his institution of higher learning that prevented him from receiving the needed care. As I helped my partner navigate his journey in higher education, it brought me to why I entered higher education. It allowed me to work with our veterans support office on that campus to provide more support to this population of students. My path in this profession was a fluke and was something other than what I knew would be my calling. I obtained a Master's in Arts Entertainment & Media Management to become a record producer; I began in higher education as the assistant director of a Latinx cultural center at a large research institution in the midwest. Here, I found my circle, my mentor, and my calling. I found that it was imperative to not only be a voice at the table but that representation matters and to create equitable change for those of historically excluded communities; I needed to progress toward my terminal degree and learn how to navigate the politics of higher education.

I moved on to become a transfer center director at an inner-city community college on the south side of Chicago, where I increased my circle while understanding the need to advocate for students. I missed the residential campus experience and decided to leave my comfort zone and take on a position at a comprehensive regional university in Southern Colorado. At this institution, I realized my worth and the importance of living my values and finding an institution that aligned with my values. At this institution, I also remembered my purpose: to ensure that leadership remembers that diversity should be more than a symbolic gesture or statement that an institution relays. Justice, Equity, Diversity, Belonging, and Inclusion should be a fabric of every part of the institution. These values embrace people from all walks of life and validate those experiences to ensure academic success. I am committed to building this community on and off campus and ensuring that any campus I am a part of supports and respects the values of Justice, Equity, Diversity, Belonging, and Inclusion. These values are critical to building a more just society and campus community. By having diverse beliefs, backgrounds, political convictions, religious beliefs, gender identity, sexual preferences, race, ethnicity, and other identities, we will build a community that encompasses the world's diversity. I seek to improve the campus climate of any institution I am a part of by creating shared learning experiences and equitable policies, and building collaborative relationships that challenge barriers, bring forth diverse dialogue, and provide educational opportunities. As the assistant vice president for student affairs and Title IX coordinator at a small elite liberal arts college in Southern California, I aligned my values with the institutional mission, allowing me to live my mission. This insulation also allows me to use a theory that guides my practice: Rendon's theory of validation; according to Rendon's theory, "validation is an enabling, confirming and supportive process initiated by in- and out-of-class agents that fosters academic and interpersonal development" (Rendon, 1994, p. 44). My mission is to enable others to use their gifts and education to follow their passions and live a life full of integrity, purpose, and vision. My mission is also to be ethically guided and seek opportunities to bring about change on a campus of higher education while creating a space that addresses injustices occurring in the world.

As I reflect on my career trajectory through higher education, the most pivotal moments in my career were the opportunities I was given to make a difference not only in the lives of my students but in creating equity-minded policies to move the needle of success for students of historically excluded communities. During these moments, I could reflect on my values and understand the positionality I held at the institution while also acknowledging the barriers in my path. The greatest lesson I have learned during my career has been that for me to do my best work I need to be my authentic self; if an institution is making decisions that go against my values, ethics, and moral compass, it is time to discern for myself if I am able to do the work I was called to do, which is to to advocate and support students of historically excluded communities. A mentor once told me to take risks, be innovative, think critically and strategically, and create my seat at the table. There will be times when I had to choose my battles and discern if that is the moment for that specific discussion. Many times at the beginning of my career I stayed quiet out of fear of being wrong or because I was not seasoned enough. This has stayed with me throughout my career and if I could advise my younger self, I would say don't be afraid to take the leap and use your voice.

TONY JIMENEZ, PhD
(FIRST GENERATION COLLEGE GRADUATE RAISED 10 MINUTES FROM THE U.S./MEXICAN BORDER IN SOUTHERN CALIFORNIA.)

As I reflect on my professional journey, currently as the dean of students for Latinx students at a consortium of highly selective liberal arts colleges on the west coast, and my previous roles coordinating the MD/PhD program at a top public medical school in the Midwest and directing diversity STEM programs at top public research universities on the west coast, my mantra is to pay it forward. My journey began with my upbringing in San Diego, as Gloria Anzaldúa articulates in her seminole book Borderlands,

> The U.S.–Mexican border es una herida abierta where the Third World grates against the first and bleeds. And before a scab forms it hemorrhages again, the lifeblood of two worlds merging to form a third country—a border culture. (Anzaldúa 1987, p. 25)

Since I was a child, I have been straddling multiple worlds. I am the son of Mexican immigrants. My father has a second-grade education, while my mom did not have the opportunity to attend school. I was raised in the Barrio, ten minutes from Tijuana. In my community, gang violence, teenage pregnancy, and drug abuse were sadly the norm. Even though higher education was not a foregone conclusion, my parents sheltered my two siblings and me. We all went to college. My journey began as an undergraduate student at a top public university in Northern California, which led me to gain admission to a social policy program in the graduate school of education at an Ivy League university. I finished my doctoral studies at a large public research university in the Midwest.

When I began my path in higher education in the mid-nineties, law school seemed the likely career trajectory. During this time, I was exposed to student affairs professionals and the difference they made in the lives of first-generation and low-income students like myself. This period was a highly political time in higher education. The Regents of the University of California and later the voters of California voted to eliminate affirmative action programs in higher education. I took this personally since Latinos and African American students were grossly underrepresented in higher education, and we were told by those in leadership positions that we did not belong (Morfin et al., 2006). Even though I was a freshman then, the social climate shifted my path to keeping the pipeline open and creating opportunities for those that would come after me.

As an undergraduate, the genesis of my student affairs career began as a work-study student in Admissions, the Education Opportunities Program (EOP), and volunteering at a rural public school in a farm working community. These positions allowed me to reach out to high school students in East Los Angeles, San Diego, and farm-working communities on the Central Coast of California. Keeping access to higher education was personal, and I would not allow misguided policies to exclude those of us in the periphery. In my graduate school years, I continued this commitment to working with high school students who were immigrants from Cape Verde and the Dominican Republic in an urban public high school in the North East and mentoring BIPOC undergraduate students in summer research programs in the Midwest. I knew my calling was to be an agent of change in Student Affairs.

When I was ABD (*all but dissertation*), I was encouraged by my mentor to seek faculty positions. However, I felt I could make a bigger impact as a clinician. Since this was my path, friends, colleagues, and faculty encouraged me to seek mid-level positions that would provide a stable income and be a leader. Even though I listened to their advice, I decided to start at an entry-level position to conceptualize this profession's complexity and diverse components fully. At the time, people thought I was foolish to seek a position below "my training" and the degrees on my wall. However, I needed to understand how student affairs from all levels functioned and how they can help or hinder student success. My first position was in graduate diversity at the school of engineering at a large public university on the beach in the west coast. The salary was low, the hours were long, and the cost of living had me living in poverty. Even though I had read about student development theory in graduate school, what mattered to leadership was results. Theory went out the door. Where I went to school did not matter. My role was to create PhD pathways to communities that had been traditionally underrepresented in STEM. I humbled myself and sought support from student affairs professionals. I did not have all the answers, but the drive to make a difference. My mentors in my first position came from all levels with decades of experience. Their pearls of wisdom laid the foundation for me to be a leader in student affairs. The lesson that I learned from my first position is to be humble. Your degrees may provide theoretical knowledge, but practical knowledge is what matters. Get your hands and feet dirty. Don't think that any job is beneath you or your expertise is based on courses that you have taken. My first position in this profession allowed me to see how organizational structures function from all levels and how critical student affairs professionals are as we prepare students to be the best version of themselves. Experience matters! To this date, some of my mentors in student affairs don't have graduate degrees, but their lived experience has allowed me to be a better leader in my current role as Dean of Students. This initial training led me to a bittersweet experience as an administrator at a medical school in the Midwest.

My career trajectory has been a roller coaster ride; the most consequential experience was also one of the toughest. As a coordinator of an MD/PhD program in a college of medicine, I was one of two Latino administrators. My background was not validated; I was implicitly encouraged not to ask questions, assimilate, be silent, and do my job. As a male of color, my colleagues never fully embraced me, but I used the opportunity to hone in on my skill sets and learn the complex nature of medical school admissions. During this arduous moment in my career, where I felt that support was minimal, I learned valuable lessons. One, be the best at what you do. Learn and see the bigger picture, even if you feel no support. The second lesson I learned is that even with difficult colleagues and a lack of direction, I use this as an opportunity to interact with challenging personalities. Be professional and resilient in the toughest of environments. What does not kill you makes you stronger.

What resulted in this opportunity was a new, highly sought-after skill-sets that allowed me to create medical school pathways for BIPOC (*Black, Indigenous and people of color*) students in my current position. Even though my second position posed many professional challenges, I was able to grow and learn and get an inside look at how to increase diversity in a field where Latinx and African Americans make up a small percentage of physicians.

This difficult experience taught me that what we learn as professionals can significantly impact the lives of our students and those they heal in their journeys. As part of my current role, I have assisted countless diverse students in being successful applicants to some of the premier medical and graduate schools. This is only possible with the lessons learned from my second position in student affairs. The lesson I learned is when you are in complex environments that do not acknowledge or validate your background or diverse perspective, use it as a laboratory and how to be a better leader and see the bigger picture on the impact of your work. In my case, I was passionate about broadening and increasing access to medical school for BIPOC students. The wealth of knowledge that I acquired has been a game-changer in my career. The sacrifices and the toxic work environment taught me how to lead and how leaders can positively or negatively impact those they are responsible for guiding. What I can deduce from this experience is that sometimes you can learn from bad leaders since they teach you how their actions or lack thereof can impact those they attempt to supervise. If I had the opportunity to advise my younger self, dedication and a strong work ethic matters, but speaking up is also essential. Be humble but be assertive. See the bigger picture and ask yourself the why, the what, and the how. Why am I doing this? What is the impact? What is the bigger picture? How can I be an agent of change? In 2007 I took a significant leap in being a student affairs professional in STEM. Even though the learning curve was steep, I became a leader in this arena, allowing me to advocate for BIPOC students.

RECOMMENDATIONS FOR NEW PROFESSIONALS

To culminate this chapter, we would like to give recommendations and advice for those entering the profession. The first piece of advice we could give future student affairs leaders would be to seek mentors who will celebrate them and provide critical feedback. No matter how great you are, failure is part of the process; seek guidance and reflection. A true mentor will not reprimand but teach and provide guidance with honesty and empathy. Also, it's a small world. People talk. Do your best, even if you think you need help finding someone. You are being noticed, and your strong work ethic will pay off. Looking back at our careers, we identified one key component that has brought us to this moment. We each found someone who invested their time, energy, advice, and commitment to our personal and professional growth. Finding a mentor who turns into your advocate and, ultimately, your friend is one of the essential pieces of advice we can share with new professionals. The second piece of advice is to be bold and take risks. Get out of your comfort zone. Doing so will make you an expert in areas you never thought possible. Today, our colleagues seek our expertise on issues of graduate STEM diversity and diversifying medical school admissions. We do not possess a degree in science, but we both have a social/educational policy background. Third, take risks in your career and leave your comfort zone. Getting out of your comfort zone will be rough and, at times, painful, but it will make you stronger and empathetic to diverse perspectives. Sometimes playing it safe may seem comfortable, but it will stunt your growth. We invite you to take calculated risks and be comfortable being uncomfortable.

REFERENCES

Anzaldúa, G. (1987). *Borderlands = la frontera: The New Mestiza*. Aunt Lute Books.

Morfin, O. J., Perez, V. H., Parker, L., Lynn, M., & Arrona, J. (2006). Hiding the politically obvious: A critical race theory preview of diversity as racial neutrality in higher education. *Educational Policy, 20*(1), 249–270. https://doi.org/10.1177/0895904805285785

Rendon, L. I., (1994). Validating culturally diverse students: Toward a new model of learning and student development. *Innovative Higher Education, 19*, 33–51. http://dx.doi.org/10.1007/BF01191156

CHAPTER 8

BEING PREPARED

How to Navigate the Course When Embarking on the Academic Leadership Journey

Karen Marie Wagner-Clarke

ABSTRACT

Leadership is a discipline widely accepted as a crucial factor in an organization's success, mediocrity, or failure (Collins, 2001; March & Weil, 2005; Northouse, 2015; Ruben, 2012). It is no different in higher education, where the impact of leaders and leadership is vital to administrative effectiveness and academic success. However, when considering leadership in higher education (HE), some contexts are, in some sense, unique to the college and university settings. For example, distributed leadership and shared governance traditions designate formal and informal leadership roles and delegate powers to faculty and staff members within committees, senates, task forces, departments, and other governing and decision-making bodies. This democratic leadership paradigm allows diverse academic voices, perspectives, and opinions. It taps many's knowledge, wisdom, and experience within the collegiate arena to identify challenges, communicate varied thoughts, promote collective decisions, share resources, and prescribe remedies institution-wide. It also creates meaningful opportunities across the academic landscape.

OVERVIEW

This chapter begins with a review of academic leadership, focusing primarily on the shared governance/distributed leadership framework germane to HE institutions. It continues with the genesis of my faculty journey in HE, highlights my academic leadership endeavors, shares reflections on my quest, and concludes with some strategies for consideration.

The hope is that the shared methods provide a helpful framework for leadership practitioners across higher education. In addition, the key concepts raised and recommendations provided in this chapter may prove beneficial for aspiring and emerging leaders preparing to navigate the HE leadership journey of continuous learning, growth, and development.

PRELUDE

Being a leader in academia is a pursuit that requires ongoing preparation and constant improvement. It is vital to meet the demands of the "disruptive" and "dramatic changes in the higher education landscape," which have affected the "nature of requirements" for higher education leadership (Ruben et al., 2017, p. 5). To meet these current requirements, HE leaders must possess vast collegiate knowledge and professional and personal competencies necessary to translate these capabilities routinely and effectively into practice (Ruben et al., 2017). They must also be constantly upgrading their capabilities; consequently, aspiring HE leaders should consider leadership a transformative journey of growth and development on a continuum. The voyage can be challenging but most effective and rewarding when it is a deliberate, focused, systematic, and reflective experience.

ACADEMIC LEADERSHIP

There is no shortage of ways to contemplate or define leadership, as proven in countless books, articles, and journals; however, one typically considers leadership as reserved for those in formal roles and positions of authority. Similarly, many popular perceptions of leadership reinforce an impression of a heroic figure at the top of the hierarchy, far from the traditional '*primus inter pares—first among equals*' and shared governance and democratic conception of academic structure and leadership. Instead, HE has a unique and systematic approach where leadership responsibility is dissociated from formal institutional roles. As a result, many perform informal and distributed forms of leadership within and across the academic arena.

Many HE managerial tasks are reserved for those who do not hold official or designated leadership roles at a relatively senior level (Macfarlane, 2011; Ruben et al., 2017; Tight, 2014). This inclusive practice of leadership promotes a shift in focus from the traits and roles of 'leaders' to the shared activities and functions of 'leadership' (Bowen & Tobin, 2015; Göksoy, 2015). In addition, it allows for recasting academic protocols and acknowledging leadership activities of faculty and professional services staff regardless of formal line management responsibilities, functions, or roles.

Case in Point: In an HE institution, typically, leadership is integral to many's daily activities and interactions. It is cross-functional and occurs at various levels, irrespective of titles and formal positions. These ongoing leadership actions are often revealed via small, incremental, informal, and emergent acts and within the large-scale transformational change from formal leaders with such titles as directors, department heads, faculty deans, chairs, and assistant chairs.

For example, leadership exercise and influence often occur at the micro, meso, or macro level.

- At the *micro* level, leadership is experienced by chairing the faculty senate, managing a committee, hosting meetings with colleagues, or leading a training class or seminar/webinar.
- At the *meso* level, leadership is exercised by designing class modules and curricula, orienting other faculty, or instructing team members on modules or course goals.
- At the *macro* level, leaders influence an entire university/college, department, function, faculty, or discipline.

This methodology broadens the scope and scale of leadership. Also, it defers from the stereotypical titles and contexts typically affiliated with formally designated leadership positions. Furthermore, it recognizes staff at all levels as integral to the institution's mission and vision. Finally, it allows those other than formal leaders to collaborate and influence a college or university's overall direction and functioning. The emphasis is on individual competence and expertise rather than position/title.

Relevance: Why Begin With an Overview of Academic Leadership?

It is germane because it is the beginning of my academic leadership journey, which has, to date, resulted in various collegiate leadership tasks and responsibilities. The shared governance methodology at the university has afforded different leadership roles that are not from a 'heroic' view at the top but rather from a distributed and democratic leadership philosophy and methodology. Moreover, its application has allowed faculty like me to serve in diverse leadership functions and projects that would otherwise likely be unavailable, at least not for one who is an adjunct professor. As Goleman (2002) declares, "There are many leaders, not just one. Leadership is distributed. It resides not solely in the individual at the top, but in every person at entry level who, in one way or another, acts as a leader" (p. 14). This approach is vital in HE as the academic community works collaboratively so that the institution can benefit from the leadership of multiple people to impart positive change.

GENESIS

My service in higher education at a private, nonprofit, nonsectarian, accredited institution began over a decade ago. Since embarking on this journey, I have served as a faculty member in various leadership roles, including spearheading the following projects/initiatives: coaching and mentoring new adjunct faculty, heading a project bridge task force, chairing the faculty senate, and leading a project team that redesigns undergraduate and graduate leadership and business courses. In lesser leadership roles, I also serve as an advisory committee member in the Doctor of Education (EdD) organizational leadership and innovation (OLI) program and as a dissertation advisor for EdD OLI students. These administrative leadership roles have collectively afforded special access to HE, its framework, underpinnings, strategies, and agendas that the early years as solely faculty did not provide.

ACADEMIC LEADERSHIP JOURNEY

My passion has always been in academia and learning. After receiving a Master of Science in organizational leadership (MSoL), I decided it was the right time to embark on the academic instruction journey and enter the HE arena as an adjunct faculty. From the onset, I realized to be most effective in the role required being proactive in furthering my collegiate knowledge, skills, abilities, and other characteristics (KSAOs) and enhancing my instruction and classroom management skills. After all, the aim has always been to engage students in the classroom, boost their learning experience, and ensure academic success on a continuum. So, from the first month of employment, I enrolled in the institution's professional development program aimed at instructional excellence for all faculty members. It included participating in various workshops, seminars, webinars, lunch and learn programs, and capitalizing on every learning and development opportunity the university offers. I was, as a result, one of the first five participants to swiftly propel through the "Pathway to Instructional Excellence" (PIE) program and complete the four stages—essential, proficient, mastery, exemplary—to achieve the ultimate exemplary teaching status. Additionally, I attended every faculty development program offered by the University's Center for Teaching Excellence and participated in most faculty-related university events. Today, I am still highly proactive in the university's learning and development workshops and initiatives.

Also, it is essential to note that I deemed it best to further my academic scholarship after embarking on the HE instruction journey. Consequently, I pursued a doctorate in education—organizational leadership and innovation (EdD OLI)—approximately eight months later. These endeavors and experiences further developed my teaching and learning competencies and augmented my experiences. They also improved my requisite capabilities for leadership excellence. These efforts did not go unnoticed! When it was realized by some key leadership players—including the university's academic directors, deans, and chairs—that I was highly proactive in the institution's learning and development initiatives and embarking on a doctorate in education, I was offered many tasks and assignments outside the traditional faculty role. Fortunately, it resulted in various formal and informal leadership positions/responsibilities discussed prior.

My leadership journey continues!

REFLECTION

Being a HE educator and leader calls for me to (a) frequently engage in metacognitive exercises, (b) actively probe cause and effect, (c) regularly question assumptions, and (d) reflect deeply on my andragogy. I deem it a valuable practice to determine what strategies and resources can be imparted to be best prepared for the demands of the HE profession.

To that end, it is difficult to understate the importance of actively probing causes and effects and engaging in reflective practices for learning. As the famous American educator John Dewey (1998) states, "We do not learn from experience...we learn from reflecting on experience" (p. 46).

Accordingly, looking back and reflecting on myself as an HE leader, I share the following advice from my experiences.

Building and Maintaining a Robust Professional Network is Vital

Networking is an extremely valuable component in professional leadership growth and development. As progress in the collegiate leadership arena continues, there is a realization of how vital it is to cultivate a robust network—internal & external—to rely on for coaching, mentorship, ideas, concepts, feedback, support, and guidance. Networking allows additional access to resources, tools, and information and helps to foster learning by connecting with others with different skills, varied perspectives, and relative contexts. It also offers exposure to new opportunities that drive personal and professional growth and success. If I had known then what I know now, I would have been highly proactive in networking.

Why? The view is that others who actively networked and broadened their social circles increased their visibility dramatically, made more impactful connections, and boosted their leadership prospects and opportunities at the institution, much more than I did in the past.

As Ibarra and Hunter (2007) assert, "Aspiring leaders must learn to build and use strategic networks that cross organizational and functional boundaries, and then link them up in novel and innovative ways" (p. 47). I advise rigorously networking (internally & externally) to increase visibility, make impactful connections, improve career growth, and accelerate your leadership journey!

STRATEGIES FOR SUCCESS

As discussed earlier, HE leadership roles require considerable collegiate knowledge and proficiency in a wide array of generic competencies and expertise specific to HE and, often, about a particular position. The reason is that, in many instances, leadership decisions and approaches directly impact the institution's future, either positively or negatively. Thus, an investment in self is warranted to learn and develop on a continuum. Moreover, it is a sound approach to becoming an asset to an institution, its mission, and its vision.

Accordingly, it is best to have a strategic personal leadership development plan (PLDP) and roadmap for success when entering the HE arena and embarking on a leadership journey.

After all, "Leadership is the capacity to translate vision into reality through planning" (Bennis, 2009, p. 188). It is a critical process for moving forward with intentionality and purpose.

Strategy #1: Clarifying Your Leadership Philosophy

A sound approach to leadership development starts with gaining clarity regarding personal and professional aspirations. Therefore, the first step is recognizing your view of an effective leader and clarifying your leadership philosophy. Step two is identifying exemplars and thoughtfully analyzing the type of leader you desire to become.

Recommendation
Ask yourself the following questions:

- What is my vision of leadership?
- What type of leader do I aspire to be?
- What is (or will be) my leadership brand?
- What are (or will be) my unique leadership qualities—competency, integrity, transparency, honesty, accommodating, inspiration, supportive?
- What do I anticipate/desire to be my leadership legacy?

These fundamental questions could help clarify your leadership vision and philosophy and serve as guideposts in the leadership development journey.

After clarifying the leadership philosophy, the suggestion is to create a personal mission and vision statement. Similar to a corporate mission and vision statement, the aim is to guide the development efforts and link the leadership initiatives with your long-term personal and professional goals. **n.b.** Ensuring that the steps taken to improve your leadership skills align with your mission and vision is crucial.

Strategy #2: Conducting a Self-Assessment

Many PLDPs are prefaced by self-evaluations, leadership inventories, and personality assessments to highlight motivations and strengths and identify areas for improvement. By conducting self-assessments, you could be (a) building self-awareness, (b) understanding tendencies, (c) recognizing behavioral patterns and motivational drivers, and (d) gaining insights into your leadership competency and style.

Note: There are myriad relevant behavioral assessment and leadership inventories available online, such as 360° assessment tools, Campbell Leadership Descriptor, DiSC Personality Test, Emotional Intelligent Leadership Inventory, Myers–Briggs Type Indicator (MBTI), the Thomas–Kilmann Conflict Mode Instrument, Leadership Competency Scorecard 2.0, True

Colors Personality Test, Leadership Practices Inventory (LPI), and Leadership Style Inventory (LSI). Determine the leadership assessments/inventories that will best suit your needs!

Recommendation

List ten to 15 essential leadership traits/characteristics.

Note: The characteristics should be a combination of HE-specific and general leadership qualities & competencies. Generating a traits inventory will aid in assessing your skills and strengths. Some of the characteristics on the list may require professional and personal growth and are, therefore, worth including in your development plan. Other traits may be core strengths that warrant noting but will be a low priority for further development.

Please note that successful leaders have many qualities in common, so it should be relatively easy to identify which traits are strengths and which will require improvements.

Strategy #3: Committing to Developing as a Leader

Developing as a leader, in my view, is individual ownership. The emphasis is on personal agency, as I do not buy into the notion that an organization or employer is responsible for one's leadership growth and development. This commitment to developing and becoming a leader (or better leader) is a lifelong practice that requires ownership (yours), intent, discipline, and a mindful engagement process reinforced by the following:

(a) Approach: Developing a learning mindset approach,
(b) Action: Engaging in learning behaviors, and
(c) Reflection: Ensuring reflective practices on a continuum, as highlighted in Figure 8.1.

Through this mindful engagement reflective practice, you can revisit your leadership philosophy and self-assessment findings to assess continuing gaps, track progress on these areas that will benefit from improvement and identify new areas needing attention and development.

Strategy #4: Creating and Establishing a PLDP

The three previous strategies are the foundation for strategy #4—Creating a clear, realistic, thoughtful, action-oriented, and time-bound PLDP.

A PLDP is a detailed roadmap to strategically guide one's career growth and professional development toward advanced leadership roles and senior

Being Prepared • 73

Figure 8.1 The mindful engagement process. *Source:* Adapted from Ashford & DeRue, 2012, p. 149.

management positions. The goal of the plan is to develop one's leadership competence and capacity further, increase intrapersonal awareness, and augment interpersonal effectiveness.

Since the document is personal, it should be in a style and format that best suits your needs. For example, it can be in the form of a spreadsheet, table, or chart. However, no matter the design, there are key criteria that every PLDP should include:

- A personal mission and vision statement (identified & discussed earlier). It is the most vital aspect of a PLDP, as it sets the overall theme for the professional development goals desired to be accomplished.
- Identified areas for development/improvement
- SMART goals with specific milestones and clear timelines
- (SMART goals are **S**pecific, **M**easurable, **A**ttainable, **R**ealistic & **T**ime-Bound)
- Specific action steps that can be measured periodically
- Established metrics to measure success
- Regular assessments and evaluations of the plan and refine/update as needed

Creating a fluid working document will help bridge the gap between your current and desired future state. To that end, how you craft and work the plan will determine how effectively you create and grow your capacity for personal and professional success in the future.

As John Maxwell (2018) states, "If you want to lead, you need to grow. Great Leaders are always great learners" (p. 76). The four shared strategies will augment enrolling in a leadership development program, a critical element of a comprehensive development plan. By integrating professional leadership development training into the process, you will be making the most out of opportunities for consistent career progress, developing leadership excellence, and being confident as you step into new roles or face different challenges.

IN SUMMARY

Leadership is a skill that must be honed and requires continuous development for excellence. Therefore, if you want to become a better leader, commit to continue developing your leadership skills and attributes. It is what transforms good leaders into great ones!

The work as a HE leader is rigorous and relentless but essential. So, as you launch your leadership journey in higher education, I will reiterate the following words once shared by a mentor: "Leading in the collegiate landscape is a journey often riddled with many challenges; however, it is fun... And now, you will get to truly see and experience how an institution of higher education works."

REFERENCES

Ashford, S. J., & DeRue, D. S. (2012). Developing as a leader: The power of mindful engagement. *Organizational Dynamics, 41*(2), 146–154. https://doi.org/10.1016/j.orgdyn.2012.01.008

Bennis, W. (2009). *On becoming a leader*. Basic Books.

Bowen, W. G., & Tobin, E. M. (2015). *Locus of authority: The evolution of faculty roles in the governance of higher education* 1st ed. (The William G. Bowen Series, 83). Princeton University Press.

Collins, J. (2001). *Good to great. Why some companies make the leap... and others don't*. Harper Business.

Dewey, J. (1998). *Experience and education: The 60th anniversary issue*. Kappa Delta Pi.

Goleman, D. (2002). *The new leaders: Transforming the art of leadership into the science of results*. Little Brown Book Group.

Göksoy, S. (2015). Distributed leadership in educational institutions. *Journal of Education and Training Studies, 3*(4), 110–118. https://doi.org/10.11114/jets.v3i4.851

Ibarra, H., & Hunter, M. L. (2007). How Leaders Create and Use Networks. *Harvard Business Review, 85*(1), 40–7, 124. https://hbr.org/2007/01/how-leaders-create-and-use-networks

Macfarlane, B. (2011). Professors as intellectual leaders: Formation, identity and role. *Studies in Higher Education, 36* (1), 57–73. doi:10.1080/03075070903443734

Maxwell, J. C. (2018). *Developing the leader within you 2.0—All new for today's generation of leaders.* Nashville, TN: Harper Collins.
March, J. G., & Weil, T. (2005). *On leadership.* Malden, MA: Blackwell.
Northouse, P. G. (2015). *Leadership: Theory and practice* (7th ed.). Thousand Oaks, CA: Sage.
Ruben, B. D. (2012). *What leaders need to know and do: A leadership competencies scorecard* (2nd ed). Washington, DC: National Association of College and University Business Officers.
Ruben, B. D., De Lisi, R., & Ralph A. Gigliotti, R. A. (2017). *A guide for leaders in higher education: Concepts, competencies, and tools.* Sterling, VA: Stylus
Tight, M. (2014). Collegiality and managerialism: A false dichotomy? Evidence from the higher education literature. *Tertiary Education and Management, 20*(4), 294–306. doi.org/10.1080/13583883.2014.956788

CHAPTER 9

WHITE PEOPLE EXPLAIN THINGS TO ME

Experiences and Recommendations on Surviving "Know-Your-Place Aggression"

Amir Asim Gilmore

ABSTRACT

As a Black academic, White people explain things to me. Sometimes, it is for my benefit. Other times, it is to remind me of my "proper place" within academia. This American phenomenon and ritual of Black people being put into their place is known as *know-your-place aggression*. As a violent yet mundane exercise of power, know-your-place aggression operates as an *absurd drama* continuously staged around you, where power-laden social processes erase Black subjectivity and *phenomenologically return* your body as inferior. I wrote this chapter out of a personal existential context to expose this aggression. Through my two vignettes, I (a) highlight why the phenomenological return occurs in academia and what it does to the Black body, (b) analyze this return through two vignettes of know-your-place aggression, and (c) provide self-care recommendations on how to survive the encounters.

OVERVIEW OF PREVIOUS POSITIONS HELD WITHIN ACADEMIC AFFAIRS

In my earlier academic positions, I was a clinical professor for Cultural Studies and Social Thought in Education (CSSTE) at Washington State University (WSU). Currently, I am a tenure-track assistant professor at WSU, and within the College of Education, I am the associate dean of equity and inclusion for student success and retention (ADEISSR).

VENTURE INTO THE STRANGE JOURNEY OF KNOWING-YOUR-PLACE

> *I remain as much as a stranger today as I was the first day I arrived.*
> —James Baldwin (2012)

Strange. That word encapsulates my non-traditional pathway to academic leadership. At 32-years-old, I am four years removed from defending my dissertation and three years into the tenure-track process—all at the same institution. I was appointed as the ADEISSR after my first year on the tenure track. My initial appointment began, like many others, during a time when faculty, staff, and students nationwide demanded racial justice in the wake of the extrajudicial killings of Ahmaud Arbery, Breonna Taylor, George Floyd, Sean Reed, and Tony McDade. The ending of my appointment coincides with a time when right-wing "free speech" advocates harness juridical-political power to intrude, curtail, and eliminate equity-oriented practices and academic freedom (see Idaho, Texas, and Florida). Strange times. With many academic institutions retreating from DEI work because they are prohibited, intimidated by current political pressures, or reached the threshold of performative activism (see Penn State's Center for Racial Justice), a part of me was elated/surprised to be re-appointed as the ADEISSR. Despite the congratulatory emails about my re-appointment, Baldwin's (2012) poignant words remain with me. Within academia, my *universal strangeness* (Ahmed, 2012) is not necessarily due to external political phenomenon, but a phenomenon buttressed by White spatial logics, rendering my Black body as incongruous and incomprehensible. I am here to describe the multilayered phenomenon: *White people explain things to me.*

Lemme tell you sum, as a Black academic leader, *White people explain things to me* for a myriad of reasons. Sometimes it is to supply me with institutional and cultural knowledge (read: put me on game). On "good" days, it is to highlight my successes and contributions to sell the appearance of a racially harmonious institution (Osei-Kofi, Torres, & Lui, 2013). On "bad" days, it is to accuse declining enrollment, the lack of academic rigor, and students' heightened sensitives on wokeness. All other days, White people explain things to me to remind me of my "proper place" within academia. The violent phenomena and ritual of knowing-your-place is a well-known U.S. tradition. Mitchell (2018) defined *know-your-place aggression* as a

> flexible, dynamic array of forces that answer the achievements of marginalized groups such that their success brings aggression as often as praise. Any progress by those who are not straight, White, and male is answered by a backlash of violence—both literal and symbolic, both physical and discursive. (p. 253)

Never be surprised by the sheer propensity of White people wanting to put you in your place—it is a therapeutic healing balm for the White psyche (Wilderson, 2020). U.S. history is full of examples (e.g., chattel slavery, Jim Crow segregation, state, and White vigilante violence), and there is no shortage of examples, even in recent memory. From disgruntled White voters hanging effigies of President Barack Obama (Mitchell, 2018), Lebron James told to "shut up and dribble" (Sullivan, 2018), Serena Williams, Sha'Carri Richardson, and Angel Reese needing to be humbled for their on-the-court "antics" (Victoria, 2023), to Tennessee state representatives Justin Jones and Justin Pearson undemocratically expelled for protesting with their constituents on gun rights (Wolfe & Razek, 2023), White people feel obligated (read: entitled) to put Black people in their place. Black presence and success, no matter its size or subtly, beckons and legitimizes violence. Know-your-place aggression exists as an apparatus of White domination to check you, teach you a lesson, and return you to a place where White people feel comfortable: beneath them. It delivers the message that you are "still just a..." (Mitchell, 2018, p. 258).

Those aspiring to be Black higher education leaders must understand that they will be targeted by know-your-place aggression. *White people will explain things to you* because Black leadership is outside the normative realm of occupational space (Yancy, 2005). The violence trafficked to you is not a matter of if but when and how often, as this ritualization is like a *fucked-up rite of passage* for Black academics. Davis' (2021) hashtag #BlackInTheIvory denuded the banality of structural racial violence levied against Black academics through know-your-place aggression as commonplace (Mustaffa, 2017). The violence will be justified and met from afar with incredulity, condolences, and naivete by White colleagues remarking "'focus on the positive,' 'give the benefit of the doubt,' '[they] didn't mean it,' and 'it was just a joke'" (Mitchell, 2018, p. 261). White academic culture teaches you what your reaction to this aggression should be: to expect it, accommodate it, and live with it (Marable, 2000). Under the guise of collegiality and civility, White people craft distorted rules of engagement that foreclose the Black body as other and solidify violent White epistemological ways of knowing and being. As Chafe (1980) reminds us, "civility within a context of oppression simply provides a veneer for more oppression" (p. 355). These asymmetric power relations conceal their deep-seated core values and enshrine notions of objectivity, neutrality, innocence, and even insolence, as virtuous intellectual standards. Therefore, White people explain things to me is not a singular event, like Whitesplaining, but an *absurd drama continuously staged around you* (Fanon, 1967), where power-laden social processes erase Black subjectivity and *phenomenologically returns* (Yancy, 2005) the Black body as inferior. We must expose this phenomenon to help mitigate the instances of it.

Consequently, I write this chapter out of a personal existential context—from a *site of exposure* (Yancy, 2005) because "the Black body is a battleground" (Yancy, 2008, p. 1) in academia. I write out of obligation to center my raced lived embodied experience as "a profound source of knowledge" (Yancy, 2005, p. 215) because U.S. society has maligned Black people as unreliable witnesses to our experiences. Being subjected to know-your-place aggression, I offer my testimonies, not to shame, but to vocalize this violence phenomenon and expose the status quo. Mitchell (2018) assiduously stated that, "know-your-place aggression shapes outcomes for all Americans—both those who are put in their "proper" place and those whose success is supported." Therefore, this conversation is also necessary for air hustlin' White academics who are perpetrators of the violence, allies of the afflicted, and bystanders actively letting others suffer. Moreover, if you are more concerned about me writing about the ways of Whiteness rather than how Whiteness has harmed me or Black academics, check your *epistemological ignorance* (Mills, 1997). By refusing to challenge these power dynamics, you become a perpetrator's best ally, rewarding them with comfort and status (Mitchell, 2018). Towards these ends, this reflective chapter will (a) highlight why the phenomenological return (Yancy, 2005) occurs in academia and what it does to the Black body, (b) analyze this return through two vignettes of know-your-place aggression, and (c) provide self-care recommendations on how to survive the encounters.

BLACK BODIES, WHITE SPACES: THE PHENOMENOLOGICAL RETURN OF THE BLACK BODY

What happens when those embodied differently come to occupy spaces rarely occupied by them?
—Puwar, 2004, p. 141

Puwar's (2004) question illuminates Black spatial realities. The connection between race, space, place, and power has a profound history in the United

States, stemming from discriminatory policies and practices of displacement, dispossession, and removal (Lipsitz, 2007). Due to strict demarcations of racialized hierarchies structured by White supremacy (Mills, 1997) and anti-Blackness (Wilderson, 2020; Jenkins, 2021), Black people are excluded from specific spaces and relegated to others. Therefore, Black people inherit social worlds rife with geographies of unequal opportunities (Lipsitz, 2011). Thus, to be Black in the United States is to exist in spaces never designed for you. Your Black body do not fit the White spaces you must navigate as a condition of your existence (Anderson, 2015). This spatial mismatch is situated by juxtaposing particular bodies within racially defined spaces (Jenkins, 2021). Within higher education, this dissonance caused by the presence of Blackness is consequential to Black people's career trajectories and leadership opportunities because it (a) limits them to occupations that White people find "suitable" for the Black body (Yancy, 2005), (b) forces them to acquiesce to racial subordination, or (c) jettisons them from career-advancing opportunities altogether.

Bodies nor spaces are neutral entities, as both are situated by shifting socio-historical constructions of race (and gender, dis/ability) and operate in tandem, contouring racialized people's "imaginations, about access to and the utility of certain spaces" (Jenkins, 2021, p. 110) (e.g., quality schools, housing, healthcare, and employment). Further, privileged positions of authority (e.g., academic leadership) have been reserved for specific bodies through racialized processes of domination, power, and exclusion (Puwar, 2004). Therefore, race is significant in deciding the space's ownership, its demography, and characteristics. The spatial logics of White supremacy and anti-Blackness provide White people the unalienable right to govern spaces and people and be normalized within those spaces. This inheritance grants White people the *reachability of the world* (Ahmed, 2007), structuring the Whiteness' spatial residence and reproduction as a moral good. Therefore, White people can never be strangers because institutions are shaped to their image and likeness. This is evident as most university presidents are primarily White (Ray, 2019) and academic hierarchies are profoundly stratified by race, as 2% of all tenured professors in the country are Black (NCES, 2021). The accumulation of White bodies allows White people to own a state of *normative absence* (Yancy, 2008). Possessing an implicit power and moral authority that Black people fundamentally lack (Anderson, 2015), White people can transcend their racialized bodies, easily move through spaces, and assume positions as the universal voice of reason. This movement is impossible by the Black body because it is a *particular body* (Gordon, 1997). Marked with a racial particularity, Black academics are viewed as race specialists that offer *minority discourse* (Puwar, 2004) to the university. The paternalistic message that is conveyed from White institutions to Black academics is, "you do that 'race stuff,' but leave the *real* leadership to us." As such, Black academics are designated and tight casted to leadership opportunities centered on race/racism, social justice, and DEI work. Thus, the act of inclusion of Black academics in leadership positions is structured to maintain exclusion (Ahmed, 2012), because we are appointed to positions that the institution believes we are best suited for.

The arrival and residence of Black bodies in White spaces disrupts the homogeneity of Whiteness (Anderson, 2015; Jenkins, 2021), creating abnormalities *(look, a negro)*. Defying historical and conceptual norms, Black academic leaders threaten the status quo by displacing the White body's exclusivity as the authority figure (Puwar, 2004). As such, the Black body cannot be universal. The totalizing White gaze (Yancy, 2005) forecloses the Black body as a problem, non-human, and spatially illegitimate (Jenkin, 2021). Foreclosed by White ideas of Blackness (Yancy, 2005), the White gaze beckons violence toward the Black body, erasing its ways of knowing and being. The White gaze invades the Black body, reconfigures it to its liking, and returns it as something else: *a nigger*. This ritual, this phenomenological return (Yancy, 2005), reduces the Black body as inferior—a plaything that "must learn to live with mediocrity and accept [their] place within the 'natural' order of things" (p. 231). This violation attacks, wounds, and scars Black intelligence, ability, and character, but above all else, destroys your way of seeing yourself. The slippage between a Black person's embodied experience and how White people understand/construct/ experience/ see that Black person (Yancy, 2005) creates the emergence of an existence gone wrong, a universal stranger. Ahmed (2012) described being a stranger as "an experience of not being White . . . the one who is recognized as 'out of place,' the one who does not belong" (p. 2). These internalized experiences of exclusion and alienation force Black people into constant surveillance and self-interrogation. The "I am" becomes "Am I?" as anti-Black racism becomes a universal experience for the Black academic leaders. Below are two vignettes of phenomenological return that begs the question, what were they trying to explain to me?

"I HOPE THIS MAKES SENSE"

Years ago, the president's office appointed me to co-chair one of the five university-wide campus climate and culture working groups. The working groups emerged in response to students of color protesting against racism on campus. I co-chaired the working group on cultural competency and allyship training. Eventually, our work grew to creating a DEI strategic plan and our working group voted to tour various academic units to discuss institutional needs and priorities. I emailed various units stating our intentions, and that is when the shit fit the fan. I received an email from a

White senior administrator saying that DEI was under the auspices of their office and as a part of their "portfolio," such requests should come from them. The email concluded with the passive-aggressive phrase, "I hope this makes sense." I was angry and insulted. Our working group, not veiled in secrecy, spent many hours crafting a strategic plan, only to be eliminated with one email. The message delivered to me: it was tolerable to exert my labor towards DEI work, but you cannot take the lead (read: ownership). DEI leadership needed to come from a White administrator. Our working group encroached on this White senior administrator's authority as a DEI leader, which was impermissible. I was returned as less than, back where I belonged by a DEI leader—oh, the irony. The real "treat" was that the administrator was aware of the message's intent and sent a Black DEI administrator to "talk to me." The levels of causcity here: a White administrator sent a Black person to "check-in on me" based on something they sent because they felt threatened by a Black man doing DEI work. *What the actual fuck?* Reflecting on this moment, I am not sure how I kept my composure. I simply endured the moment because who I was supposed to talk about this? The administrator's supervisor? Within the university, there is no auditor for the know-your-place aggression levied towards Black people. Besides, I was a clinical professor on a one-year contract, I did not have the power to "make waves," nor did I want to jeopardize my career. If I reported this event, it would simply be reduced to a HR "workplace disagreement." From that day, I learned my lesson about my place.

"SO I DON'T HAVE TO HIRE A CLOWN?"

On my way to a meeting, I was approached by a faculty member about a situation dealing with accusations of racism from White students. Students of color felt antagonized and alienated. Conversations stalled, and morale was low. Unable to reconcile the situation, the faculty member looked at me, and jokingly said, "Amir, I do not know what to do. Do I have to hire a clown?" This was a visceral cut that only I could experience. Accusations of racism are not a clown matter, nor am I a clown. However, the question implicitly implied that. Knowing where this conversation was headed, I agreed to talk to the class about racism. Ecstatic, the faculty member responded, "Great, so I don't have to hire a clown?" Another cut. The message delivered was taking shape: *this is a joke*. I attended the class, ready to facilitate a discussion about racism, but the joke was on me. When I asked the students, "do you know why I am here?" I was mostly met with silence, something that I expected. The silence was broken by the faculty member saying, "Well, I brought him here because I think he's cute." The White students laughed. Another cut. I was publicly humiliated. The message was quite clear: *this was a joke.* Why hire a clown when you can make me into one? My body was invaded, distorted, and returned to me as something else: a nigger. White students learned that racial humiliation is permissible. Students of color learned that they, too must learn to live with this mediocrity (Yancy, 2005). I live with the shame of not speaking up in that moment. I could have "blown up" and caused a scene, but would have been the outcome of that? If you stand up for yourself, you are labeled as the angry Black man—a stereotype that lives with me because I know how the Black male body is *seen*. I know that I must work twice as hard to maximize the distance between you and the idea of you (Ahmed, 2012). As such as, I acquiesced to the moment and smiled through the pain. Could I have reported it? *Surely*, however, reporting an incident like this always carries a risk. A risk that your complaint backfires and more violence comes your way. You risk being labeled as *the problem* because you are exposing an issue that many will claim that does not exist at your institution (Ahmed, 2012). You risk jeopardizing your career—compelling you think, "is it really worth it?" So, what do you do in a situation like this? *I don't know*, however, I wish people were accountable of their words.

LOOKING BACK, WHAT ADVICE WOULD YOU SHARE WITH YOURSELF AS A NEW HIGHER EDUCATION LEADER? HAVE LESS GRACE

The advice I would share is that grace and forgiveness cannot be extended to everyone. Sometimes, people need to be held accountable for their misdeeds. Black forgiveness of White transgressions is a phenomenon layered by race and racism. We are continually praised for our capacities to endure racism and forgive, yet those same capacities are weaponized against us by egregious violators that never want to be held accountable. Conditioned preserving White social comfort, being ambivalent to racial microaggressions will devour you. Have less grace for White transgressions, demand higher standards, and save your soul.

ADVICE FOR FUTURE BLACK HIGHER EDUCATION LEADERS

As I close, I have three pieces of advice to share. **Number one**: *have a support network*. White supremacy and anti-Blackness do not take a day off from putting you in your place. Whether it is friends, family, or colleagues you can trust, you need a crew to ride the rough seas with you. **Bonus:** *if you can afford a therapist, get one*. **Number two:** *protect your energy*. You must name know-your-place-aggression to limit your energies around people and situations that will drain you. This will allow you to re-orient yourself in fulfilling ways and get work done. **Number three:** *rob White people of their naiveté.* Baldwin (2012) denoted that the White people keep Black people at a "certain human remove" (p. 170) because it preserves their simplicity and avoids accountability. When targeted by know-your-place aggression, promptly ask, "why do you feel comfortable doing/saying this to me?" The redirection orients the gaze from you onto the structures and people trying to dispossess you of your humanity.

REFERENCES

Ahmed, S. (2007). A phenomenology of Whiteness. *Feminist Theory, 8*(2), 149–168.
Ahmed, S. (2012). *On being included: Racism and diversity in institutional life.* Duke University Press.
Anderson, E. (2015). The White space. *Sociology of Race and Ethnicity, 1*(1), 10–21.
Baldwin, J. (2012). *Notes of a native son.* Beacon Press.
Chafe, W. H (1980). *Civilities and civil rights: Greensboro, North Carolina, and the Black struggle for freedom.* Oxford University Press.
Davis, S. M. (2021). *The creator.* Black In The Ivory. https://blackintheivory.net/creator
Fanon, F. (1967). *Black skin, White masks.* Grove.
Gordon, L. R. (1995). *Black faith and antiblack racism.* Humanity Books.
Gordon, L. R. (1997). *Existence in Black: An anthology of Black existential philosophy.* Routledge.
Lipsitz, G. (2007). The racialization of space and the spatialization of race theorizing the hidden architecture of landscape. *Landscape Journal, 26*(1), 10–23.
Lipsitz, G. (2011). *How racism takes place.* Temple University Press.
Marable, M. (2000). A conversation with Ossie Davis. *Souls: A Critical Journal of Black Politics, Culture, and Society 2*(3), 6–16.
Mills, C. W. (1997). *The racial contract.* Cornell University Press.
Mustaffa, J. B. (2017). Mapping violence, naming life: A history of anti-Black oppression in the higher education system. *International Journal of Qualitative Studies in Education, 30*(8), 711–727.
Osei-Kofi, N., Torres, L. E., & Lui, J. (2013). Practices of Whiteness: Racialization in college admissions viewbooks. *Race Ethnicity and Education, 16*(3), 385–405.
Puwar, N. (2004). *Space invaders: Race, gender and bodies out of place.* Berg.
Ray, V. (2019). *Why so many organizations stay White.* Harvard Business Review. Retrieved from https://hbr.org/2019/11/why-so-many-organizations-stay-white
Sullivan, E. (2018, February 19). *Laura Ingraham told Lebron James to shut up and dribble; he went to the hoop.* NPR. Retrieved from https://www.npr.org/sections/thetwo-way/2018/02/19/587097707/laura-ingraham-told-lebron-james-to-shutup-and-dribble-he-went-to-the-hoop
U.S. Department of Education, National Center for Education Statistics. (2021). *Full-time faculty in degree-granting postsecondary institutions, by race/ethnicity, sex,*

  and academic rank: Fall 2018, Fall 2019, and Fall 2020. https://nces.ed.gov/programs/digest/d21/tables/dt21_315.20.asp

Victoria, K. (2023, April 3). *Stop trying to humble Black women in sport.* Girls United. Retrieved from https://girlsunited.essence.com/article/stop-trying-to-humble-black-women-in-sports/

Wilderson, F. B. (2020). *Afropessimism.* Liveright Publishing Corporation.

Wolfe, E., & Razek, R. (2023, April 8). *Tennessee House GOP expels 2 Democrats in retaliation over gun control protest, on 'sad day for democracy'.* CNN. Retrieved from https://www.cnn.com/2023/04/07/us/tennessee-democrat-house-representatives-expelled-friday/index.html

Yancy, G. (2005). Whiteness and the return of the Black body. *The Journal of Speculative Philosophy, 19*(4), 215–241. www.jstor.org/stable/25670583

Yancy, G. (2008). *Black bodies, White gazes: The continuing significance of race.* Rowan & Littlefield.

CHAPTER 10

STRIVE TO SERVE

Jacob Ashby

ABSTRACT

Leadership research has focused on theories such as traits, skills, styles, transactional, transformational, and servant leadership. The key focus in each of these theories is that in order to be an effective leader one must have followers. Servant leadership helps team members find fulfillment, builds respect within teams, and focuses on personal relationships. This approach has been demonstrated to increase buy-in, employee motivation, and results. This strategy has helped the author to build incredible relationships across three higher education institutions. Furthermore it has allowed the author to both successfully advance in leadership roles as well develop a record of accomplishment. Leaders should be authentic to their leadership style, practice humility, and put people first. If leaders strive to serve and keep the principles of servant leadership in their approach, they will find success in higher education.

My career started in business. I was hired as a manager and served in a role where I was not passionate. Without disclosing the company, I found myself selling addictions including alcohol, unhealthy food, soda, and nicotine to individuals who often could not afford what I perceived as the important things in life in a very rural, and socioeconomically challenged region of the United States. Despite the challenges these individuals faced they would come in and spend their hard earned money on addictions. This really caused me to reflect on what I was doing, what I was passionate about, and what I could promote to individuals across the socioeconomic spectrum. After thorough reflection, I realized the privilege that I had been given in life was my education. I recognized that education is the one means to move on the socioeconomic pathway that is not left to chance. While there are stories of social mobility in athletics how many similar stories do we have where an athlete tears their ACL and never moves up the socioeconomic ladder? National data demonstrates that individuals who complete a degree earn more over the course of their career. This recognition of the value of education not only became my career passion, but also sent me back to school to learn more. I started a position in higher education and also began pursuing my Master's degree at West Virginia University. I began working in student affairs at a local community college serving as a part-time academic advisor. As I completed my Master's degree I also began to provide in class instruction as an adjunct professor. I continued to advance my career and eventually earned an administrative position overseeing assessment and institutional effectiveness for another community college in the same state. I moved into this role because it gave me an opportunity to utilize the leadership skills I had developed in business in higher education. Later, I was promoted to the title of Assistant Dean, Assessment and Articulation. Finally, I was approached to serve in an interim position as the Associate Vice President for the Center for Teaching and Learning during the unprecedented global pandemic. Currently, I am the Executive Director for a regional center within the state system where I am responsible for providing leadership and a vision for the center. This meteoric rise in higher education was directly influenced by the experiences I was provided to demonstrate my leadership. While working in assessment and institutional effectiveness I was challenged with implementing a program review assessment process and navigating the college Middle States Commission on Higher Education institutional accreditation. Finally, I led our Center for Teaching and Learning and coordinated, along with other academic leaders, the response to the COVID-19 pandemic. While these three major leadership initiatives had a dramatic impact on my ability to grow my leadership skills, there were a lot of other small leadership opportunities within the governance structure of the institution, my job duties, and within the state that aided in my growth and helped me to build relationships to become a stronger leader. Throughout my journey I have benefited from having strong mentors and individuals who were willing to invest equity in me whether that being providing opportunities to demonstrate leadership, listening to questions or concerns, sharing their experiences, or providing me with guidance. One thing I have learned is that these relationships and relationships in general are the key to being a successful leader. I would like to now focus on the three specific opportunities that helped to shape me as leader and informed my philosophy. When I was hired to work within assessment and institutional effectiveness I was immediately faced with a leadership challenge. At the time I felt overwhelmed, but my supervisor provided me with support and training. I was tasked with implementing an academic program review process for the institution which had never been done to date. The framework for the process had been developed, but I would now have to work with faculty to navigate the process and complete the review of their programs over the course of a year. Generally in my management roles prior to higher education, I relied on relationships to get subordinates to do what needed to be done. In this case, I was new to the institution and starting from scratch. In thinking about how to support faculty most effectively I decided to begin every program review with a face-to-face kick-off meeting with the program manager where I walked them through the entire program review process and articulated to them all the ways I could support them in completing their reviews. This strategy had a bifurcated purpose. First, it allowed me to get to know the program managers at the institution. Additionally, it allowed me to demonstrate to the program manager that I was there to support them through the process. Over time, I continued this practice and by the time I moved on from this role the institution was in the third 5-year cycle of program review. I had moved our process from implementation into a new assessment platform. I navigated multiple transitions in Deans and program managers. Furthermore, we had continuously improved the process to be more effective. The process was now ingrained in the institutional culture. Despite these accomplishments, what I was most proud of was the success of the initial kick-off meetings. These meetings helped me build rapport and amazing relationships with our faculty that exist to this day. As an assessment leader, many people recognize that when you walk into a room there is a negative sensation that impacts faculty subconsciously. Still faculty successfully navigated the process and articulated to me how supported they felt throughout. In leaving the position, faculty at the institution were both very happy for me, but very sad to see me leave. This is because of the relationships I was able to build with faculty across our wonderful campus. As I continued my time in assessment and institutional effectiveness, I was approached by college leadership to serve as a co-chair for our institution's Middle States Commission on Higher Education (MSCHE) reaccreditation process. I was somewhat familiar with the MSCHE process having written a previous institutional update, but had not participated in a reaccreditation process let alone co-chaired one. I attended training with MSCHE, I read and re-read the standards, I familiarized myself with the requirements, and I reviewed examples of other institution's work in the area all to familiarize myself with the process. However, what gave me confidence that I would be successful in leading the institutional re-accreditation process was the relationships I had built over the 5 years at the institution. The institution was in a leadership transition with three Vice President vacancies, an interim President, and a new President who was coming on board as we were beginning our work. Furthermore, the decision for who would chair the accreditation process and the general start of the process was behind. I met with my co-chair and we created a short video to get people involved and solicit participation. Moreover, we both made a concerted effort to get out around campus and talk to people to get them involved. There was a campus wide call for participants, but we leveraged our relationships to ensure that the people needed to complete the self-study process were on the right sub-committees. As we navigated the process, people relied on our leadership for guidance. I was able to get individuals to participate who were hesitant because of existing relationships. I was able to work with the working groups and assist them with their research and writing for their assigned standards. After the report was complete, I was able to work with college leadership and the larger college community to review the report and get things finalized. Finally, I was able to work with the external review team to help them understand the value and quality of our institution and ensure they had what they needed during the review. While I did not work alone and had the help of many folks along the way, my leadership supported the successful process. I focused on the people involved in the process and worked to ensure they felt supported and heard. In the end our institution was found in compliance with all 14 standards of accreditation with commendations on 2 standards, Institutional Assessment and Student Support Services. Finally, in 2020, I was asked to take on an interim role as the Associate Vice President for the Center for Teaching and Learning. The former leader of the area was transitioning back to a faculty role in July 2020 and I foresaw this being a short-term opportunity to further demonstrate my leadership skills at the institution. My wife and I were also expecting our second son due in June as I started to navigate the transition, and coordinated with the former Associate Vice President (AVP) to determine strategies to keep the area on the right path in the short-term until a permanent replacement was identified. In March 2020, the unprecedented COVID-19 global pandemic closed our college for what many of us thought would be few weeks. As July approached I had a newborn and also was transitioning into a role that was significantly different than what I had originally expected. Because of the pandemic and possible enrollment declines the college requested that I serve as the AVP for the Center for Teaching and Learning for the entire 2021 academic year. The position directly oversaw library services, testing services, and tutoring and writing center services in a remote fashion. Prior to my time in the role the institution had never provided comprehensive virtual services in the school's history. Furthermore, I worked with the Director of the Testing Services area to navigate both virtual and face-to-face testing services from the beginning of the pandemic. To demonstrate effective leadership, I relied on the relationships I built with the staff and more specifically my direct reports. During my time as the Interim AVP for the Center for Teaching and Learning, we were able to secure additional funding for online tutoring, hire multiple grant funded support positions, provide expanded virtual chat support for student research, provide additional opportunities for placement testing using an online vendor, implement an online proctoring platform, and transition all faculty professional development to a virtual format. When we started to re-open face-to-face services, I worked with the Directors of each area to determine the strategy for navigating our way back to campus and to determine how we would balance our new virtual offerings and our face-to-face offerings. After sixteen months in the position, I applied for the permanent role and was a finalist but not the chosen candidate. The failure to be chosen for the position forced me to reflect on my leadership approach during my time in the role, my leadership goals, and my experiences at the institution. My former direct reports continued to articulate to me that I was able to listen to them, help them feel supported, and advocate for their areas with leadership. Their feedback along with my experience in the role helped me to continue to look to expand my career moving on to my current Executive Director role. Each of these experiences helped to teach me the importance of focusing on people and relationships when serving as a leader. Although leadership theory focuses on traits, skills, styles, and strategies for leadership, it is often reiterated that we cannot be leaders without followers. With this logic focusing on the individuals you lead and building strong relationships with them is key to leadership success. If I had one piece of advice to offer my younger self it would be to live by Maya Angelou's quote, "I've learned that people will forget what you said, people will forget what you did, but people will never forget how you made them feel." This is why I think it is most important for leaders to strive to serve. Leaders should focus on serving the individuals they lead by building relationships with them, learning about their obligations outside of work, understanding their culture, caring about their aspirations, and being altruistic. Having earned my doctorate with a focus in Leadership in Higher Education, I have had the opportunity to study leadership theories and principles. Understanding these concepts has been useful to me as I have been forced to navigate leadership opportunities including those detailed above. However, as with any theory, leadership theory has limitations in how it is applied to real life situations and people with different needs and desires. The principles of servant leadership are no different. "According to Greenleaf (1977), servant leaders are leaders who put others people's needs, aspirations and interests above their own."

(Sendjaya & Sarros, 2002, p. 57). Moreover, servant leadership consists of ten characteristics including listening, empathy, healing, awareness, persuasion, conceptualization, foresight, stewardship, commitment to growth of people, and building community (Spears, 1995). While different perspectives on servant leadership exist, its principle focus is on the needs of the followers. The key principle is that a servant-leader is a servant first ensuring the needs of others are the highest priority (Greenleaf, 1977). This occurs by putting the obligation to serve above the desire to lead. In other words, "The servant leader operates on the assumption that "I am the leader, therefore I serve" rather than "I am the leader, therefore I lead" (Sendjaya & Sarros, 2002, p. 60). This may all seem idealistic in nature, but below I will provide three principles that I have embraced in my leadership experience that are directly informed from servant leadership principles.

BE AUTHENTIC

Growing up, my family taught me the principles of caring for others. My mother loved to quote from Mathew 7:12, although not directly, telling my sister and I to do unto others as you would want done unto you. My mom was a college professor and I watched her over many years dedicate her career to helping students achieve their goals. She also dedicated her home life to ensuring my sister and I had what we needed. Moreover, my father was the type of person who would finish cleaning up the broken limbs in his yard and then he and I would head around to the neighbors to help them clean up their yards as well. He was the type of guy to help friends move, who took care of his mother, and who put his family first. This background demonstrated that caring about people was engrained in me from a young age and is an authentic component of my character. Thus, in my leadership roles I often find myself connecting with employees authentically. For example, I have checked in with employees who have had personal family concerns to see what they need. I regularly ask my employees what their career goals are and how I can help them achieve those. Furthermore, I try to learn about my employees' cultures and backgrounds to find areas where we can connect and I can demonstrate that I care about them as a person and not just an employee.

Sendjaya and Sarros (2002) provide the story of Herman Miller CEO, Max De Pree for context. In the story:

> He arrived at a local tennis club just after high school students had vacated the locker room. Like chickens, they had not bothered to pick up after themselves. Without thinking much about it, I gathered the towels and put them in the hamper. A friend of mine quietly watched me do this and then asked the question that I've pondered many times of the years. "Do you pick up

towels because you're the president of the company. Or are you the president because you pick up towels." (De Pree, 1989, p. 218–219)

In De Pree's case, gathering up the towels was a demonstration of servant leadership. As with De Pree, for me the desire to serve must come naturally. Caring about people was something I was taught from a young age and is part of my disposition. If you are serving to lead, then your followers will notice. Leaders should be reflective about who they are and most importantly be authentic in their leadership approach.

PRACTICE HUMILITY

My parents also taught me to be humble. While the quote has multiple attributions, my father used to always tell me, "Act like you have been there before." I grew up in athletics, most specifically soccer, and my father expected me after scoring a goal to pick up the ball and either hand it to the referee or take it back to the center circle and set it down. This was an expectation from the time I was young. I received praise for my performance in private, but when we were around others humility was the expectation. This same principle applies to leadership. Humility allows us to recognize those who have helped us to complete tasks, helped us to grow, and most of all display thankfulness. As a leader if you practice humility it will spread among your team. In the bible, Jesus demonstrates humility in the Gospel of John by washing the feet of his disciples. During the time washing someone's feet was regarded as one of the most demeaning tasks someone could undertake. In the Gospel of John, Jesus says, "Do you understand what I have done for you? You call me a 'Teacher' and 'Lord,' and rightly so, for that is what I am. Now that I, your Lord and Teacher, have washed your feet, you should also wash one another's feet. I have set you an example that you should do as I have done for you." If you practice humility in servant leadership, this practice will rub off on your followers. I have had success using humility to keep ego, both mine and others, from interfering with team goals. Practicing humility is an important tip for successful servant leadership.

PUT PEOPLE FIRST

Finally, and most importantly, I would suggest those hoping to become a leader put people first. Sendjaya, and Sarros (2002) state it more eloquently saying, "As stewards, servant leaders regard their followers as people who have been entrusted to them to be elevated to their better selves and to be what they are capable of becoming" (p. 61). Walt Bettinger, CEO of

Charles Schwab shares a story when he completed a business course where the professor told him that he had taught him everything he needed to know except one of the most important questions. What is the name of the lady who cleans this building? The assignment had a significant impact of Bettinger and taught him the importance of people in practicing servant leadership (Rittenhouse, 2018). When provided with leadership opportunities, take the time to build relationships. Get to know those you lead personally. Learn their culture. Understand their goals. Understand their family obligations. Most importantly, show you care. If you are able to do this, you will build lifelong relationships that will help you as you continue to grow in your leadership endeavors.

My leadership experience has taught me many things. Most of all, always be authentic, practice humility, and put people first. These principles are the foundations of "striving to serve."

REFERENCES

Greenleaf, R. K. (1977). *Servant leadership: A journey into the nature of legitimate power and greatness.* Paulist Press.

John: The Gospel According to John. (n.d.). *Biblehub.com.* https://biblehub.com/john/

Rittenhouse, L. (2018, June 4). How a cleaning lady inspired awesome leadership. *Forbes.* Retrieved March 11, 2023, from https://www.forbes.com/sites/laurarittenhouse/2018/06/02/how-a-cleaning-lady-inspired-awesome-leadership/?sh=4eec62d139d9

Sendjaya, S., & Sarros, J. C. (2002). Servant leadership: Its origin, development, and application in organizations. *Journal of Leadership & Organizational Studies, 9*(2), 57–64. https://doi.org/10.1177/107179190200900205

Servant Leadership: The Philosophy & Practice of Caring Leadership. (n.d.). *www.mheducation.com.* https://www.mheducation.com/highered/ideas/articles/servant-leadership

Spears, L. (1995). Servant leadership in the Greanleaf legacy. In L. C. Spears (Ed.), *Reflections on leadership* (pp. 1–16). John Wiley & Sons.

CHAPTER 11

UNPACK, UNLEARN, UNLEASH

Tasha Wilson

ABSTRACT

Leadership is an exploratory term that encompasses one's ability, experience, expertise, and overall character. Leadership is the action you take to influence and inspire. To provoke change, leaders must continually seek knowledge. Historically, institutions sought out individuals who were aesthetically acceptable to the traditional social norms. Until recently, there has been a demand for diverse representation in leadership. Systematically speaking, it is time to take a transformative method in recruitment and retention strategies. Although we have made progress, there is still more work to accomplish. With emerging trends on the horizon, innovative approaches are essential as it relates to organizational structure while examining personal bias and perceptions relative to leadership and professional development. Give yourself permission to unpack historical barriers, unlearn restricted thinking patterns, and unleash the leader within.

BRIEF OVERVIEW OF PREVIOUS POSITIONS/ROLES

I always knew that whatever profession I pursued in life it would intrinsically align with who I am. As a person who was always curious with the connection between human behavior and environment, I knew that I had to be in a field that gave me the freedom to be a catalyst for change. I value the transformative power of education and how it maximizes the need for collaboration and engagement. My professional background is a myriad of social work and education. Having a double masters in two prominent areas of concentration led me to obtaining a plethora of multifaceted roles within unconventional spaces in the realm of student affairs. I often sought after inaugural roles that had a clear depiction toward advancement. Some of the roles I held required me to supervise a team of student leaders and professional staff, while having the responsibility to oversee operations and compliance. The various roles I held ranged from residence life, athletics, dean of student life, counseling, diversity, equity, and inclusion (DEI). My experiences were well-rounded in nature due to being employed at Historically Black Colleges and Universities (HBCUs), and at Predominately White Institutions (PWI)—both public and private. Mission and size played an intricate part in the culture and climate of the institutions I worked for. Hence, some were more bureaucratic than I had anticipated. Working at institutions that tokenized my Blackness and diminished my expertise made me feel like a glorified stereotype. There was a lack of genuine interest and effort to collaborate with me on campus wide initiatives and projects. The actions of my counterparts seemed driven by a diversity checklist.

JOURNEY IN THE FIELD/TRAJECTORY TO LEADERSHIP

Your mindset can be your most powerful tool or your greatest limitation. The way you approach and assess situations essentially determine the intended outcome. Do you view uncertainty as an opportunity for growth? Or do you retreat to comfortability as a safety net? My journey in the field challenged my thinking, my beliefs, and my actions. I initially accepted positions that I felt most familiar with. The responsibilities were comfortable and sustainable and did not require me to tap into my full potential. I was accustomed to approaching life from the lens of survival mode. I was more focused with my "right now" instead of the bigger picture. As a first-generation college student, I was not given a manual on how to navigate the real world after receiving my undergraduate degree. It was apparent that my degree completion would not only impact my personal life but also those who were connected to me. Having that visual in my mind was daunting yet liberating. Recognizing that I had the ability to create my own path and prepare a blueprint for the family lineage that would come after me. This taught me the importance of being relentless in my pursuit of creating the life I have always desired. Embracing the unknown and transforming obstacles into opportunities. Being a ground breaker requires having a vision, taking risks and executing innovative approaches. Essentially, having a "bounce back" mentality and a tenacious spirit while blazing trails.

In efforts for me to take advantage of my journey in the field, I had to unpack survival tactics of shrinking back and minimizing myself whenever faced with a challenge. I worked in spaces that often viewed my uniqueness as a burden so playing small became my default response. It was a mechanism where I once believed that mediocrity was the safest route for me to accept until the "right" moment presented itself. Instead, I had to consciously view those challenges as opportunities for me to make a decision that would perpetuate my life for the better. Essentially, making a one eighty degree turn from where I first started in student affairs. Unlearning everything I assumed leadership required and rethinking what being a leader actually entails. Being more intentional, more strategic, and more certain of what I wanted to aspire in my career. Standing tall, asserting myself and walking into rooms with confidence. Knowing my worth and believing that I am worthy of being successful. No longer allowing others to decide who I am or what I want to accomplish. Not giving others the power to validate my experience or endorse my ideas as a gaslighting tactic. My trajectory to leadership is unconventional. I would consider it to be far from linear in comparison to my fellow colleagues. Some institutions welcomed the idea of me aspiring to evolve from an entry level role toward senior leadership. While others were resistant to the possibility. For those who were reluctant to change, I took a moment to assess how the change may impact the overall functionality of the department, as well as, the relationship dynamics among the team. I created written plans to explain the change, discuss benefits and elicit ideas. I believed that having anecdotal records and data analytics to support my reasoning for the evolution showcased my commitment to the institution and its future outlook.

Historically, my experiences regarding leadership were homogenized. There were not a lot of individuals I could relate or identify with, until the year of 2008. That year, I met two women by the names of Ms. Nicole Gould and Dr. Emerald Fulmore. They served as the supervisors for my graduate assistantship in the Athletics Compliance office. Their mentorship helped me start viewing life outside of the box and considering areas within student affairs that resonated with me the most. On the first day of my graduate assistantship, I remember Ms. Gould and Dr. Fulmore asking me where I saw myself in five years. I had never considered what life would look like for me professionally until that moment. What I appreciate about that moment was that Ms. Gould and Dr. Fulmore did not expect me to have an immediate answer yet wanted me to take some time throughout the week to ponder on it and provide them with a thoughtful response. They prompted me to create a list of the skills I excelled in, a list of activities I enjoyed, and a list of things I desired in a work environment. The experience with Ms. Gould and Dr. Fulmore helped shape me as a leader because it taught me the importance of being multifaceted and exploring the impact of having transferable skills that extend beyond a specific role. They implemented the lists I created into my graduate assistantship to personalize the experience and tailor it as a foundational framework for my next job opportunity. From 2010–2014 I served in an inaugural position that focused on students who were experiencing academic challenges due to personal trauma. My supervisor throughout that duration of time was Mrs. Chikeia (Boykin) Teal. From the beginning she saw greatness within me and my capacity to lead. Mrs. Teal was the mentor and supervisor I needed at such a pivotal time in my life. She was approachable, communicative, and exuded a presence that showed up in rooms prior to her arrival. Seeing her confident aura and humble posture with her leadership inspired me to emulate her example. Mrs. Teal started intentionally scheduling time throughout the week to teach me critical skills that were necessary for me to soar in leadership roles within higher education, such as personal advocacy, interview techniques, and facilitating presentations. Mrs. Teal taught me the importance of believing in myself, having the confidence in what I can contribute to any workspace, and to be a lifelong learner. Mrs. Teal always reminded me to not become complacent and to always position myself in a role that provokes evolutionary change. She taught me how to be marketable. I had to learn how to leverage between flexibility and adaptability in the workplace. Even if it meant taking the risk of functioning outside of my comfort zone and leaning into the unknown. Being open and willing to new trends, making the necessary adjustments, and establishing solutions. The tools were always there but they needed to be sharpened. With a productivity plan and patience, I would be able to fully ascend into the leader within.

Both experiences impact my leadership style and approach in various ways. Building my confidence level as a leader has taught me to immediately deal with conflict, be open to feedback, and align my words with my actions. I recognize that visibility is critical in fostering relationships and building trust. I authentically show up as myself and do not emulate the persona of someone I am not. Engaging in conversation and actively listening to the needs of others helps me become more efficient and effective as a leader. I ensure that strategy serves as the tool to measure goals and purposeful action. Having reference points enhances traceability for desirable results. Having a comprehensible framework optimizes the skills and competences I implement in the work space.

LOOKING BACK

As a Black educated woman in the United States my exterior is often judged before my expertise and experience are acknowledged. Whenever I enter spaces that highlight the visibility of my exterior being the opposite of what is primarily present, I am immediately put on display. Assumptive stigmas are associated with who others believe who I am based on my appearance, my dialect, and overall aura. Essentially, causing queries to arise regarding the validity of my accomplishments. As a new higher education leader, those experiences caused me to question if I had the stamina, grit, and willpower to immerse myself in the field for the long haul. Having feelings of doubt caused me to reflect on my childhood. As a child I used to be shy, timid, and insecure when being in front of an audience. In wanting to prove to myself that I can overcome the fear and doubt projected on me from those who only knew me from face value is what propelled me to seek out mentorship. I needed to foster relationships with mentors in the field that would help equip me into an innovative, emerging leader. Looking back, the advice I would share with myself is to "Embrace being a trendsetter. Eliminate the noise and keep going. Don't allow the actions and behaviors of others to discourage you from pursuing your goals." If I knew then, what I know now, I would have done things differently. I would have not allowed the assumptions and opinions of others to take precedence of how I navigated throughout the trajectory of my career. I would not have settled as often as I did when applying for positions. Instead of looking for roles that felt safe and comfortable, I would have taken more initiative in pursuing roles that did not stifle the gifts and talents I had to offer. At the beginning of my career, I would have been more intentional in networking and joining professional organizations that were within my scope of expertise.

TIPS/STRATEGIES

To be successful as a new and potential higher education leader it requires you to adopt the Triple U method which consists of the following stages—unpack, unlearn, and unleash. For one to unleash the leader within they must first get to the root and unpack any barriers (professional or personal) that may be preventing them from entertaining the idea of seeking out leadership roles. Often the unpacking and unlearning stages can happen simultaneously. When identifying barriers one can also make the connection as to how those barriers have influenced limited beliefs or internal assumptions. Essentially, behaviors and responses that must be unlearned. This is a method that I created during a time in my career where I encountered a cross road. I was unsure of which direction I wanted to take in higher education and was uncertain as to how I would get there. The beauty of the Triple U method is that the stages are continuous and are applicable to all areas of your life.

A recommendation that I believe would be helpful for new and potential higher education leaders is to never stop learning. To be an effective leader, one must be willing to stay current with what is happening in the world around them and how it impacts the population they are serving. If you have an aspiration to grow in people management and strategic decision-making it is imperative to discover professional development opportunities that cultivate your skills on a continual basis. Another recommendation is to always update your resume or CV often. It is vital to keep into the habit of setting aside time to ensure that your documentation is current with the work that you are doing throughout the year. Preparation is key. Life can often abruptly change, and it is best to be prepared for unexpected prospects. Lastly, partner with local and national organizations as a way to foster relationships from around the world. Networking is an excellent way for others to familiarize themselves with who you are and the work that you are most passionate about. A first impression is a lasting impression. Asserting yourself and showcasing your leadership abilities by joining committees gives others the interpersonal advantage of knowing how you function in diverse settings. I can personally attest that most of the leadership roles that I held in higher education were shared with me from individuals I have collaborated with on projects through professional organizations.

SECTION III

LEADERSHIP TRANSITIONING

CHAPTER 12

UNDERSTANDING ORGANIZATIONAL STRUCTURES, LEADERSHIP THEORIES, AND IDENTITY MATTERS FOR EFFECTIVE HIGHER EDUCATION LEADERSHIP

Heather D. Maldonado

ABSTRACT

Institutions of higher education in the United States are complex organizational structures that have multiple divisions and people from diverse backgrounds and areas of expertise working within them to achieve a common, often altruistic, mission. This chapter provides an overview of common higher educational organizational structures, explores the traditional "great divide" between Academic Affairs and Student Affairs, discusses three key leadership theories (i.e., transformational leadership, situational leadership, and servant leadership) that assist in cross-divisional collaboration, and provides commentary on the importance of understanding identity in effective leadership. This chapter is designed to provide a high-level, introductory overview of these key concepts for new leaders to assist them in designing their ongoing professional development plan to gain skills in critical areas of effective higher education leadership.

AUTHOR OVERVIEW

I currently serve as the vice president for student development at Keuka College. Prior to my current role, I worked for over fifteen years in the Academic Affairs division at SUNY—Buffalo State College (now Buffalo State University) with my last position being the assistant provost for student success. During my nearly twenty-year tenure with State University of New York (SUNY), I was active in shared governance, having been elected to the College Senate, the SUNY University Faculty Senate (UFS), and ultimately being elected as the SUNY UFS president (a role I needed to decline due leaving the SUNY system to accept my current position at Keuka College).

My journey in the field began with a Resident Assistant position at SUNY Geneseo and the realization that a career in higher education existed. After graduating from The Ohio State University with my masters degree in Higher Education & Student Affairs, I worked in professional roles in Student Affairs for seven years: in Pennsylvania as a hall director, in New Jersey as an area coordinator, and in New York as an assistant director of residence life. After nearly fifteen years in Academic Affairs, I returned to my Student Affairs roots when I accepted my current role as Vice President for Student Development. Key experiences in my career journey include taking "reach" assignments that allowed me to build cross-divisional relationships, running for a College Senator position, earning her PhD and engaging in the same teaching/scholarship/service activities as my faculty colleagues, completing the HERS Leadership Institute, and serving as a Middle States Commission on Higher Education (MSCHE) peer reviewer. These experiences expanded my higher education network and understanding of the divisional roles and functions within institutions, developed my professional competencies, and well-positioned me for the next set of challenges and opportunities.

Advice I would offer to new higher education leaders to help them become more influential, impactful, and satisfied in their career includes:

- *Take professional risks* from "reach" assignments to launching innovative projects—so you can learn and build your network. There is a lot to be learned as you develop new skills or join a cross-divisional implementation group, but there is also a lot to be learned when you fail to

successfully complete a project or realize your collegial circle is not as wide as it needs to be to accomplish your goals. Enjoy your successes but study your failures so you know how to work, relate, and influence differently the next time you need to execute successfully.
- *Build strong teams* by gathering people who think differently than you, that are critical thinkers who are not afraid to share their thoughts and critique an idea or process, and who bring strong and different skill sets to the group; also, only hire exceptional people (in skill and disposition) because a bad hire is more costly in every way (e.g., staff morale damage, failing to achieve goals, cost of firing/rehiring) than no hire.
- *Be authentically you* because your team and your organization need you to bring the knowledge, expertise, and disposition — that only you possess—that they noticed in your hiring process to the work you do for your institution. Bring your culture and life experiences. Bring your vulnerability. Bring your humor. Bring your candor. Bring you to your work—while remembering to engage and share within professional boundaries—and you will create space for others to do the same which will allow your team to become inclusive and filled with synergy.
- *Eventually you will "swim with sharks."* Good mentors (like mine — thank you, Dr. Janet Ramsey) will tell you that the leadership journey is not always smooth sailing—and one of the biggest challenges you will likely face is people who actively try to undermine you in your work or professional advancement. Build strong networks within and beyond your organization, take care with how much you share with others about your work and personal life, and know that not everyone is looking out for your best interest. Often these behaviors happen because others are threatened by you—which means you are competent and influential—so just thank those sharks you encounter on your leadership journey for noticing your impact.

UNDERSTANDING ORGANIZATIONAL STRUCTURES, LEADERSHIP THEORIES, AND IDENTITY MATTERS FOR EFFECTIVE HIGHER EDUCATION LEADERSHIP

Institutions of higher education within the United States are complex organizational structures that have multiple divisions and people from diverse backgrounds and areas of expertise working within them to achieve a common, often altruistic, mission. While this sounds like a utopian business model, the reality is often one of territoriality, misunderstanding, and ego—all of which get in the way of serving students, creating a positive work culture, and achieving the goals of the institution. This chapter will explore common higher education organizational structures that shape how institutions function. Understanding these structures is imperative to being able to effectively influence organizational change through the application of key leadership theories to bring about institutional transformation required to keep colleges and universities relevant to today's societal and student needs. Today's most successful leaders—within and beyond higher education—recognize the critical importance of understanding identity, voice, and belonging as they lead their organizations given the generational changes in the workforce and the related expectations of employers. By taking a broad view of higher education organizational structures in the United States while having an awareness of leadership theories and the role of identity in successful organizations, aspiring leaders will be well-positioned to gather the appropriate experiences and accumulate a portfolio of successes that will advance both organizational mission and professional success.

ORGANIZATIONAL STRUCTURES

The history of higher education in the United States dates to the seventeen hundreds and there are many works dedicated to detailing its history (see Altbach et al., 2019; Lucas, 2006; Thelin, 2019) and organizational development (see Birnbaum, 1988; Manning, 2012; Tierney, 1988). At present, the U.S. higher education landscape includes private not-for-profit, public not-for-profit, and private for-profit institutions who deliver many combinations of "micro-credentials," certificate programs, two-year and four-year undergraduate degrees, graduate degrees, and life-long learning continuing education credits (and non-credits). These institutional types have varying governance structures—from Boards of Trustees with fiduciary responsibility to faculty governance with the responsibility to participate in shared governance and make policy recommendations to institutions' administrations to the campus executives and the employees in their divisions for the implementation of policies and procedures—that all contribute to institutional operations and health. Further, higher education institutions are bound by accrediting bodies that ensure institutions are fulfilling their missions and provide quality academic programs to students.

Institutions that are large, public, unionized, and have strong faculty governance bodies are often the most complex types of higher education structures to lead. This is due to the large population size and its various constituent viewpoints that must be brought into consensus within knotty sets of overlapping regulations, bylaws, and processes that are usually found in complex, established organizations such as public university systems. However, small, private, non-unionized, or with weak faculty governance bodies can often present their own unique set of challenges. Small institutions often need to rely on the same faculty and staff to populate multiple committees or do the work of shared governance simply because of the organization's number of employees. Private institutions are frequently tuition-driven (not unlike public institutions which are increasingly becoming the same due to governmental defunding of higher education in the United States) which can create distinct operational and leadership challenges in times of decreased enrollment, even within institutions that are not mandated to follow union labor contracts. The critical point for aspiring leaders in any type of organization is to determine what the power structure is, who the key players are, and how to utilize the appropriate organizational systems and relationships to bring about change. Additionally, aspiring leaders should work to understand the shared governance structure at their institutions and leverage Faculty/College Senates to assist in helping administrations transform institutions (see Cramer, 2017) to ensure they can achieve their mission while adjusting to changing social and economic conditions that may threaten organizational health if left unaddressed.

While the variety of institutional types and how work gets done from institution to institution does not deviate much from the variety that might be found in any other type of industry's organizational culture, one of the key differences of organizational culture specific to higher education is the seemingly perpetual gulf between Academic Affairs and Student Affairs/Development divisions. Aspiring leaders in higher education need to understand the root causes of the common phenomenon of Academic Affairs and Student Affairs struggling to align their divisional efforts. It is in understanding both divisions' points of view and expertise that leaders can intentionally develop change management processes that inspire both faculty and staff to create operational improvements in alignment with institutional strategic plans.

The Academic Affairs/Student Affairs divide stems from the origins of American higher education itself, given the European traditions from which it draws its roots. The U.S. higher educational model began in the 1600's in the German tradition of *in loco parentis with* strict discipline and faculty as authority but then evolved in the 1800's to include residential college developed from the British tradition wherein students required more extra-curricular oversight and development. The 1900's saw the diversification of the student body as various laws, policies, and programs widened beyond the privileged White male students of earlier times. As a result, there was a growing need on campuses for professionals to address the additional out-of-class social and development needs of students which gave rise to Student Affairs/Development as a profession (Long, 2012) which, at many institutions, currently requires minimum requirements of masters degrees to be qualified for entry-level positions in the field.

Student Affairs/Development professionals today are highly credentialed and experienced staff who assist their institutions in meeting accreditation requirements by implementing—and assessing—programs to support the student experience and assist students in developing their non-academic skills. Often, it is these professionals who work non-traditional hours, live on campus, and serve in emergency on-duty rotations to assist students in crisis at any hour. However, these professionals' expertise is regularly undervalued, as evidenced by them being excluded from representation in shared governance structures, not being invited to serve on committees related to the student experience, and being equitably treated compared to faculty peers (e.g., being paid less for adjunct teaching, not being permitted to adjunct). When this happens it is a devastating blow to both employee morale and institutional effectiveness (Walsh and Metcalf, 2003), and organizational structures and culture should be revised to mitigate these outcomes. Aspiring leaders of higher education have an underutilized corps of experts who are dedicated to student success on campus who are committed to the institutional mission, so fully comprehending the work, knowledge, and skills of Student Affairs/Development professionals to help bridge the divide with faculty can only improve institutional effectiveness.

LEADERSHIP THEORIES

Navigating the complex organizational structures of higher education, including the Academic Affairs/Student Affairs divide, can be challenging for even the most seasoned leader as every situation brings its own unique context and potential consequences for any chosen course of action. Experienced leaders have their past successes and failures to draw upon as they encounter new situations they must lead their institutions through, but most also rely on leadership theory to guide their work. Leadership theories also provide guidance for practice, so it is important for new and potential leaders to have awareness of key frameworks to maximize their effectiveness in their roles. An overview of three frequently cited leadership theories in higher education follows, although it should be noted that these theories have each received empirical critique of their effectiveness.

The three leadership theories discussed in this chapter focus on transformation, situations, and service. Transformational leadership theory is helpful because it resonates with the mission and vision of many, if not most, institutions of higher education: to be transformational; it is hard to find a better way for an organization to achieve an institutional mission of transformation than transforming the people who constitute the organization. Situational leadership theory is useful to those who acknowledge that leadership in higher education is about the cultivation of human capital — a process that involves significant personal and situational complexity due to the varied life experiences and skills people bring to their place of employment. Servant Leadership theory synthesizes the importance of achieving transformational goals and while acknowledging how critical interpersonal relationships and self-awareness are to achieving those goals. These theories are all generally helpful, but they become even more critical to understand in practice when leaders of intergenerational teams need to support the world of work preferences of Gen X, Gen Y, and Gen Z—who seek out personal growth opportunities, open dialog, and a friendly relationship with authority figures all leading to collective, impactful action — in order to retain team members.

Transformational leadership theory (Bass, 1985; Burns, 1978) includes four elements: *individualized consideration* wherein the leader is attentive to their team members' concerns and needs; *intellectual stimulation* wherein the leader creates a space that invites curiosity and independent thinking that leads to learning; *inspirational motivation* wherein the leader can articulate an inspiring vision that motivates team members to act toward goals with purpose; and *idealized influence* wherein the leader embodies ethical behavior, trust, and respect to their team. By engaging these four elements well, a leader can transform both individuals and the organization. Experiences applying transformational leadership theory in situations such as listening to concerns related to reorganizations, providing professional development opportunities, creating strategic plans, and serving as a mentor and role model all create pathways for staff to be heard, developed, and supported while working to achieve the goals of the organization.

Situational leadership theory (Hersey and Blanchard, 1977) outlines ways in which leaders can modify their leadership style depending on the needs presented in a given situation. The four situational leadership styles are: *telling (directing)* wherein the leader makes decisions and provides close monitoring of execution with the intention of compelling action on task or project; *selling (coaching)* wherein the leader is the primary decision maker but shares contextual information related to the decision to help their team commit to the decision and required action; *participating (supporting)* wherein the team members make decisions with guidance and support for the leader to create task mastery and accomplishment; and *delegating (empowering)* wherein team members are trusted to make decisions, implement, and suggest improvements to move toward embracing best practices. A second model of situational leadership (Goleman, 2000) notes six styles—*coaching leaders, pacesetting leaders, democratic leaders, affirmative leaders, authoritative leaders,* and *coercive leaders*—which share alignment with Blanchard and Hersey's model. Situational theory has a twin focus on what both the leader and the team members bring to the working relationship and, as a result, is a model that can be applied differently to the same pair of people across different situations as the context changes. Applying situational leadership theory principles allows leaders to recruit talented team member who may be at various points of their professional development and coach them all—given their different attributes and responsibilities—to become better professionals and to achieve organizational goals, as well as improving organizational health and cultivating strong leaders for succession planning.

Servant leadership theory (Greenleaf, 1970) explicitly states that serving others is the top priority of leaders. The tenets of servant leadership include: *service to others* wherein leadership arise from the desire to help others rather than to gain power or influence for personal gain; *holistic approach to work* wherein people can bring their authentic selves and all elements of their identities to their professional lives in order to improve their work and the outcomes of the organization; *promoting a sense of community* wherein it is believed that organizational success can only be achieved in—and by—the community so cultivating community is a primary responsibility of a leader; *sharing of power in decision-making* wherein participatory, empowered environments in which all voices are heard are fostered by the leader. Servant leadership theory details ten critical characteristics—*listening, empathy, healing, awareness, persuasion, conceptualization, foresight, stewardship, commitment to growth of people,* and *building community*—that are essential for a servant-leader to possess to successfully serve their organization. Servant leadership principles are well aligned with the employment environment needs of younger generations of employees which is exceptionally helpful for aspiring leaders to recognize as they create positions to recruit the most promising talent and foster work cultures that retain these talented employees to develop the strongest possible employee base to serve students and the institutional mission.

The three leadership theories highlighted in this chapter—transformational leadership, situational leadership, and servant leadership—provide models for aspiring leaders to be intentional in their work with their teams at their institutions of higher education. There are many other leadership theories within and outside of higher education (see, e.g., Bolman and Deal, 2008; Harris, 2022) that aspiring leaders can review to help improve their practice. When these theories are carefully applied by a leader with self-awareness, knowledge of their team's identities, and a commitment to the institutional mission, it is possible to achieve strategic goals and organizational transformation.

IDENTITY

In addition to having knowledge of organizational structure and leadership theories, leaders also need to understand themselves and be in tune with the experiences and expectations of those under their area of responsibility in order to best motivate and support their teams in achieving professional goals and institutional strategic plans. Theories related to identity development (see Crenshaw, 2017; Cross, 1991; Erikson, 1963; Ferdman & Gallegos, 2001; Helms, 1995; Horse, 2005; Josselson, 1991; Kim, 2001) provide insight into the ways in which people make sense of who they are in the world based on their values, beliefs, and personal traits. Leaders should aspire to understand both their own identities and the identities of their team members by engaging in formal professional development (e.g., courses, conference attendance, coaching) and informal personal reflection (e.g., reading, journaling around background and privilege, discussions with trusted peers) to develop self-awareness and team awareness. This is critical personal work for aspiring leaders as identities both shape and are shaped by social interactions and roles in society—including at institutions of higher education. Identity informs perception and perception in turn shapes how individuals view themselves, their work, and those with whom they work. Aspiring leaders should strive to understand identity development, intersectionality of identities, and the impact of identity on team behaviors, attitudes, and relationships with others. This awareness—including a leader's self-awareness of their own identities—allows for the intentional development of the diverse strengths of the team, inclusivity for all voices, and creation of a sense of belonging within the organization that will accelerate professional and institutional goal achievement.

CONCLUSION

The organizational structures of colleges and universities in the United States are varied and complex, and the people who work within these institutions bring diverse identities to the workplace and their work. These are two key realities within higher education that aspiring leaders must understand in order to develop the comprehensive strategies required to achieve strategic goals within and across divisions at colleges and universities. Leadership theories provide guidance for successful approaches that can be employed to direct, coach, motivate, and empower team members to work in transformational ways in service to their institution. This chapter was designed to provide a high-level, introductory overview of the key concepts related to higher educational structures, leadership theories, and identity matters. Aspiring leaders are encouraged to use this chapter as a foundation by which they design their own professional development plan to go deeper and learn more about these critical areas required for effective higher education leadership.

REFERENCES

Altbach, P. G., Berdahl, R. O., & Gumport, P. J. (Eds.). (2019). *American higher education in the twenty-first century: social, political, and economic challenges* (3rd ed.). Johns Hopkins University Press.
Bass, B. M. (1985). Leadership: Good, better, best. *Organizational Dynamics, 13,* 26–40.
Birnbaum, R. (1988). *How colleges work: The cybernetics of academic organization and leadership.* Jossey-Bass.
Bolman, L. G., & Deal, T. E. (2008). *Reframing organizations: Artistry, choice, and leadership* (4th ed.). Jossey-Bass.
Burns, J. M. (1978) *Leadership.* Harper & Row.
Cramer, S. (Ed.). (2017). *Shared governance in higher education* (Vol. 1). State University of New York Press.
Cramer, S. (Ed.). (2017). *Shared governance in higher education* (Vol. 2). State University of New York Press.
Crenshaw Kimberlé. (2017). *On intersectionality essential writings.* The New Press.
Cross, W. E., Jr. (1991). *Shades of Black: Diversity in African-American identity.* Temple University Press.
Erikson, E. H. (1963). *Childhood and society* (2nd ed.). Norton.
Ferdman, B. M., & Gallegos, P. I. (2001). Latinos and racial identity development. In C. L. Wijeyesinghe & B. W. Jackson III (Eds.), *New perspectives on racial identity development: A theoretical and practical anthology* (pp. 32–66). New York University Press.
Goleman, D. (2000). Leadership that gets results. *Harvard Business Review.* March-April: 1–15.
Greenleaf, R. (1970). *The servant as leader.* Indianapolis, The Greenleaf Center.
Harris, C. A. (2022). *Lead to win: How to be a powerful, impactful, influential leader in any environment.* Avery.
Helms, J. E. (1995). An update of Helms's White and people of color racial identity models. In J. G. Ponterotto, J. M. Casa, L. S. Suzuki, & C. M. Alexander (Eds.), *Handbook of multicultural counseling* (pp. 181–198). Sage Publications.
Hersey, P. and Blanchard, K.H. (1977). *Management of organizational behavior: Utilizing human resources.* Prentice Hall.
Horse, P. G. (2005). Native American identity. *New Directions for Student Services, 109,* 61–68.
Josselson, R. E. (1991). *Finding herself: Pathways to identity in women.* Jossey-Bass.
Kim, J. (2001). Asian American racial identity theory. In C. L. Wijeyesinghe & B. W. Jackson III (Eds.), *New perspectives on racial identity development: A theoretical and practical anthology* (pp. 138–161). New York University Press.
Long, D. (2012). The foundations of student affairs: A guide to the profession. In L. J. Hinchliffe & M. A. Wong (Eds.), *Environments for student growth and*

development: Librarians and student affairs in collaboration (pp. 1–39). Association of College & Research Libraries.

Lucas, C. J. (2006). *American higher education: A history* (2nd ed.). Palgrave Macmillan.

Manning, K. (2012). *Organizational theory in higher education.* Routledge.

Thelin, J. R. (2019). *A history of American higher education* (3rd ed.). John Hopkins University Press.

Tierney, W. (1988). Organizational culture in higher education. *Journal of Higher Education, 59,* 2–21.

Welsh, J. F., & Metcalf, J. (2003). Faculty and administrative support for institutional effectiveness activities. *Journal of Higher Education, 74*(4), 445–468.

CHAPTER 13

FROM STAFF TO FACULTY

Navigating the Transition and Thriving in a New Role

Nadia Ibrahim-Taney

ABSTRACT

The transition from staff to faculty is a significant one that comes with both challenges and opportunities. As a student affairs administrator who moved into a faculty role coaching and advising students in cooperative education and careers, I experienced this transition firsthand. In this chapter, I share my personal journey and insights on how to navigate the transition from staff to faculty successfully and authentically.

HAVING A DIRECTION-FILLED CAREER DOESN'T EQUAL A DIRECTION-LESS LEADER

Some might say I'm a "Jill-of-all-trades," some might say I've had a meandering career. Me? I say my career has taken me exactly where I've needed to go, when I needed to be there. The same holds true for my education journey. As highly accomplished student affairs practitioners and educators with a diversity of experience and expertise, I know it can be challenging for us to remember our careers aren't always linear. *Having a direction-filled career doesn't mean you are direction-less.*

For example, I hold a Bachelor of Science in administration of justice and sociology from the University of Louisville, as well as multiple master's degrees, including a Master of Education in higher education administration from Suffolk University, a Master of Arts in education leadership and management from Roehampton University, and a Master of Science in marketing from the University of Cincinnati's Carl H. Lindner College of Business. You can say I really love education and earning degrees! It's a wandering journey with each of these experiences being exactly what I needed at the time I needed them and somehow, I've made use of each in building my career from staff to faculty.

In my current role, I serve as an assistant professor and educator at the University of Cincinnati's College of Cooperative Education and Professional Studies. In this role, I teach and advise undergraduate and graduate students in information technology and cybersecurity. I mentor and support over 350 students each year, ensuring compliance with mandatory cooperative education procedures, policies, and professional practices. Through classes, workshops, and individual coaching appointments, I help students strengthen their job search collateral, resulting in higher placement rates and higher student levels of empowerment and confidence when navigating work placements. Through partnerships with academic advising and retention support teams, I strategize to support at-risk students holistically before, during, and after their co-op experience.

Prior to my faculty role, I was the assistant director of career development at the Carl H. Lindner College of Business at the University of Cincinnati. In this staff role, I was heavily customer service focused, helping to cultivate and retain employer relationships annually through company visits, phone/virtual calls, and in-person meetings. Having never worked externally with employer partners before, this was entirely new terrain for me and required daily research to learn how to meet employer needs. Thanks to my social science undergraduate degree I earned 10 years previously, I knew a thing or two about how to conduct research and synthesis information accurately and quickly, helping me upskill into this role seamlessly.

This role taught me how to work one on one with multiple generations of students including Gen Z and Millennials. Understanding the nuances and different needs of each generation progressing through academia throughout my tenure is essential in helping me make meaningful connections, supporting people the way they best appreciate support and relating to folks humanly and authentically. In this role, I conducted approximately 500 individual coaching appointments per year with a caseload of 1,700 students. While my masters in higher education semi-prepared me for advising and mentoring students, nothing can replicate the real-life issues and challenges students bring to your desk each session as a student affairs professional, such as depression or even suicide ideation. In my opinion, the best way to hone your student affairs expertise is by doing the work- sitting with students, listening for what is said, listening for what isn't said, and making connections authentically and personally.

During my time as assistant director, I had a few additional interim roles too. As staff, we are all too familiar with jumping in and executing "other duties as assigned" when the need arises. As a member of the LGBTQ+ community, I expected my student affairs path would eventually lead me to supporting and mentoring LGBTQ+ students because representation and visibility of marginalized identities in academia matters. So, I took on an interim program manager role supporting the LGBTQ+ Inclusive Excellence program at my college during a full-time staff member maternity leave. I managed student leaders, provided direction and strategy to engage the university and local community through events and social media, and partnered with the Counseling and Psychological Services (CAPS) division to facilitate a workshop on how to have difficult conversations and coming out to family and friends. All things I had never done before but learned on the job, which is one of the most valuable approaches I think we can take in our career journey. Push your boundaries, go outside your scope of work, and try new things. I think this mental openness has served me well in helping me narrow in on what I really want to spend 40 hours a week doing.

My second interim role came in 2020 as an interim instructional designer. This was another role that put me exactly where I needed to be when I needed to be there and while I probably had no business doing it from an experience, expertise, or time perspective, I did it anyways. I augmented a team of two instructional designers to assist faculty and adjunct instructors with the transition and creation of online and hybrid business courses via the Canvas Learning Management System due to COVID-19. I proctored daily drop-in hours via Webex for faculty and adjuncts, problem-solving technical issues related to content delivery and creation, and helped produce asynchronous help tools for faculty and adjunct instructors to use in the development of their courses. This work developed my instructional skills, comfortability creating teaching curriculum and was the first time I seriously considered making the move into a faculty position. Which leads me into the next section of my journey

NAVIGATING THE COMPLEXITIES
OF STAFF-TO-FACULTY TRANSITIONS

The transition from staff to faculty is a significant one that comes with both challenges and opportunities. One of the most significant challenges I found moving from staff to faculty is adjusting to new expectations and responsibilities. As a staff member, my focus was primarily on supporting students through programs and services, while as a faculty member, I'm responsible for teaching, research, and service. My advice to folks making this staff-to-faculty transition is to start with what you know best and lean into your skill set you developed in your staff roles. For me, that was advising students and departmental service as that is what I spent time doing as a staff member. Faculty elements like teaching and scholarship were new to me, so I was gentle and kind with myself as I upskilled in these areas. I scheduled my learnings to be slow by building up my skill set with very intentional trainings, classes, and lectures. The key to my success was not committing to too much too soon in my professional development plan and holding myself accountable to the things I did commit to. As I transitioned into my new role, it was far too easy to push professional development to the back burner in favor of more urgent and critical needs but without the commitment and execution of my professional development plan, I would have never learned how to successfully navigate the newer elements of being faculty. Sometimes to go fast, you must first go slow.

Despite these challenges, there are many opportunities for personal and professional growth that come with the transition to faculty. As a faculty member, I get to develop my teaching and research skills, and pursue new interests and collaborations. To thrive in this new role, I found it's essential to seek out support and guidance from colleagues and mentors, stay open to feedback and constructive criticism, and be willing to learn from your mistakes. I can't tell you how many mistakes I made (and to some extent continue to make) in my faculty role. This is where building strong relationships with colleagues, staying up-to-date on current trends and effective practices in your field, and actively engaging in professional development opportunities can play a significant part in your success as faculty. As faculty, a big part of my job is my own continuous learning in my functional area and dissemination of information to the academic community and my students. These activities are hard to do alone, and, in my experience, I find I enjoy researching and service more when I collaborate with the brilliant people around me. People and purpose might be the greatest and most influential allies I had in my transition to faculty.

As faculty, some of my proudest and most profound moments have come from contributing to research and scholarship opportunities, mentoring students, and engaging in service activities that benefit the broader community. The transition to faculty also provided me greater autonomy and flexibility in terms of setting priorities and pursuing individual interests and passions so that now, I really do feel like what I am doing day in, and day out is in full alignment with who I am as a professional. And who I am is in service to my students, my research community and myself. It has taken nearly 20 years to fully design and create the career and professional persona that feels authentically me. It's been a journey and as I've evolved in my career over the years, and presume to continue to do, I know this work will never really fully be done. The magic of discovering ourselves and letting others discovery us is through the journey. This inner personal work has been some of the most rewarding aspects of my career journey.

My current research area focuses on neurodiversity in the workplace, especially neurodivergence in the STEM student community. Neurodiverse is a term typically used to describe neurodivergent people. For clarity, neurodivergence is a noun and refers to cognitive functioning which is not considered "typical." For example, autistic, or people with attention-deficit hyperactivity disorder (ADHD). Neurodivergent is an adjective that describes people who have a neurodivergence. For example, a person with a neurodivergence would say they are neurodivergent or identify with the neurodiverse community. A person who does not have a neurodivergence would say they are neurotypical. I chose this area because it's what my students were presenting to me as a need I could help with. I simply let my research area be guided by pain points I'm experiencing with my students. I've had the opportunity to work with folks individually who are challenged by their neurodivergence in getting hired and retained in professional organizations. The time, energy, and resources I receive as faculty to research helps me ultimately be a better support mechanism for students and advanced the advocacy of neurodivergent individuals across the hiring and careers spectrum. What I am doing at work matters and being able to see that firsthand is such a rewarding experience!

My career journey has been made up of loads of little experiences just like this. Where one or two students brings a problem, issue, or concern to our sessions together and it pushes me to think curiously and creatively. As faculty, much of my work resides in the curiosity or innovation of thought, which is very different than the practical nature of staff roles. Considering how you want to use your time in working and helping students will help you decide if a faculty or staff role is right for you. It's about how you want to advance the advocacy and success of your students- which is why we all go into student affairs in the first place.

THE WISDOM OF EXPERIENCE: ADVICE FOR NEW HIGHER EDUCATION LEADERS

Be in Service to Others

I've held several service positions within the University of Cincinnati (UC) over the years, including serving on Faculty Senate. As a member of the LGBTQ+ Faculty & Staff Association, I co-chaired the board for two years, managing budgets and developing innovative programming to support and retain diverse employees while also attracting new staff and faculty to the university. As the president of the UC Association of Administrators, Managers, and Professionals, I was responsible for leading and managing board members and moderating an equity and inclusion panel to promote awareness of diversity and belonging at my university. As a mental health champion, I encourage students to find advocacy and support for mental health and as a QPR trainer for the counseling and psychological services, I help educate the UC community on suicide prevention virtually and in-person.

All to say, be in service to others. Being in service to others can be incredibly beneficial on a personal and professional level. Service can take many forms, including volunteering in your department/college, helping colleagues, or supporting students. Serving others can help you grow as student and academic affairs professional by increasing your sense of empathy, compassion, and social awareness. It can help you develop new skills, gain new perspectives, and learn about different cultures and lifestyles. It's also not a bad way to foster professional development as service provides opportunities for networking, building relationships, and developing new skills. It can help you develop leadership skills, build your reputation, and increase your visibility within your profession.

For me, being in service to others promotes personal fulfillment. Helping others is incredibly rewarding and gives me a sense of satisfaction and pride knowing I'm making a positive impact on the lives of others. I believe serving others can enhance overall well-being too as I've noticed a reduction in my stress, increase in my work/life happiness, and improvement in physical health. Serving others has helped me develop a sense of gratitude too and has generally increased my overall level of life satisfaction. Now, too much of a good thing can go bad quickly, so be intentional and purposeful in your service and commit fully to the opportunities you resonate with.

Be in Service to Yourself

Taking care of yourself is critical to your overall well-being and success in student affairs (and any career path for that matter) and it complements being in service to others. It is important to recognize that self-care is not selfish; it is necessary for maintaining good physical, emotional, and mental health. When you take care of yourself, you are better equipped to handle the demands of daily academic life, and it can increase productivity, efficiency, and focus. By being in service to myself, I feel more energized, focused, and positive, which helps me achieve my goals more effectively and allows me to show up more authentically at work.

As you are moving through your career journey in student affairs or academic affairs, remember to think of you first. Consider your personal and professional needs, opportunities for growth and your community you surround yourself with who appreciate you and support you. While much of our work focuses on our students, it's challenging to keep ourselves at the forefront of our careers, but I encourage you to do so anyway. Taking care of yourself is instrumental in building and engaging in relationships with yourself and others around you and increases your ability to communicate effectively, empathize with others, and be present in the moment. When you take care of yourself, you are better equipped to take care of others, which is what we spend a lot of our time doing in student affairs careers so it's a learned and practiced skill you will evolve with throughout your entire career.

MAXIMIZING YOUR POTENTIAL: DEMONSTRATING IMPACT, EMBRACING CHANGE, AND COMMUNICATING EFFECTIVELY

Tip #1: Track Everything To Show Impact

As a professional in career development, I cannot overemphasize the significance of tracking your activities and accomplishments in the pursuit of career growth. When you maintain a comprehensive record of progress and achievements, it gives you the opportunity to showcase your value-add and impact to superiors or potential future employers. This ultimately sets you apart from other candidates when seeking a promotion or employment in a new or current organization. Furthermore, during performance evaluations, you can draw on documented accomplishments to exhibit contributions you've made to your division/college, students, and colleagues. This presentation of a tangible record of achievements can go a long way in negotiating a salary increase or promotion.

Lastly, tracking your progress also enables the identification of areas requiring improvement and establishes goals for future development. This self-awareness creates a roadmap towards achieving your career objectives. Reviewing past accomplishments and taking note of successful endeavors enhances confidence levels and serves as a reminder of your individual strengths and capabilities. This reinforcement is especially valuable during periods of uncertainty or career challenges, which from my experience happens often in higher education.

Tip #2: Embrace Change and Take Calculated Risks

Embracing change and taking calculated risks are vital components of achieving career success. Professionals who are willing to step outside their comfort zones and take calculated risks are often the ones who thrive in today's fast-paced, ever-evolving job market. By embracing change, we acknowledge the inevitability of fluctuation, and rather than fearing it, we recognize it as an opportunity for growth, learning, and development. Professionals who are open to new ideas and opportunities are more likely to expand their knowledge and skills, explore new paths, and discover different approaches to achieving their goals.

Calculated risks require careful evaluation and consideration of potential outcomes, weighing the potential benefits against the potential costs or negative consequences. They necessitate a deliberate plan of action, taking into account potential risks and benefits. In my career, I took on additional tasks and responsibilities very intentionally and purposefully. Learning how to take calculated risks will help you stretch yourself, try new things, and seize opportunities that you may not have previously considered. All this leads to adding new skills, abilities and experiences to your resume which help you move into new and diverse functional areas throughout your career.

While failure is an inevitable part of taking risks, it is also a valuable opportunity for growth and learning. Reflection on past failures provides the opportunity to identify mistakes, recognize what went wrong, and learn from them. By using failure as a learning experience, you become more resilient, adaptable, and better equipped to handle future challenges- which is a huge boost to your success and a tenure career in academia!

Tip #3: Develop Excellent Communication Skills

Whether it's presenting to a group, writing reports, or engaging in one-on-one conversations, the ability to communicate effectively can make a significant difference in your higher education career. Developing excellent communication skills is a crucial aspect of achieving career success, and it requires mastery of several components. To begin with, effective communication involves the ability to articulate ideas in a clear and concise manner, as well as the ability to actively listen to others. Developing your active listening skills, in particular, requires attentiveness and the capacity to understand the perspectives and needs of others, which is fundamental to building trust and rapport with colleagues. Whether you are working with students, faculty or staff (or perhaps even alumni or external university partners) developing advanced communicational skills will serve you well in your career.

Another critical aspect of effective communication is the ability to adapt communication style to different situations and audiences. Communication styles can vary depending on factors such as the purpose of the communication, the intended audience, and the nature of the message. By understanding the nuances of different communication styles, you can tailor your message to be more effective and impactful. Moreover, given today's globalized and diverse academic environment, excellent communication skills are even more essential. Student affairs leaders who can communicate effectively across cultures, languages, and backgrounds are better positioned to collaborate with international colleagues and students, build inclusive workplaces, and foster diversity and inclusion. Therefore, mastering communication skills is crucial for creating a positive and thriving work environment.

THE ROAD LESS TRAVELED: CHARTING YOUR OWN, UNIQUE COURSE

As student and academic affairs professionals and emerging leaders, we chart our own unique paths and make meaningful impacts on the lives of those we serve. Whether our career journeys have been straightforward or meandering, we can all learn from each other's experiences and insights. I want to take this opportunity to acknowledge you in your efforts to learn from those who came before you and I hope my thoughts and beliefs shared in this writing are in service to helping you create your own great path forward. So now go forth on the road less traveled, charting your own course and leaving a lasting impact on the world of higher education.

CHAPTER 14

FROM UNIVERSITY ADMINISTRATOR BACK TO FULL-TIME FACULTY

Transitioning and Mentoring the Next Generation of Leaders

Mark Gillen

ABSTRACT

Having held numerous administrative responsibilities over my career, including the last 19 years in academia, I discuss three primary beliefs that have provided a pathway to working with a team, including the importance of building relationships, knowing yourself and your job, and supporting future leaders. However, this is only part of the story. Having been out of administration for four years I explore the issues that support successful rebalancing of my job expectations while continuing to use my administrative skills and experience to support the next generation of administrative leaders.

I have been in academia for 19 years, after beginning my doctoral studies in my mid-forties. In that time, I have served as program director for two different institutions for a total of eleven years, internship coordinator for eighteen years, department chair for nine years, and associate dean for a year. This chapter covers some of the lessons learned from my administrative roles as well as thoughts on how to disengage from administrative work and return successfully to full time faculty status.

My administrative journey began long before I started as a university faculty member and then faculty member/administrator. My first formal administrative work began in my second year as a classroom teacher. As the youngest and newest teacher in my K–5 building I was none- -the-less elected as lead teacher by my peers, well, almost all my peers. There was another teacher who expected to be elected lead teacher and thus began my lesson in learning about leadership. Though in truth, I am not sure I recognized the skills I was learning or how to thoughtfully apply those lessons.

My next most influential leadership experiences came from working as an outdoor wilderness guide leading groups on trips ranging from seven to 30 days. There was some initial training that focused mainly on the hard skills required to survive in the wilderness, but not the facilitation skills necessary to live together. The group facilitation and leadership skills came as a sidebar, but they were essential in allowing me to successfully navigate spending every waking moment with groups in high stress outdoor experiences. The skills I learned from these experiences came together in three jobs that tested my understanding of administration responsibilities and group facilitation. The first was the decade I spent working in the juvenile justice system as the lead counselor and later executive director for a day treatment program. Next, I worked for a small private college directing their outdoor programming for students and community focused on team building. Then, I directed the second largest university outdoor program serving more than 2,000, with seven outdoor clubs, advising more than 150 student club leaders.

Successful non-profit and higher education administrators must be purposeful in their actions while remining dedicated to institutional short and long-term goals. Facilitating connections and creating relationships while maintaining a clear focus built on consensus is vital. At the small private college, I took what I had learned about building relationships with people and continued to apply them to the administrative requirements of the job. It was in this position, while doing a training for ropes course instructors, that one of the college faculty first pointed out the foundational group theory ideas that I was asking the trainees to apply in their work with groups. Up until this point I was unaware that such group theory even existed. At my next institution, with a much larger pool of volunteer leaders, there was a strong but balanced emphasis on administration and advising that made me consider how I was doing my job, not just what I was doing. My doctoral program reinforced my counseling and relationship building skills, group counseling theory and skills and my administrative journey in higher education solidified my understanding and application. However, my interest lies not only in how to work as an administrator but also the importance of mentoring the next generation of leaders when transitioning back from administrative duties to a faculty role.

PURPOSEFUL ADMINISTRATION

Performing efficiently and effectively as an administrator requires some primary beliefs and skills. Gunsalus (2006) stated that choosing to take on an administrative role can be traced back to a desire to make a difference while expanding your experience. Sutton (2007) suggested a similar goal for undertaking administrative work but added that having clear goals and understanding of yourself was vital.

Build Relationships

The cornerstone of good administrative work is engaging others. The job of administrator relies upon solid teambuilding to address the issues that groups face, including dealing with difficult people and situations, satisfying institutional objectives, and financial oversite. Sutton (2007) characterized this as collaborating with the person right in front of you, in the right way, right now. Fortunately, as a trained counselor, and someone who teaches others how to be a counselor, I am steeped in these effective beliefs. If you can't find a way to build a relationship and find common ground, then groups do not function effectively. Creating a professional relationship is different from a friendship. You may not like the people you work with, but as a successful administrator, you do need to find ways to partner with them professionally.

The first seeds of a professional relationship must be planted with key individuals before any issues arise. Building relationships means getting out of your office space and meeting with others on their turf. Learn to hang out with others, not because you need something now but because you need to make good will deposits that you can draw upon later. For example, many times I pick up the phone and call someone across campus about an issue. They not only answer the phone, but because I made an earlier connection with them, they assist me to work efficiently through the issue. Examples like this occurred daily in the university outdoor programs which had links to many other departments including budget and finance, human resources, fleet vehicle and risk management. I recognized early on that having a working relationship based on mutual respect was vital to maintaining programs and required that my administrative staff and I build strong professional connections with office staff and administrators in those departments. The payoff came when those relationships helped us handle a call from the risk management and fleet services folks when a group of students on a ski trip made poor choices driving down the highway. The ongoing relationship allowed us to find a response that met all of our needs while reinforcing the boundaries and expectations with the students while allowing them to keep using fleet vehicles.

One thing that cements relationships is consistency and structure. When an administrator can offer calm, clear, consistent actions, it encourages others to engage while reducing their anxiety. An example of consistency and structure occurred early on in my tenure as department chair. I wanted to use some situations as examples on a collaborative approach to work with faculty and staff on responses that everyone could live with. A member of the department mentioned that previously they found that "asking for forgiveness after doing something was more effective than asking for permission or support." I thanked them for sharing that perspective, but then explained that sharing ideas on the front end allowed me, and the entire department, the opportunity to understand the issues more clearly. As a result, that could lead to a better outcome for all, so I encouraged them to ask for support on the front end of an issue. This shift did not happen overnight, but with a few successful forays people began to seek me out, raising small issues for consideration before they became big problems.

As I mentioned earlier it is vital to make others a part of relationship building. As program director and department chair, I worked with a program associate who was a master at creating relationships and a willing collaborator. Watching how he created and managed relationships across campus, reminded me that everyone in the system is important and plays a role in enhancing administrative work. Choosing when and with whom to engage, being clear on expectations, and supporting others to do their work helps guide people to shift their behavior (Sutton, 2007).

Know Yourself and Know Your Job

To be an effective administrator it is vital that you first know yourself so that you can better understand how to do your job. The assistant director I worked with at the large university outdoor program says he appreciated that I was real, in other words what you saw was what you got. As a leader I tried to be consistent in my interactions with everyone. For example, when someone wasn't happy with a policy or issue, I tried to not take it personally. When I did take it as a personal attack, I would take a break from the situation providing time to deescalate. One of my favorite questions as an administrator has always been, "Do you need an answer on this right now?" An important component of knowing yourself also involves understanding the boundaries of the job. As a new department chair, I spent time carefully reviewing the expectations laid out by the university and faculty governing body related to my job. When difficult issues arose, it was helpful to be able to point to policies and procedures that clearly outlined my responsibilities for curriculum assignments, budgeting, and other related issues. However, while my responsibilities were clear I also strongly encouraged all department staff and faculty to discuss, make decisions and equitably find the best pathway, with my feedback, for themselves.

I always had a lot of ideas, good ideas. Many of those good ideas came to fruition but many others are still just good ideas whose time has not yet come. Often those good ideas shifted and changed because program or department staff and faculty had better ideas, which I needed to be prepared to listen to. Being open to new ideas keeps you nimble as an administrator. A thoughtful administrator asks questions and pushes back on faculty and staff regarding ideas, but as a middle manager you must also be willing to push back on those above you to be effective. However, engaging others to consider options requires confidence, good listening skills and group facilitation. A couple of ideas help the process.

It's valuable to keep the focus on the program and not the people involved. To accomplish this, know your goals, and be patient. Asking the questions, "What do we want this program to look like in three to five years?" and "If we all left the program this year would the stakeholders (students, alumni, higher administration) continue the program as it is because it is meeting the needs?" helps to clarify whether action is needed, what that should be and where we are headed.

Equally important for a successful administrator, are budgetary parameters. Budgets must be integrated into visioning and planning sessions because in higher education nothing changes without funding. Everything that happens starts and ends with support in terms of time, energy, and money. If your department decides to take on a new task then deciding which current tasks will you let go of, or reshape, is fundamental to dedicate time for the new idea.

Mentoring

As an administrator, you can put in a lot of hard work, consult with your team, collaborate to deal with issues and be an advocate, but if you don't spend energy mentoring the next generation of leaders there is little chance the work will transfer into the future. Mentoring junior faculty to understand and engage in leadership, even before they realize that is what you are doing, is key. Buller and Cipriano (2015) determined that there are four roles in mentoring. The four roles include a confidant who listens with discretion; a coach who provides skill building opportunities; a mentor who provides opportunities and allows for consequences to occur; and a sponsor who removes obstacles for advancement.

Mentoring others to take my job as department chair provided an opportunity to outline the program's future by creating opportunities for others to engage, bump into boundaries and then determine, with support, how to navigate to an acceptable conclusion. Effective mentoring begins with helping others to slow down so they can see the big picture. A previous mentee and current administrator and colleague recall a couple of lessons that helped her make that transition. One example—waiting to respond to an email request when possible. Sleeping on your response can minimize the emotion in the response and eliminates the need to circle back around to mend fences. Another technique my colleague shared was getting more information to be sure more voices are heard, and ideas considered. However, there is a limit to this idea and a responsible administrator will recognize when it is vital to decide to avoid analysis paralysis. Other ideas to reinforce when mentoring include building on existing success and remembering that ultimately it is not about you, it is about the program.

NAVIGATING THE CHANGE FROM ADMINISTRATOR TO FACULTY

Tichy (1997) posited that individuals who have served as department chairs rarely return to faculty positions, however, they represent a critical institutional resource. Smith et al. (2012) surveyed department chairs and unlike Tichy's research found that 65% planned on returning to their faculty roles but only 40% received any support or guidance on how to smoothly make that transition. One way to remain engaged when returning to a faculty role is continuing to mentor the next generation of leaders. I think of this as low-key collaboration and consultation regarding policies, procedures, and leadership options to assist new leaders as they take on their roles. This can also provide some continuity for all staff and faculty while increasing the likelihood for successful transition. Former administrators can become force multipliers offering input that allows for greater accomplishments from the next leaders. Likewise, previous administrators can stay engaged, shifting from leading to supporting.

Another immediate suggestion I share with incoming administrators is to spend no time or energy defending previous administrators or administrative decisions. There are always some faculty or staff who have not been happy with a policy or procedure and the first thing they do is complain to the new boss hoping to influence change. Spending administrative capital on these issues is of little value. My only recommendation to the next generation has been, "do not spend time or energy engaging in defense of me by my critics. It will not change what happened." What is important is to listen to their concerns, slow down, take what they have to say seriously and then consider what you want or need to do with the issue.

Gunsalus (2006) suggested that taking on administrative duties as an opportunity to make a difference and expand your scope of practice is equally important when returning to a faculty position. As a former administrator you have a unique understanding of the institution's operations and expectations that can enhance your program and department. If mentoring is not available, you can advocate for this support. You understand how to consult and collaborate with others, and you can utilize your relationships. At the same time, you provide a role model, sounding board and mentor for the next administrator without all the responsibilities. While your department may not have a plan for transition and succession you can set the stage for thoughtful success.

Leaving administrative work increases your capacity to explore new roles within the academy and at state and national levels. It allows you to refocus and expand your teaching, service and scholarship while utilizing the skills and connections that you have built. While many may view a return to faculty as a demotion, I tend to think of it as an opportunity. However, to fully take advantage of this opportunity requires that you balance allowing others to lead your program or department in a new way while seizing upon unexplored opportunities for your growth and potentially the growth of your program.

Providing administrative successors opportunities to lead and succeed before they take on the role formally and you return to a faculty position is vital. Involving all faculty in decision-making provides a process that supports future leadership. Once you have moved on from your administrative duties your support and enthusiasm for the next administrator suggests vital integrity and a successful transition for faculty and staff (Wilson, 2016). Purposeful change also allows you, as a returning faculty member, to carefully evaluate what areas you will need to support, and what strengths you bring to the team while filling a new role. This allows you to let go of previous responsibilities and expectations and carefully engage in a new scope of activities and planning that will continue to make a difference.

REFERENCES

Buller, J., & Cipriano, R. (2015). *A toolkit for department chairs*. Rowman and Littlefield.
Gunsalus, C. K. (2006). *A college administrator's survival guide*. Harvard University Press.

Smith, D., Rollins, K., & Smith, L. (2012). Back to the faculty: Transition from university department leadership. *Innovative Higher Education, 37*(1), 53–63. https://doi.org/10.1007/s10755-011-9186-8

Sutton, R. I. (2007). *The no asshole rule: Building a civilized workplace and surviving one that isn't.* Business Plus.

Tichy, N. M. (1997). *The leadership engine: How winning companies build leaders at every level.* Harper Collins.

Wilson, A. K. (2016). Successful succession planning for chairs: Perspectives on passing the torch. *Department Chair, 27*(1), 5–6. https://doi.org/10.1002/dch.30087

CHAPTER 15

WAITING TO EXCEL

Alea Cross

ABSTRACT

I know he's not popular these days, but I truly feel like Jeff Beszo was right, "It takes about 10 years to be an overnight success." How I define success now is completely different from how I understood success when I was an emerging leader. At the start of my career, I was completely focused on being well accomplished to take care of my family. Young, wild, and mostly free, age 21, I was caring for a father with COPD, and I was raising a child from my teenage years full-time, navigating my relationship with an absent mother, searching for love, and being the best professional I knew to be. What I now know at age 34 has allowed the hindsight of life to unveil three things: (a) Life is a pie we must evaluate well, (b) Boundaries are not to restrict you, but free you, (c) People pay you to do a job; your talent makes room for you to excel. Reflecting on these 13 years, learning these lessons allowed me to exhale with life; so, I can truly excel in life. As a Black woman, I found it freeing to learn and be Nikki Giovanni's *Revolutionary Dreams*.

TIES TO THE GREAT MIGRATION

I am a proud Millennial who has an intergenerational background. My father, born in 1936, is a Mississippi boy who started working as early as he could coordinate walking and his hands. His family was one of the few families within Attala County that owned the land they lived on and a business. My paternal grandfather Lucious was a preacher and owned a timber mill. I share these factors as significance because I am four generations removed from slavery; so, the pride to have academic success from a family who was functionally literate and experienced racism du jour mattered a lot in decisions I made as a first generation student to complete a college degree. My mother, born in 1953, is a Mississippi girl who raised 14 siblings as the oldest child. Though she lived closer to city life in the country, her resilience would matter most in her middle school and high school days as secondary education in Mississippi began integration. Growing up, I distinctly remember my mother lamenting not having a prom because White families didn't want the Black students dancing with White kids. Remnants of Jim Crow still lingered as we took family visits to the south. I remember driving at night, packing lunches, and only stopping at Boom Land before we arrived in Kosciusko safely to family who exclusively lived on winding roads where they could see each other's homes. It wouldn't be until 2021 where I learned about the Green Book that was optimized by many Black families to navigate the roads from the north and south that served as an emerging renaissance to the Great Migration. My father would arrive to Milwaukee finding refuge from racism he swore would've killed him. My mother fell in love with my father over a weekend, came to Milwaukee byway of my aunt who lived in Milwaukee's Bronzeville for a "vacation." She found a job and never left. 1978, my parents would be married. After struggling to conceive and six miscarriages later, my mother would birth me, October 26, 1988 at 3:02 p.m. I know you're probably asking, *why do these events matter, Alea?* Well, who I come from and where I come from have influenced my relationship with education, success, and life choices.

Hindsight, I find my life story quite impressionable to history when I consider why we have to talk about education, equity gap, and a beloved community as politically as we do. The 1916 project has a quote that reads, "You don't have to be Black to see the importance of slavery to the American story. It has fundamentally shaped who we are. Erasing that erases history (2019)." My paternal great grandfather, Richard, and great grandmother Mary had twelve children. Of those children was my grandfather, Lucious Cross, who as the old Baptist would read "would begat" my father (born 1936), Thomas Cross, who would "begat" me, Alea Cross ('88 was a good year). Great Grandfather Richard would be the first recorded family member out of slavery making me the fourth generation out of slavery. In August of 1619, a ship appeared on a coastal port in the English colony of Virginia. It carried more than 20 enslaved Africans who were sold to colonists. This journey of how American created industry, informed education, and taught the American dream would be 400 years of unfolding and unlearning. The U.S. Supreme Court issued its historic *Brown vs. Board of Education of Topeka, Kansas*, 347 U.S. 483, on May 17, 1954. Tied to the 14th Amendment, the decision declared all laws establishing segregated schools to be unconstitutional, and it called for the desegregation of all schools throughout the nation. My father would be 18. 1965—President Lyndon B. Johnson issued E.O. 11246, requiring all government contractors and subcontractors to take affirmative action to expand job opportunities for minorities. Affirmative action as a practice was partially upheld by the Supreme Court in Grutter v. Bollinger (2003). In 2003, I was 15. Even today, Affirmative action often gives rise to controversy in American politics:

> Only in the 20th century did elite colleges and universities begin to actively prioritize diversity and expand access by adopting tools such as affirmative action—a narrowly tailored practice of considering race and ethnicity as part of a holistic evaluation of a student's application. College enrollment and completion rates have risen significantly over the past four decades. However, students of color, especially Black and Latinx students, are more underrepresented at selective universities today than they were 35 years ago. In fact, a Black student enrollment disparity exists at 45 of the 50 flagship state universities, meaning that the percentage of undergraduates who are Black is lower than the percentage of high school graduates in that state who are Black. (President et al., 2022, para. 1)

I grew up with brave and functionally literate parents who depended on me to sign legal documents as early as 4th or 5th grade. As a first-generation college student, I had to figure out post-secondary education on my own with a few great people who filled in the gaps.I knew what I wanted- success, but spent a good chunk of pivotal time learning how to do school before learning how to be a rule breaker to not only create success for myself, but others. I attended public schools until it was no longer the best option for me. My mother haphazardly learned about the Milwaukee Parental School Choice program where I was able to finish Middle School and complete High School. With a private school education, I was able to graduate second in my class of 112 students to attend a prestigious Jesuit College through TRIO in the inner city as a first generation student. As I've discussed my journey in higher education, I understand how impressionable and vital it was to see other Black professionals within the student affairs discourse community. Having the ability to see others who look like me designed an influential roadmap for a profession I'd select. This selection also informed the difference between economic health and what an occupation's title meant in the discourse community. Being able to normalize leaders who lived and led within the community, for me, as an emerging leader, positively impacted my practice within student affairs, how I make work-life balance decisions, and qualify my experience as I get promoted within higher education.

INVITED TO THE BBQ: EARLY CONNECTIONS TO HIGHER EDUCATION

As a freshman, I will never forget the day I met Carla. She was a West Caribbean woman with chunky coils, rocking a campus tee shirt. Definitely looked like a student. Little did I know she already had her master's degree and was the hall director of my freshman dorm for the summer TRIO program?! Very poised and charismatic, it was enjoyable to randomly bump into her without necessarily needing anything. When the summer session ended, she made an intentional effort to see how I was doing and encouraged me to participate in the student leadership program. Within that program, I'd be introduced to residence life and student life, among other leadership opportunities on campus. As the hiring season opened up for student leaders, Carla invited me to the "BBQ." Well, it wasn't a BBQ... though it felt like one. I saw a rainbow of melanin-(ated) Black professionals come through to talk about what they did over light snacks and games. I'm probably over-exaggerating for the right reasons, but all we needed was the electric slide. It was a vibe. Honestly, it was the first moment where anything outside of a lawyer, doctor, accountant, or teacher made sense for me to feel successful. When I consider Westside Boogie's mantra, "[Make] more Black super heroes," I'll introduce DJ and Cheronda fully later in the text. Attending that "BBQ" made me feel like Black excellence could have levels.

Carla cued me into space, whereas DJ and Cheronda taught me how to thrive in space. I didn't realize how humbled and grateful I'd be 4 years later with connecting my next steps as a profession to my college degree. Later in my college days, a certain National Pan-Hellenic Council (NPHC) professional from Malcolm X's hometown would be my next influential supervisor. DJ had a swag about himself. Very professional and strategic. He never minded empowering my voice. And believe me I was loud and proud about normalizing space for Black people in the college setting. We programmed around loving Black people's hair, what was Black excellence as a spectrum, and the influence of hip-hop. I wanted the college to not only see me, but also the community I came from as a Milwaukee native. Cheronda was a Black French woman, well at least her last name gave me that sentiment. She was fair-skinned with eyes that lit up any room. Cheronda wanted you to put details to any vision that aligned with life-purpose, because she believed the details mattered for the type of professional and person you'd be in life. From this experience, I gained working knowledge in residence life, multi-cultural programming, and career development.

M.A.A.D CITY: NAVIGATING ROLES

After college, it wasn't like I didn't know what I wanted to do. The plan was definitely going to grad school to work in Higher education within the realm of Residence Life, Career Development, or Student Programs. Honestly, I didn't want to feel like I was boring as I adulted; so, after applying to over 100 places of employment, I got 3 call backs. City Year Milwaukee, Public Allies, and a start-up high school interviewed me. My father didn't understand at the time, I had been holding on to so much responsibility, that I just wanted a moment to make a choice independent of raising a child that was transplanted into the home (that I'd soon adopt from family circumstances), taking care of him (father went from home hospice to home care during my last 6 months of college), or needing to do the "right-logical thing." With a 750 credit score, I took out a loan and did a year of service through City Year Milwaukee as an Americorp member. Before Abbott Elementary, City Year Milwaukee was the educational parody in life rather than the TV show. Like Janine Teagues, I was a proud corps member ready to put on my red jacket, white button up, and khakis. I was moved by the spirit of believing in a cause greater than self and really unlearning what life should be to embrace where I was: I was a Black woman on the cusp of a quarter life crisis learning how to thrive outside of my trauma to be who I authentically wanted to be. I sequentially met the modern day Niggerati. Naturally, I type cast myself as Zora Neal Hurston, but I had a dynamic squad with me, Larry, Mo, Janessa, Jennifer, and Serena were my equals with wanting to change our part of the world without muting our pain. Working at the schools 12 hours a day between school and Community Learning Centers (CLC) was enough to make you believe in others depending on your excellence to thrive (notice how I didn't say survive). After my Corps Year ended, I was ready for the next adventure that would influence me on a whole other level as I slowly started to navigate my way back to higher education.

Working at a Black high school where 65% of staff was Black was monumental for me. I didn't have to code switch (I stopped caring about it anyway) in the workplace because everyone got it. When I received the assignment: *cultivate students in a way they want to go "to and through" college*, I quickly aligned with the plan as a paraprofessional, substitute teacher, assistant to the Dean of Culture, etc. Let's just say sis was wearing a lot of hats. But one that radiated purpose for me was *advisor*. I loved the idea of tracking students' academic progress, aiding their exposures to college to know what to do, who to meet, and how to thrive. When I created college tours, we weren't going to the gift shop. I needed them to meet the Black Student Union leaders, connect with Black faculty, and most of all learn from near-peer mentors what college life was actually like navigating different majors. Growing up, education was my way out. Yeah, I could've just gotten any job, but my father encouraged me to figure out my dream; so, it was a culture shock to be raised to believe in education, legacy, and liberation, then meet Black students who didn't want to learn. In retrospect, I don't think it was they didn't want to learn, but students definitely wanted to understand the value of learning. They were young, gifted, and Black with limited exposure. With my 10th grade girls, we talked about everything that influenced their life choices that connected back to the trajectory of their education. Between our dialogues, my student programming, and our "class outings" I found a love for academic advising, because I learned how to "coach" others to their purpose, serve as a "navigator" for their academic and career plans, and "aid" normalizing leaders from all walks of life. Call me the "*The Incredible Jessica James*" before Netflix. Leveraging my full-time work, while going back to school for graduate courses, I wasn't ready to leave secondary education alone just yet, but I knew Career and Advising would be my dynamic duo for career placement once I landed in higher education. Losing my Father in 2014 changed a lot for me. It was the first time I wasn't so sure a career to survive was what I wanted over the relationships I needed to develop to thrive. When you grow up with someone who thought the best in you, was always present for you, and they leave, you become numb. It would honestly be a six year journey of grieving before I'd ever feel safe or would trust anyone with both personal and professional spaces of my life.

If there's one thing I love about Milwaukee it's her mood swings. Milwaukee can be hot as Arizona one day and the very next day frigid cold as the "D" on 8 Mile. Milwaukee can be as diverse in community offerings as much as it can be hyper-segregated by its environmental physical and constructed landmarks. Milwaukee is the place I love, as a native, and I lament that it took me 18 years to visit and explore local places like West Allis, Wauwatosa, Bayview, and the Southside. Imagine being college-educated, but being limited to the exposure of your own city. Now factor the awe of being a 21 year old who's allowed to visit outside their 5 mile radius being a part of a non-profit youth organization? I know now through a child's lens it was larger than life. As a Youth Engagement Specialist, I wanted students to know life was bigger than they could imagine. One low impact moment for me was working with a funeral home to "host" a *funeral* to talk about violence and poor-decision making they experienced because of the zip code. I was actually grateful to the Serenity Funeral Home for opening its doors and connecting with members from the police community to talk about very real consequences the kids could avoid by choosing better options within the communities they would return to every night with access supports. One high moment for me was asking students who they believe they'd be in 15 years and connecting them to 40 leaders under age 40 to provide examples of people who look like them and come from similar circumstances. Providing a safe space for the youth to network with near-peer mentors meant everything to me, because it's exactly the tribe building that got me where I am today.

SPIN THE BLOCK

I feel like better leaders are built during their time of "becoming." Growing up with a Type A personality, I felt like I was rewarded for my dysfunction. It was far easier to receive support for my high achievers mentality. At the time, I received limited support for my ability to navigate life as a whole. The focus, again, was survival to support my family while having the ability to do what I love. I think the course of events that I will describe challenged me think of life as a whole. Thinking in a survival mode mentality, I was limited in being able to juggle the items I valued in my life. When life took me through moments of insecurity and uncertainty to recalibrate, I feel like I became my most functional and human self. Leadership, for me, becomes why am I serving, who I am serving, how does the value provide purpose? Whereas leadership can be seen as I am a leader and I delegate duties to be accomplished. I believe the later version diminishes humanity where we need it most. Having the ability to have vulnerable experiences made me look at the humanity that is needed to lead. I knew out of these experiences if I learned to lead myself, I could without doubt lead others in a functional way.

Let me be honest, I think of biblical trope, Joseph when I hear someone say, "I haven't forgotten about you." Joseph had been a dreamer who found himself in jail to become an interpreter. Isn't it life's hassle to be young, gifted, and Black and seemingly underappreciated? For what I loved about Milwaukee and pursing my career here, I did find myself wanting to leave for its limitations. Saturated by colleges, but an acutely small discourse community, I found myself within a year of graduating and not employed within higher education. So, I became regretful to stay in my city and thought about setting myself back a year, just to get hired in another state and complete my degree at another college. It wasn't until I met this older White lady at my grad program that catalyzed my ability to stay on track to graduate and get my job in higher education post-bachelors. She was exceptionally tall, curvy, and full of life. I had only met Lisa on one occasion and she let me express 15 different moods in 2 hours while reviewing my resume. She didn't say much outside of *"Don't leave Wisconsin, make these edits, and I'll see you soon."* When I left the Career Service Office, I wasn't sure what to make of her comments. I just updated the resume and thanked her again for her time. About a week later, she shared with me there was a positon opening up to be a Coordinator for the college's bridge to bachelor's program. I applied and interviewed with their satellite campus. This position not only taught me how important Admissions, Advising, and Career Services should work to support the experience of students (esp. Black and Brown students), but how important it is to choose your life goals. I enjoyed working with community-based organizations like College Possible to funnel students into programs that work to transform their lives. I guess I was shocked by having to choose for myself: Do I continue this work in a particular environment, or do I quit the job to complete my degree and seemingly start all over? After a few conversations with women I truly saw as *sheroes* (read, SHE-roes), I quit my job to be underemployed for exactly 6 months to complete my degree. One of my mentors shared that she couldn't have been more proud of me, which is counterintuitive to what I learned about success. I say Redonna Rodgers name fully and proudly for the encouragement she gave me before passing. Success, previously, was "grinding things out to get to where you want to." Through this moment, I learned that success is as strategic as quitting.

I'll never forget Mike. Mike looked like Brad Pitt. Like, *Ocean's Eleven* Brad Pitt. I truly thank him as my graduate instructor, for investing in me and making me apply for an academic and career advisor position. He shared the posting with me in November, and I was hired by my first four-year public institution. My first day was my Father's Birthday- February 21. Being able to put two theories actively together (academic and career), created the formula I use to this day for advising students and coaching my staff. From the first meeting, helping students understand their program, tracking themselves, accessing services, increasing social capital, and doing something every semester that gets them closer to the job they didn't think they could have is the dream I work to manifest for students. I think this methodology reigns so true because of my collegiate struggles. I had people who had me think about how I was navigating an educational system to be successful. How those professionals shared they *had not forgotten about me*, didn't forget about me, and worked to meet my needs as an emerging professional mattered. Having the ability to give that experience through implementation to everyone I met, coached, or created programs for mattered. I will honestly share, I wish I could've kept this job longer, but learning professionally that culture and climate matter for success, it caused me to set my sights on a position that aligned with what I needed to be my best professional self.

So, again, I didn't think my city or state was going to do it for me. I applied as far as I could go with a child headed to middle school.... Hawaii just didn't seem far enough. And certain realities sank in for me when my mother was diagnosed with breast and ovarian cancer. I reframed my need to focus on what I was running too and not away from. 8 months into my position, I applied to an art and design college where it was the first time I declined a position because my knowledge base didn't align with the salary. When I tell you I never did that for any job, it was as rewarding as it was unnerving; so, when the hiring manager said, "I understand, I'll be in touch" and had the Dean of Students reach out to me, this moment helped me understand that while jobs pay you to do a job, your excellence makes room for you. The dean wasn't asking me to do another entry level job or even middle-level job. I was asked to apply for a director's position. For my birthday-October 26, I quit my job to start another position that following week as the Director of Advising. And I was truly grateful to not only be qualified for a position but also be seen for my body of work. Serving as a Director, I felt like I had the influence I needed to make the incremental changes to improve student success. I created programs for First Year Experience (FYE) students and continuing students, assessed program success as well as advising efforts, and trained professional staff about belonging, academic success, and holistic advising through a diversity, equity, and inclusion (DEI lens). This was extremely important as I would be the only Black woman on the student and academic sides of an institution that had a growing population of Black students and limited efforts for recruiting and retaining Black faculty. Reframing the retention and recruitment to not only focus on students, but address the reflection of staff representative, and true equity at a predominately White institution (PWI) would keep me there for three years.

Maybe it was the pandemic... Honestly, it was the pandemic. I got really frustrated with having to separate my Blackness from my work experience. We were asking if the students were okay and no one asked me if I was okay or the other two Black male faculty members on staff. I was frustrated and fatigued with correcting individual macroaggressions when it was the institution as a whole that had to change. It wasn't enough to resist when I just wanted to be at peace and unbothered with a lot of controversy that kept me at home. Choosing to leave that space with an option was freeing because I know I made the space better than I arrived; and I was able to keep good rapport with faculty and staff I knew cared about my message and professional practice. As the New Year started in 2021, I began my role as an advising manager within Wisconsin's most diverse public two-year institution with COVID (I'll leave that there). Within this role I am grateful to manage advisors who support last-dollar scholarship students, students behind prison walls through Correctional Education, Community Education (General Educational Development [GED]/Adult High School in addition to English as a Second Language [ESL]), and grants through community partners. Within 2021, I would have experienced 5 significant deaths, one including the death of my mother. Which really put a fire in me to not just think about how I want to live, but why I want to live intentionally. I share these nuances to not create somber overtones for anyone who reads this but to share a reality we often ignore about feeling a sensation of success. We must set our goals to endure the process to reach our goals *and* feel content for what we have achieved as we navigate the continuum of life. Being where I am now and feeling like I can safely occupy space professionally as much as I do privately matters in how I identify with success and personal fulfillment these days.

TEN YEARS FOR *OVERNIGHT SUCCESS*

How you take up space personally matters in leadership. I truly believe how we live impacts how we lead. As a leader that believes in restoring humanity in this area of practice, I want to share three reflective points that have shaped how I challenge workspaces, lead with others, and live revolutionary. Previously, I spoke about learning humility as much as humanity through moments of vulnerability and uncertainty. I feel these moments made me a better leader because I truly had to balance what I valued in action in a purpose-filled way.

For me, a leader assesses because it's important to know what is needed and why it's needed. I cannot tell you how many times, I've said, "I need to do..." when the reality was I didn't. I was speaking to my imposter syndrome of not feeling like I was enough instead of tapping into how great I was and creating space to amplify my voice in a space that was needed. Personally, if you are suffering from trauma and not managing it well, it's hard to publicly make good decisions. When you know where you are, you have awareness to ask better questions to seek the support you need. This strategy works in your personal space and becomes applicable in your professional endeavors whether you are leading a team or leading a project. Integrity is an invaluable quality of any functional leader. Whether it was personally or professionally, I wanted to be seen as being "helpful." Well, sometimes being seen as helpful can be detrimental because you can be enabling. Being an enabler can be debilitating for what you are truly assigned to do. I truly believe the revolutionary act is being free to be who you are, not who others challenge you to be as a leader. Finally, finding what's intrinsic to you as a leader allows you to thrive in environments that you find to be a challenge. How you assign your purpose versus how an institution aligns your skills are not always agreeable. Learning as a leader to keep your power can help you learn why you stay in certain spaces through work fatigue or welcome new opportunities for synergy between personal fulfillment and professional purpose.

When I consider the advice I would share to an emerging professional, I think I'd focus on these three reflective points intentionally:

1. *Be in a space to assess well.* What do you want your life to look like as a whole? If I'm honest with myself, I felt like I was in survival mode upon graduating with my bachelors moving into my professional space. Even though family and money were a high priority, and I had people who encouraged my way I felt were friends, my struggle was my focus rather than sustainable solutions to fix areas of my life that would allow me to flourish how I wanted. So, even though I valued living holistically, it wasn't something I practiced. Learning how to prioritize what I valued and actively doing the work to be a success privately allowed me to be the success I've become publicly within professional spaces. So my recommendation (advice is expensive): Know what you want and do the active work. Evaluate your life as a "pie" (See Figure 15.1). We have to be in a space to assess well all aspects of our lives and how they interdependently impact each other. I think we admire a lot of dysfunctional leaders for their charisma and prestige. We forget that decisions impact longevity. I want habits that are adaptable for longevity in every aspect of my life. This worksheet I've shared has helped me not only look at what I valued at the time, but also the values that impact other spaces to know how well I was "doing" in life.

    What do you choose for your life? How do you assess where you are? What are the steps to get you closer to where you want/need to be? Use Figure 15.2 to assess for yourself.

2. *Free yourself with boundaries.* As I hinted within sharing my story, life has not been easy for me. Learning my limits has helped others learn theirs with me. I recommend learning how you want to be treated in spaces because the integrity of self will inform how you perform and will be retained in professional spaces. There's literally a graphic with informed research about how women of color "exit institutions" (See Figure 15.3).

    The intersectionality of being Black and anything else will always have you question how safe you feel to perform and thrive in work environments. Know what your boundaries are to thrive. There will be influencers and decision leaders who see you and assist with having spaces decolonize and address their fragility. There will also be influencers and decision leaders who will aid your move to another workplace for a better experience. Be okay with both sides of the coin as you make informed decisions to leave or stay at

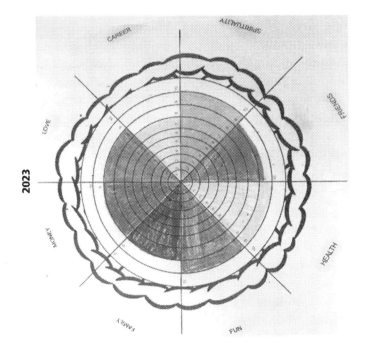

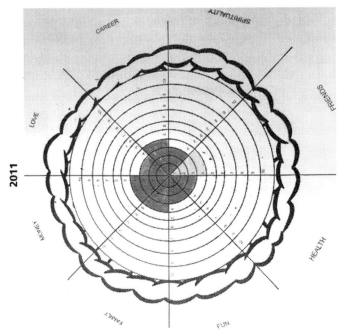

Figure 15.1

Waiting to Excel ▪ **145**

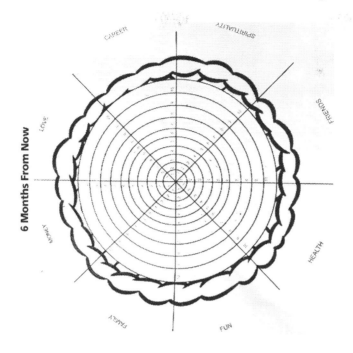

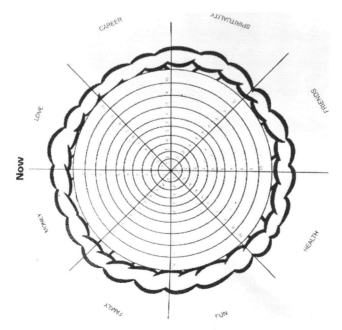

Figure 15.2

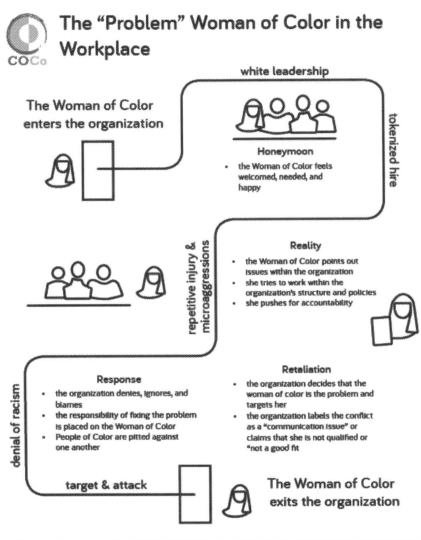

Figure 15.3

places of work. Don't let the environment diminish your mission is all I'm tryna say (yes, tryna not trying). When I was introduced to *Nikki Giovanni's Revolutionary Dream* (2016) I stopped "fighting the world" so I could channel the peace I wanted to create within myself with healthy boundaries for others to coexist with me.

3. *What Pays You Won't Always Allow You to Excel.* One thing is for certain, two things for sure, a job pays you to *do the job.* Which is why, I'm not entirely upset with those who "quiet quit." When you're not fulfilled you can feel stifled. I recommend going above and beyond anyway for your name's sake. You can't pay me enough to do a good job because I know my *work ethic* and *worth ethic* make room for me. When the right people see your integrity and your work, they will truly speak your name in places you haven't seen yet and serve as connectors for your next position and/or institution. Even if people don't influence for you, who you are alone with your work will be so attractive that you will walk into the space you need to be at God's divine time and order for yourself. Make yourself known by your impact. Period.

REFERENCES

New York Times, The. (2019). The 1619 project. *The New York Times.* https://www.nytimes.com/interactive/2019/08/14/magazine/1619-america-slavery.html

Page, K. (2019). The "Problem" woman of colour in nonprofit organizations. COCo. https://coco-net.org/problem-woman-colour-nonprofit-organizations/

President, J. C. V., Cusick, J., President, V., Director, M. C. A., Coleman, M., Director, A., Director, S. N. A., Nadeau, S., Shepherd Director, M., Shepherd, M., Director, Director, E. L. A., Lofgren, E., Gordon Director, P., Gordon, P., Director, J. P. S., Parshall, J., Director, S., Ndumele, N. L., & Zhavoronkova, M. (2022). *5 reasons to support affirmative action in college admissions.* Center for American Progress. https://www.americanprogress.org/article/5-reasons-support-affirmative-action-college-admissions/

"Revolutionary dreams" by Nikki Giovanni. Stuff Jeff Reads. (2016). https://stuffjeffreads.wordpress.com/2016/03/14/revolutionary-dreams-by-nikki-giovanni

CHAPTER 16

PRACTICING FROM A PLACE OF AUTHENTICITY

Dawn Shafer

ABSTRACT

I came to student affairs work after a lengthy career as a clinical social worker. While this was helpful to aspects of my role as a student affairs dean for a Master of Social Work program, it also contributed to my initial reluctance to show up as my authentic self. The clinical world prepared me well for being a psychotherapist and using myself as a mirror and receptacle for the emotions and experiences of others. However, when I came to student affairs, I needed to unlearn the part of my training that prevented me from sharing aspects of myself, including my constellation of social identities. It was only when I was able to claim these aspects of myself that I could really begin to engage with students in a more deep and meaningful way. This chapter overviews and explores the importance of representation and authentic connection as a means for cultivating a great sense of belonging and inclusion with higher education. It also offers discussion about how to manage the need for balance and boundaries within this context.

I am a working-class scholar and practitioner. I am the first in my family to complete undergraduate, masters, and doctoral degrees. I am a cisgender,

White, bisexual, single mother. I have points of privilege and points of marginalization and my identities inform and influence everything that I do, professionally and personally. I start this chapter by naming some of my social identities to provide context for the way that I approach my student affairs work, which is, I hope, from a place of authenticity.

I came to student affairs work after a lengthy career as a clinical social worker. While this was helpful to aspects of my role as a student affairs dean for a Master of Social Work program, it also contributed to my initial reluctance to show up as my authentic self. The clinical world prepared me well for being a psychotherapist and using myself as a mirror and receptacle for the emotions and experiences of others. However, when I came to student affairs, I needed to unlearn the part of my training that prevented me from sharing aspects of myself, including my constellation of social identities. This unlearning was vital as I sought to engage with students in order to form relationships and to provide support, advising, and advocacy. It was only when I was able to claim these aspects of myself that I could really begin to engage with students in a more deep and meaningful way.

I wish that I could say that I came to this realization on my own after personal deep reflection. Instead, the journey to understanding how who I am impacts how I show up for students originated in a colossal mistake. During my first semester as the assistant dean of student affairs, I was invited to a student group focused on anti-racist and anti-oppressive practices, specifically within social work education. Each attendee was invited to share their reasons for coming to the meeting and how anti-racist practices are important to them personally. I listened to students share their personal reasons and stories and when it was my turn to share, I remember saying something to the effect of "it's important to me to understand what's important to you as students." While it was true that this was part of my reason for attending, it was clear that it was not satisfying for students, nor was it a thorough answer. My response furthered a divide between me and the student body president, deepening her distrust of me and contributing to a difficult first year in my position.

To be honest, I'm not sure that I was prepared to do anything differently at the time. It was only with the gift of hindsight that I have come to understand this as a pivotal moment in my own development. As I now enter my tenth academic year as a student affairs dean, my answer to this question would be much different. If I were to answer now, I would reference my own positionality, my duty to use my unearned race privilege to forward sustainable systemic change, and my commitment to anti-racism and liberation both professionally and personally. Ten years ago, I did not have this language because I was much earlier in my own journey and to say so would likely have been inauthentic. Through our student affairs work, our closeness to students, and our proximity to large systems we are changed, just as our students are changed through their time in our programs. The goal, I think, is to lean into that change, to explore who you are and what you stand for, and to use the knowledge gained in that personal inquiry to support students along their journeys.

I was asked by the editor of this book to share my journey within the field and my trajectory to leadership in student affairs. My journey to my current position was not traditional. I was not academically driven during high school or college; in fact, I only went to college because, after wandering aimlessly for 2 years after high school, my parents insisted that I return to Pennsylvania and "get it together." I returned to my hometown of State College, Pennsylvania and enrolled at Penn State. While I was the first in my family to attend college, I was only able to do so because of my parents' sacrifices. My father worked for PSU so that I would have the tuition benefit and ultimately had to pull strings for me to even be admitted. Soon after graduating, I moved to California and worked a variety of bachelors level jobs until I discovered my desire to become a therapist. I obtained my Master of Social Work degree in 2003 from San Diego State University where I was able to marry my clinical interests and passion for working with college-age students by completing both of my graduate practicums in college and university counseling centers; this would later serve me well as I transitioned to student affairs.

Upon moving to Maryland, I found that I had to choose between clinical work and student affairs work, which was a rude awakening. I initially held out for student counseling center jobs, but they were few and far between and I knew that I wanted to complete my clinical licensing hours. As such, I went to work for a prominent institution in Baltimore, where I spent the first ten years of my career. Working for a large and respected institution provided opportunities that I may not have had elsewhere and allowed me to continue working with students while building other skills and areas of expertise. After becoming licensed as an LCSW-C, I became a clinical supervisor for MSW students and eventually co-facilitated the student internship program. I also became a clinical supervisor for new graduates, strengthening my portfolio of leadership and supervision.

After almost ten years, I accepted a position as the program manager for a student wellness program at an affiliated university on their graduate and professional campus. While I was only in this position for a year and a half, it helped me to cultivate skills in program development and assessment, short-term counseling, event management, and student driven programming. This was the bridge that led to becoming a student affairs professional.

Student affairs work at graduate and professional schools is unusual in that they often seek faculty and staff within the same discipline to serve in these roles. While this was the case for me, there are colleagues at my institution who possess masters and doctoral degrees within student affairs. Much to my surprise, having a terminal degree within the discipline (MSW) and student affairs experience qualified me to apply for the Assistant Dean for a Masters of Social Work program.

I had never imagined that I would be an Assistant or Associate Dean...of anything. Even the decision to apply was fraught with angst and self doubt, yet I also felt like I wanted to stretch my wings and see what others paths may be out there. To say that I was shocked when I was offered the position would be an understatement. And yet, here I am. It took me a long time to understand my value in this position and to accept that I had earned the right to be here and to help and guide the students in my program. I am still unpacking my own imposterism and fears of inadequacy, which is likely related to some of the social identities that I referenced at the beginning of this chapter. But what I understand now that I did not before, is that there is a place for sharing these feelings and experiences with my students.

Seven years ago, I embarked on a doctoral journey that took much longer than I had anticipated. Four years ago, I began my dissertation process, which again, took much longer than I had anticipated. Going through my PhD process while working so closely with students created a parallel process that I am still unearthing. My dissertation was a qualitative study of the experiences of first-generation masters' students. Being a first-generation student, studying first-generation students, while working with many first-generation students provided more immersion than I could have imagined; spending my days so closely engaged with the first-generation experience was humbling, illuminating, and unifying. I was privileged enough to start a program for first-generation master's students during this period and the relationships that I developed with students in the program have been some of the greatest gifts of my professional life. These relationships were fostered from shared experiences, the value of relationships, and prioritization of authenticity and genuineness within these relationships.

I am still on my own journey and am still a work in progress. I make mistakes regularly; I own them, apologize, and try to do better. I am no longer invested in viewing myself as an expert but now see myself as a fellow traveler. That isn't to say that I don't have expertise, I do. Or that I don't have knowledge and hard-earned wisdom to share, I do. Through this work, I have come to value the importance of showing up in a way that is authentic to who I am and using genuine dialogue and, hopefully, connection, to cultivate brave spaces that foster inclusion and belonging. And with that, I offer the following recommendations for consideration.

RECOMMENDATIONS

Practice From a Place of Authenticity

Be yourself. Say what you mean, tactfully. Higher education needs us to show up as our authentic selves, as much as we feel safe to do so. Students need role models who may move in the professional world in a different way than they have seen before. Should we be professional? Of course. Should we interrogate what "professional" means, and the ways that it is sometimes coded language? Absolutely.

For me, being authentic has also meant acknowledging my relationship to power, from both places of privilege and of marginalization. It has meant knowing my limitations, knowing when to speak up, and knowing when to sit down and listen. It has meant aspiring to be an ally and using my power to uplift the voices of folks who are often excluded from conversations. I have made mistakes and talked with a shaking voice. I've had to apologize and have had to do a lot of interrogating my own beliefs. All of this has led to more genuine connections with students and colleagues (some, not all), opening the door for discussions that would not have otherwise been possible.

Representation Matters

Who you are and how you show up in this work matters. Higher education continues to be an institution predominantly based on White dominant ideologies. Students from historically marginalized identities often feel a sense of otherness, particularly if they do not see faculty and staff who look like them or have shared experiences. As a White person, I cannot pretend to understand the experiences of my BIPOC students. But I do know what it is like to be first-generation, to grow up working class, and to be a part of the Queer community. I am intentional about sharing these aspects of my identity and creating visibility and community. I am an aspiring ally to communities of which I am not a part. Part of that entails learning as much as I can and then using my own privilege as much as possible to address and undo past harms.

All of Your Past Experiences Matter

Earlier in this chapter I detailed some professional experiences that may seem unrelated to student affairs. While my path was not linear in many respects, the experiences that I gained outside of higher education were valuable. Each of those professional experiences were the connective tissue that eventually led me to my current role. Never underestimate the value and relatedness of the things that you have done that have brought you to your current state. Practice talking about the ways that past skillsets are transferrable to your student affairs aspirations.

Do not be afraid to tell the world how great you are. The world has conditioned many of us to downplay our accomplishments, particularly those of us from historically marginalized identities.

We tend not to want to sing our own praises for fear that others will think we're bragging or not being humble. Your professional career is not the time to practice humility. Be assertive. Know your value. Ask for what you want.

Set and Keep Your Boundaries

While giving of yourself is valuable, setting limits and boundaries is also important. Student affairs work happens at all hours of the day and can be exhausting. Not only is it okay for you to take time for yourself, but it is also your ethical responsibility to do so. For us to be effective in our roles, we need to be healthy and reasonably content in other areas of our lives. We are always modeling for students; by setting limits and boundaries for yourself, you are teaching them to do the same thing.

CONCLUSION

My journey as a student affairs practitioner has taught me a lot about myself and what it means to show up in spaces as my authentic self. Being willing to take the risk to do so has been a journey in and of itself. I acknowledge that I am writing this chapter during a time in my career in which I have built significant capital. This, in combination with my privileged identities, affords me some protection that others may not possess. This chapter is not a call to sacrifice your emotional safety or to share your identities without caution. Rather it is meant as a call to be the student affairs practitioner and mentor that you needed during your journey through higher education. Someone who showed up authentically, valued your relationship, and saw you for your whole self.

SECTION IV

LEADERSHIP IN ACTION

CHAPTER 17

WHAT YOU REALLY NEED

Empathy

D'Shaun Vance

ABSTRACT

Walters and Seyedian, (2016) conducted a study, assessing the needs of students from their academic advisors. The results showed academic advisors lacked certain soft skills such as empathy. Empathetic cultures retain the best people and enjoy higher productivity. If empathy leads to retention, then be practiced in higher education to recruit and retain students and employees on a college campus. Empathy is a trait higher education leaders need to be successful in building relationships with the students and coworkers. Having a culture of empathy within higher education will show compassion and a genuine interest in the students, employees, and other stakeholders. This type of environment will allow for new people to come in and feel comfortable, current stakeholders will want to celebrate accomplishments, and encourage others to do the same.

DEFINITION OF TERMS

Empathy: the action of understanding, being aware of, being sensitive to, and vicariously experiencing the feelings, thoughts, and experience of another of either the past or present without having the feelings, thoughts, and experience fully communicated in an objectively explicit manner

Developmental: the advising process in which academic advisors focus on in cultivating whole students, not just giving instructions on what to do and how to do it, but taking on a role in the student's life, leading to movement and progression in the advisor and advisee relationship with both taking accountability for the growth of the student

Proactive: informing people you are there for them while building relationships with before a problems happens so if in the event something does happen, they know to come to you for advice and help

Prescriptive: the advising process in which academic advisors tell students what to do with little to no input from the student

Dump: the process by which an individual shares information or expresses emotions to a trusted person without them sharing their feelings back, but offering advice

INTRODUCTION

Leading, this is what we are all called to do in whatever it is we are called to once we figure out our purpose. Leading is not a title, more so a way of life. People with the "working" titles of Program Assistant, Program Associate, Program Coordinator and others alike are just as much leaders in their own right as dean, provosts, and presidents. Titles do not make a person a leader, but the impact they have on those who are entrusted in their care. Being referred to as a leader without having an impact or influence is like a fruit tree bearing no fruit; ineffective, useless, and replaceable. So, this is not for those who had 'leadership' titles, but for those who are doing the impactful and influential leadership work.

Furthermore, I view leadership, as a lifestyle, not a title. My name is Dr. D'Shaun Vance and I've been working in higher education for six years directly and indirectly for another three years. During my indirect years, I was working in finance, attending conferences to recruit students to work at the bank where I worked and creating recruiting pipelines with Historically Black Colleges and Universities (HBCUs). I found it quite ridiculous there was an HBCU a few miles literally down the street where the company did not have a recruiting presence, let alone a contact. I made it my mission to get college students who looked like me, a Black man, jobs in the financial industry and not just where I worked. This was important because there are and were many students who get overlooked for jobs because of their background, the schools they went to, or even their names appearing Black. I wanted to start being the change and felt I was in position to do so. I used my networks and influence on behalf of deserving, but overlooked students. For students I recruited or interviewed who may not have necessarily been fit for roles I was interviewing or recruiting for, I would pass them along to colleagues within my company or to friends and colleagues outside of my organization to ensure these students were not just passed and looked over. However, doing this work only as a piece of my work and not on a full-time basis bothered me and it was time for a change. This bothered me because I felt the impact I was making, seeing the results of the students who I recruited get interviews, internship, and job offers at all types of companies. I felt called to work with students and not doing so from the time I woke up to the time I clocked motivated me to push for a career change.

 I met with my manager and told him I wanted to transition out of finance and into higher education. He saw the work I was passionate about and supported the career shift. I left my village I built in Charlotte, sold my brand new home, and moved back to the DC area where I am from and started my higher education career. In 2017 I started working in higher education and began an immediately fulfilling career as a Student Services Coordinator. After about three years, I made a transition from that role to another role in the city, managing dual enrollment, the process by which high school students are able to take college credits and earn credits from ten universities. From there, I left working in higher education to begin pursuing my Doctorate in Education with a focus on Higher Education Leadership. I also started some higher education consulting while doing my dissertation research. I consulted with four institutions in various areas before returning to work at an institution. Now, I work at one of the institutions that was a part of the dual enrollment program I helped manage, overseeing academic affairs for their Health Science programs.

THE JOURNEY TO AND THROUGH

My journey was not clear to higher education, but my vision in the field is. I left finance because I felt like I was not helping people. The first day in higher education I KNEW I was going to help people. My first task was coordinating a summer program for 90 students, for FREE. The students who were able to participate in the program were only responsible for their transportation to campus. Everything else once they got to campus was free for an entire week. This program introduced high school students to college life and majors. I was able to connect with the students, build relationships, and use this moment as a recruiting tool to get them to apply and enroll at the institution. Curating this event effectively needed to have a lasting impact on these students to peak or increase their interest in the school. I will credit this experience and ability to recruit to my time in finance recruiting future employees. This led to me becoming the lead for admissions and recruitment in the department. My ability to do certain tasks allowed me to be trusted to lead more operations within the department.

I was also trusted to lead a portion of academic advising for 700 students, student leader training, global education, endowed scholarship selection, and literally anything else I was asked to lend a helping hand with. My eagerness to be in higher education preempted my willingness to take on different tasks, seemingly unrelated to learn as much as I possibly could. Being a touch point at so many parts of a student's matriculation placed me in a unique position to grow as a person, a leader, and a trusted counselor to the students.

EMPATHY

Johnny C. Taylor Jr., the president of the Society of Human Resource Management has been preaching the word "empathy" to his company and others throughout 2021. He said, "people remember how you make them feel, the ability to display empathy is and will remain a critical part of leadership" (Taylor, 2021). According to Merriam-Webster Online, empathy is defined as, "the action of understanding, being aware of, being sensitive to, and vicariously experiencing the feelings, thoughts, and experience of another of either the past or present without having the feelings, thoughts, and experience fully communicated in an objectively explicit manner" (Merriam-Webster, 2021). Empathy is a trait higher education leaders need to be successful in building relationships with the students. Student-facing departments can have the best advising platforms, practices/procedures, advisors with decades of experience, but without empathy, the quality of leading will suffer in value and effectiveness.

From my experience, not showing you care for students shows whether the leader recognizes it or not. The students can pick up on it and begin retreating and acting out. Now, acting out can be no longer coming to this individual or individuals for help, avoiding the office at all costs, talking about the leader to other leaders, switching majors, and the list can go on. The students are able to recognize when someone does not care about them or their situations. Their concerns or cries for help go unresolved, showing the lack of empathy and advocacy on behalf of the students. Students can see when leaders treat others more justly than themselves, causing them to retreat; not attending events, classes, etc.. Because if a "leader" is doing this, what is everyone else thinking or doing that supports this behavior. The leader now cannot reach not only this student, but others who are close to the student, have seen how they treated that student, or any other students this one impacted student has informed of their negative interaction, further diminishing their effectiveness in their role as a leader.

For higher education leaders, the office where they conduct their affairs is the perfect place to build empathy since this is where students and advisors alike spend most of their time. Having a culture of empathy within higher education offices exhibits compassion and a genuine interest in the students. This type of environment will allow for new students to come in and feel comfortable, current students will want to celebrate accomplishments, seek help willingly, and encourage others to come into the office. Taylor defines empathy as the ability and willingness to open our minds to the perspectives of others, with empathetic cultures retaining the best people and enjoying higher productivity (Taylor, 2021). If empathy leads to retention, then the skill is one higher education leaders should be practicing as quality interactions aide in the improvement of retention on college campuses. In an environment of empathy, students would not have to beg their leaders to intervene, rather higher education professionals would love to do so on behalf of the students.

Being an academic advisor has been the biggest blessing shaping my experiences in higher education. I could speak on several different experiences each week that have shaped me as a leader. I started as an academic advisor at the age of 24, so I was the closest in age to the students compared to the other 6 colleagues who worked in the office. With me being close to my students in age, it was easier to establish an avenue of respect, with the students not addressing me by my first name, but as Mr. Vance because of the position I was in and how I was there to help guide them through college. On the flip side, I was able to connect and build lasting relationships with them, speaking with and catching up with them in person or over the phone on a consistent basis. I was transparent, real, and allowed the students to have a safe space. My office was always filled with students, being called "Club Vance" by my direct manager at the time and others in the school. Leading with empathy when interacting with students and advocating for ALL students produced this environment; an environment that no longer exists because I left the position.

Since the environment no longer is extremely welcoming to students, it upsets me. I worked hard to allow them to feel and be free in the office. I even had the students fundraise to get a couch put into my office because they were always there and the couch is gone. It upsets that the student-centered and student-first environment I established is nonexistent. This was something I prided myself on, making it easier for the Office of STUDENT

Affairs to be a place they would come to enjoy, but now it just seems like the principal's office.

Each student and their scenarios were different, but there is one that stands out exemplifying empathy. There was a young man on the basketball team who was one of my students. Our department had an "assigned" athletic academic advisor. She would have all the athletes come to her for advising based on her contacts and history with the athletic department. She would advise them on being "compliant" with NCAA and university regulations, but never really had conversations with the students about what THEY wanted for their futures long term. She trained me on how to use the adivsing systems and not how to be an advisor. I appreciated her techniques on the technical side, but the way she treated and at times screamed at students stood out negatively to me, knowing I had to make a change so all students could be successful and not just a certain population or those who she thought she had the only answer for.

STUDENT EXPERIENCE

One day, the student on the basketball team came to me after going to the self-proclaimed "athletic" advisor and said, "Vance, I need the real and I know you will keep it 100 with me." Now, the student and I had a relationship because I had hired him back to back summers to work the aforementioned summer program,there was history and comfortability there. He was now a senior with an extra year of eligibility left and was trying to figure out which master's degree program he should sign up for within the school. The other advisor brushed him off because he "changed his major too much" and one of the degree programs he was considering was one of the majors he changed from. However, after very in-depthand real conversations, the student and I came up with him going back to his original field when he first applied, finance.

He applied to the program, was accepted, and got his final year of eligibility cleared and was ready to go. Because he was on the basketball team, he would miss a lot of class and assignment concepts due to traveling. I connected him with another student, who I worked closely with as I served as her advisor as a student and while she was senior class president. She was a sharp individual who loved helping and connecting and the two of them was gold! They would FaceTime while he was on the road, whether on the bus to games or in hotel rooms explaining class concepts.

When he returned from one trip, I was in the office alone and he came in and said, "Vance, you saved me, thank you for believing in me. I want to help someone the same way you helped me. Show me how." My compassion and empathy jumped out for him. I thought to myself, how are we as higher education leaders not taking input from those who really need to be giving it? We should not be prescriptive in leading, but developmental and proactive. This young man had a plan and it was my duty to make sure he fulfilled it. The following year he went on himself to get another master's degree, which was paid for, at a large institution in the south in Urban Education and Leadership. He works with the young men on the basketball team directing their day to day operations. He also is the Marketing and Finance Director for an NBA player, who expressed to him, this would not be possible if he would have never gotten the Masters of Science in Finance degree, a degree he almost did not pursue.

Situations like this student, because there are tons more, excite me about being a leader. The shared responsibility in their success propels me out of any comfort zone I may have had for the day. Students are always seeking guidance and I am happy to be a part of their journey. Even, checking in on their success journey once they have left my office or inbox, hearing their updates brings a joy I cannot explain. I can use stories such as these to inspire future generations of leaders in higher education for them to know they can be impactful, they can change lives, and they are here to make a difference.

EMPLOYEE EXPERIENCE

Currently I manage employees on a day to day basis. I oversee a lot of the academic functions within the school I work for, so a bunch of functions means a bunch of people. There is this one guy on the team who is around my age. He is an amazing person and does his job really well. The problem: HE HATES IT HERE! He has also dealt with a lot of death, personal situations, and other things I needed to help him through and keep him motivated. He has said, "If it was not for you, I would have been left." He is waiting until he finishes up his masters degree in Criminal Justice to make a move away from higher education and with a few credits left, he can see the light. Him finishing matters to me because he came to asking, "how to get out," and all I could think of was the conversation I had with my manager to switch into higher education. Someone helped me, and I am here to help others reach their full potential. As a leader, the goal is to get the best out of those you are leading and his best is not where he currently is, so we are working to get him where he needs to be.

When I first started in the role, I met with each of the direct reports and one question I asked was, "How can I help you get to where you want to be"? His very candid answer was, "By helping me get out of here and find a new job." While some may take that the wrong way, it was the way in which he said it, I needed to unpack. There was a concerned undertone there and I wanted to help him address this. I wanted to make sure he was being engaged in ways that would benefit him and his intended career trajectory so much that when he finishes school, he is set in a perfect position.

Working with him has taught me how to be flexible, not with just direct reports, but myself as well. With all of the moving parts in his life, he is always coming to me with some sort of ask or exception. Some have seen them as excuses, but because I lead with empathy, learned him as a person, and am understanding, I do not look at the things he does as excuses, but rather opportunities to learn flexibility. His work has not fallen off and is actually able to take on more than he is supposed to and does so without question or hesitation, so yes, I willingly accommodate his exceptions when asked. Being empathetic has allowed him and I to connect and push each other to grow in ways many would miss because they see his asks as excuses and not opportunities to learn empathy.

Now, I am not naive, but because he is a great worker and I know what his ultimate career goals are and I have been helping him achieve those. Being close to graduation, I have introduced him to people in my network who are able to help him or introduce him to people who can. To me, this is what being a leader is all about; placing people in places to succeed and leaving them or them leaving you in a better place than when the relationship initially started. Him being close to being in the career he wants brings the both of us joy, because it is a milestone we have been working on since I was hired a year and a half ago. Being able to contribute to the success of others is the reason I love when my alarm clock goes off each day, whether a student or co-worker.

ADVICE TO MY FORMER SELF

In higher education, we have to learn how to work with people from *all* walks of life. Coming from the finance world, I was not prepared for the shift in the amount of people I would interact with on a day to day basis. So, to my 24-year-old self, I would say do not stop attending conferences and training events. When I got into higher education, these completely stopped. I am sure going to conferences would have catapulted my ability and knowledge on how to work with people in the many situations higher education presents. Conferences allow you to speak with others about problems, concerns, industry trends, and how to address each from several perspectives.

Having several perspectives while learning how to be in higher education is a value add. Just seeking help from those within your institution can be biased or just may not work. The colleagues in your institution may have limited views, especially if they have been with the institution for a number of years and are just stuck in the "university way." The "university way" may work for some things, but with the world changing daily, collaboration outside of the university at conferences and training events can and will help to push the university forward.

More advice I would give my former self would be to collaborate more outside of the department I work in. In both of my university roles, I worked very closely with those just in the specific schools I was a part of. Increased collaboration between schools and departments campus-wide should lead to cross-facilitation and enhanced programming. These connections can grow to also impact students positively, creating minors, certificates, and dual degree programs. These interactions with others can also help introduce students to other parts of campus, programming, and curriculum. This would especially benefit all of the students who would come to you not necessarily knowing what they want to do, so being introduced to others to have candid and honest conversations will and can help.

RECOMMENDATIONS FOR FUTURE HIGHER EDUCATION LEADERS

What truly helps me in this field is learning people for who *they* are. As a leader, you can have two people who have the same profile, but could not be more different. There can be two accounting major students coming to you for help. However, you cannot give the same advice to student A that you gave student B. They are their own people and getting to know each student, employee, or other stakeholders and how to handle their situations is imperative. It can be after meetings, events, or advising sessions, but be intentional to set time aside to have those extra conversations that are not about work or school, but to check in, catch up, learn something new about a person. This will show you actually care and they are not just a number on a roster or an employee with goals to meet, but the people you are speaking with and getting to know will understand by your actions they are people, people who matter.

This next recommendation is because of the first one: *Go to therapy.* As you speak to a number of folks as an empathetic leader, they will dump their life on you for as long as you let them. You will see happiness, sadness, anger, frustration, grief and being a higher education leader, you take these things on by default. You may not feel as if all of the stories and dumping is impacting you, but one day it will hit and then as you were the person to talk to, you will now need a person to talk to. Carrying the emotions of others and always giving of your time, energy, effort, and advice will get heavy. Please, find a therapist you trust to speak with to make sure you are mentally able to continue to do so. Allow the therapist to provide tips and tricks on working with people on a daily basis.

Lastly, before I leave you all, the last piece of advice I have is find a mentor. I still do not have anyone I call a definite mentor in the field. I have a lot of trusted people who have given great words of advice, but a mentor should be that person to help you navigate the field, consistently bounce ideas off of, confide in, and maybe even shadow. I do feel people would say yes if I asked them to be my mentor, but it also has to be a great fit professionally and personally. Just because someone gives great advice does not mean they should be a mentor. Take the time to vet anyone you want to be a mentor; ask them questions, watch them work, watch how they lead and then determine if this is someone you definitely want to follow.

REFERENCES

Merriam-Webster. (2021). Empathy. In *Merriam-Webster.com dictionary*. https://www.merriam-webster.com/dictionary/empathy.

Taylor, J. C. (2021, April 12). *Message from the president*. SHRM. https://www.shrm.org/executive/resources/people-strategy-journal/spring2021/Pages/president-message.aspx.

Walters, L. M., & Seyedian, M. (2016). Improving academic advising using quality function deployment: A case study. *College Student Journal, 50*(2), 253–267.

CHAPTER 18

PSYCHOLOGICAL SAFETY
Setting the Tone for Team Effectiveness

LaToya Jordan

ABSTRACT

This chapter is centered on the significance of psychological safety on teams higher education teams. It provides practical advice for aspiring leaders on how to create a culture of psychological safety that promotes team effectiveness, creativity, and innovation. We begin by defining psychological safety as a sense of confidence in a team's ability to share ideas, questions, concerns, and mistakes without fear of negative consequences. From there, we explore the reasons why psychological safety is crucial for team effectiveness, especially in higher education. We explain how psychological safety can improve communication, increase creativity, amplify innovation, and enhance development. This chapter outlines several strategies for higher education leaders to promote psychological safety within their teams or departments, Tactics include: modeling vulnerability, actively listening,, and delivering feedback in a supportive manner. We also address potential barriers to establishing psychological safety and suggest ways to overcome them. Overall, this chapter discusses why it is important for aspiring higher education leaders to create psychological safety within their teams or departments. In support of this critical need, we also share various tools and strategies.

The Handbook for Aspiring Higher Education Leaders, pages 167–174
Copyright © 2024 by Information Age Publishing
www.infoagepub.com
All rights of reproduction in any form reserved.

As a talent strategist, coach, and educator, I typically use the professional journey of my clients to help illuminate relevant inflection points that link to the purpose of our work together. It's not often, though, that I take the opportunity to leverage the same tactic to reflect on my professional journey. What started as a passion for students and student communities evolved into employees and employees environments. I began my professional career as an academic advisor in athletics, working directly with high-profile student-athletes. First and foremost, my goal at the time was to make sure my advisees were seen as humans with depth of experiences. They were studentswho happened to be highly skilled athletes, not the other way around. After developing student-athletes, I shifted to the role of assistant director of residence life at a large urban school, where I was responsible for six upper-class residence halls in the heart of the city. In this role, the goal was to ensure students felt safe, seen, and in community with each other amid the city's intense and electric environment.

Upon completing my PhD in social-organizational psychology, I transitioned from working with students at large institutions to working with employees at Fortune 500 companies. In these corporate roles, I led various functions within HR (talent management, succession planning, DEI, and leadership and employee development). As a corporate executive, I was responsible for multiple aspects of human capital strategies and organizational cultures. At the same time, I returned to academia as an adjunct professor teaching at small and large institutions for undergraduate and graduate students. Now, as a consultant and executive coach, I specialize in supporting women of color executives in higher education. I bring decades of experience in talent strategy and leadership development to spaces where there is also a shortage of resources and support. When I reflect on the common thread of my time at universities with my time in corporate spaces, it is my sincere desire to ensure individuals feel seen, heard, and valued in these spaces.

Thinking back on my leadership advancement, two pivotal moments have shaped my leadership journey. I recall a specific incident when a colleague learned the news of my promotion to an executive role. While we were previously peers, I was now at a higher level role than he was, but I held him in high regard as he was someone who mentored me when I first started at this company. He also worked very closely with senior leaders so I was eager to gain his counsel on my approach to the new position. In a private moment, when I asked him for advice, he turned to me and said in a stern tone, it was time for me to start to act more like a senior leader and leave the other behavior behind. I was so dismayed by his response. What did he mean? What specifically was he referring to? Have people been talking? I went on a mental tailspin about this brief, but impactful advice. I started second-guessing all of my actions. I began wondering if people were talking about me and, worse, if I belonged in the role.

I started to tweak my leadership style to align with the leadership models that I observed across the organization. In the same vein, I also started dressing the part, donning. It felt so unnatural to me to behave in a stoic, highly directive approach. And the look of the corporate leader felt bland and lacked my personality. But the words "act more like a senior leader" rang loudly in my ear, so I stayed the course. In the end, though, I wasn't enjoying myself in this new role. The pivot point came when an employee walked up to me and thanked me for representing within the senior ranks. At that time, I slowly started to add a bit of my style to my executive wardrobe, including wearing African fabric skirts. This particular employee, an African American man, remarked how proud he was to see me wear these fabrics while attending these critical meetings. I could not believe what I was hearing. I wore these clothes to reignite my spirit and had no idea the impact it was having on others. I became a version of "acting like an executive." So, I had a decision to make on the model I wanted to project. With that, I vowed to show up authentically as me going forward, no matter the role or the environment I was in. Being authentically and uniquely me mattered not just to me but to all those who were watching and learning from me.

The second pivotal moment in my leadership journey happened unexpectedly. At the end of a routine leadership meeting, functional leaders shared some quick updates with the group. One item related to downsizing a particular group caught my attention because there were no questions or conversations about this decision. Everyone simply nodded in agreement and moved on to the next item. I was struck by the individuals who would lose their jobs and needed to better understand the decision. After the meeting, I went to the functional leader and their boss to gain better clarity on the direction. While I recognized that it was their decision to make, I also was clear that my leadership role in HR and DEI gave me the responsibility to ask the appropriate questions to better understand the matter. Opting out of engaging in this situation would be counter to what I was called to do as a leader. Something internally clicked for me that leadership was more of a "verb" than a noun such that leadership required action. It wasn't enough to be in the role but it was critical that I actively engaged within the role. That required competence and confidence. Once I was clear that I was comfortable with my levels in both areas, I changed my posture as a leader. The trajectory of my leadership changed at this point because I began to genuinely stand in my power as a leader, particularly across my peer group. I used my voice to ask questions or offer other viewpoints. I was no longer sitting in the seat, but I was standing and stretching and taking up more space. After that experience, I felt much more comfortable speaking up and leveraging my experience to make an impact within the role.

ADVICE TO MY YOUNGER SELF

As a new leader in higher education, looking back, there are few pieces of advice I would give myself. First, I would remind myself of the uniqueness I bring to the role. So instead of fitting into a perceived mold, I would create my own mold. Often, there is a great deal of anxiety as a new leader to fit in and "not rock the boat." But I would remind myself that the best thing I could do for me, and those I serve, is to show up authentically. The second piece of advice I would give myself is to seek mentors inside and outside of the university. I recall being a young professional so keen on being respected and valued that I did not proactively look for a mentor because I was so busy trying to prove myself. The fact is that these two constructs are not mutually exclusive. You can prove your value to an organization while also being mentored. Additionally, often mentoring provides a pathway to greater success and supplies a sounding board to help illuminate an enhanced sense of value. So, I would remind myself that there really is no downside to receiving mentoring, especially as a new leader. The final piece of advice I would give myself as a new leader is to be brave. I would tell myself to take ambitious leaps with the expectation to fail, but more importantly to learn. One thing that we do not realize at that time, but in some ways, new leaders have less to "lose" at the start of their careers. It might be the most optimal time to take chances on new approaches or strategies.

This latter advice, to take big, bold leaps requires an environment where you feel safe to fail. As a new leader, this is critical. "Humans' ability to grow is infinite... when they feel safe." This famous quote by Carl Roger is at the core of the tenets to success as a leader. The notion of creating psychological safety is often overlooked by many leaders as their focus is typically on executing goals. But paying attention to creating a safe environment is a game changer in any workplace. Generally speaking, psychological safety is a shared belief by members of a team that the team is safe to take risks within a particular context (Edmondson, 1999). Specifically, in spaces that are highly hierarchical, or with a great deal of reverence towards titles of roles (e.g., governmental and/or higher education institutions), the idea of fostering an environment where employees feel safe to express themselves is often unheard of and/or disregarded in service of maintaining the power structure. But as research shows, such psychologically safe environments are foundational and critical to the performance of the team, bringing out the best in people and therefore the best work. Thus, it is imperative that higher education leaders do whatever is in their power to ensure psychological safety permeates their team culture.

Carl Rogers, a clinical psychologist, first introduced the term "psychological safety" in 1954 within a study on fostering creativity in individuals (What Is Psychological Safety? — Psychological Safety, n.d.). It was in 1965 that Edgar Schein and Warren Bennis termed it as a group experience that reduces interpersonal risk (Schein & Bennis, 1965). As a graduate assistant within a student life department, I recall the fear that permeated throughout the staff at meetings. The leader would have a strong, negative reaction to questions or push back on ideas. Less hostile versions of that environment continued to be present in other departments where I worked. It wasn't until I joined a small team as an academic advisor in athletics that I experienced the true freedom to express my opinions and contribute freely. While I didn't have a name for this new environment, I immediately felt the difference in this new work space and was grateful for it.

As I have shifted to being a leader, the memory of what it was like when I felt stifled to share my opinion and I've continued to be committed to having a safe environment for my team. Ensuring an environment exists where individuals to feel safe to take risks is paramount to team effectiveness and should be a top priority to any leader. Research has shown its impact on employee engagement, innovation, and retention (Gallo, 2023). This culture of safety determines how the employees and teams learn, how they function towards toward goal attainment and how they interact with each other. When leaders can provide a safe space to take risks, their team members are able to bring their authentic self to work and are not afraid to ask bold questions or to suggest bolder solutions. Thus, psychological safety is a crucial phenomenon that institutions and leaders need to apply considerable attention.

According to Edmundson, there are three keys leadership tips to foster psychological safety on teams (Edmondson, 1999):

1. *Frame the work as a learning problem, not an execution problem*—this shifts the approach from an execution posture to an iterative, learning posture, creating value-add regardless of the final end product or output. As a leader, consider how you outline work expectations. Is there a way to relate the output to gaining new insights on the problem in addition to the specific outcomes? This minor adjustment in framing the work will reduce the focus on getting to a specific, "right" output and instead will lean more heavily on learning throughout the process to gain better insights. In turn, this approach will also encourage employees to feel free to ask questions, try innovative ways to solve the problem, and even take bold leaps in service of learning something new. Creativity tends to be an outcome of this way of thinking about the work, where employees feel more boundless in the way they work. The actions as a result of this change in the problem framing is where the growth mindset begins.

As I've moved into higher-level leadership roles, this is a posture I have taken whenever possible. Initially, I struggled with the idea of completing work for "learning sake" because work or deliverables were not always given to me from my bosses with room to learn. But, when possible, I would tease out aspects of the project where there was room to focus on gathering new information as a key goal instead of getting "it" right. This would allow the team freedom to try novel approaches, talk to different stakeholders, test a unique assumption all for "learning sake" but inevitably in service of the project outcome. In turn, I've found the team to be way more energized to move things forward with some novelty or curiosity baked into the work than just pushing them towards a perfect outcome or solution.

2. *Acknowledge your own fallibility*—a leader that owns up to their shortcoming creates a comfort level for employees to do the same. They feel safe to admit mistakes and listen to other's ideas. One of the greatest gifts a leader can give to their team is to show their uncertainty, vulnerability, and imperfection. In other words, their humanity. Why? Because this creates space for involvement by your team. As a leader, I have found using phrases like "I am not an expert in this and would love your input," or "I may miss something so I need to hear from you," or "Can you help me think this through" allows my team to comfortably offer their perspective. What's more, their sense of ownership of the work increases and I experience them to be more proactive in helping solve challenges. These behaviors adds to the quality of the results and increases employee engagement. While these outcomes have been phenomenal consequences of a psychologically safe work environment, one of my favorite aspects of this approach is that frees me up from feeling like I have to have all of the answers. This has led to a sense of relief, lightening my load related to some unwritten expectation and responsibility that as the leader, I must also be the expert. In turn, by removing that unconscious stressor, I show up more present and subsequently more effective as a leader.

3. *Model curiosity*—be a curious leader! This final tip is my favorite! Within this approach, ask lots of questions to signal approval of questioning and provide opportunities for input from team members. This is a marvelous opportunity to lean into divergent thinking. Asking questions creates room for employees to voice their ideas. In making space for diverse perspectives to be heard, a leader models openness to gathering input from the collective team leading to team members feeling seen and valued. I have found this to be such a critical component to teaming and employee engage-

ment and therefore, worth making considerable effort to drive this dynamic home. Even if you have a strong opinion on the topic, I will pause from sharing my perspective and, instead, model a bit of curiosity in order to hear other ways to tackle the challenge, which has provided me with a lens on my team's thought process. In doing so, I found my team to be more eager to share and more committed to the work and the outcome. I have found that this approach also clears up assumptions that I, or others, may have on the team and gives me a range of insights to make more educated decisions.

While the merits of establishing psychological safety may appear obvious, it could be challenging to create within certain organizational cultures. Barriers to fostering this environment are often based in the individual fear of speaking up. This fear could be grounded in the anxiety of being seen as ignorant or incompetent. It could also come from a worry that questions or push back could lead to a reputation of being negative or disruptive. At a system level, developing a psychologically safe culture could be challenged by formally entrenched hierarchy or policies that reinforces norms that counteract that of a safe environment. For example, written or unwritten rules about expected behavior in decision making, the approach to divergent thinking, or the style of communication, if navigated carelessly could all negatively affect the efforts to increase psychological safety. These types of barriers may lead to a longer timeline in building a safe culture, but they are not impossible to overcome.

As higher education leaders look to create and maintain a culture of psychological safety within their teams or departments, the following are a myriad of best practice approaches (Test Gorilla, 2023; Jimenez, 2022):

1. Establish specific norms that will create a culture conducive to psychological safety such as:
    a. Encourage transparency amongst team members
    b. Foster open communication and active listening
    c. Show respect for different opinions and embrace conflict
    d. Build a culture of recognition and appreciation
    e. Treat mistakes as correctable rather than an opportunity to play the blame game
2. Be mindful of negative patterns within the team and be prepared to recognize if teams are suppressing ideas and different opinions
3. Adopt a progressive mindset by:
    a. Make sure you are fully engaged with your teams and include them in decision making
    b. Be self-aware of your biases and be open to feedback

    c. Invest in self-development skills such as self-awareness, vulnerability, empathy, and compassion
    d. Be an advocate for diversity, equity, and inclusion in meaningful ways
    e. Provide different way for employees to share their thoughts when regular methods are not working

The case for psychological safety has been made countless times. As a new leader, it is important to take stock of the value of creating such an environment and then adjusting one's behavior to achieve it. As I consider my leadership journey, I realized that psychological safety has always been a part of my leadership style. I simply did not know it. I knew it was important to hear from the full team. I knew it was critical for team members to feel seen and heard. The positive outcomes were not as obvious to me. To know that it leads to higher engagement, increased retention, innovation, and trust makes creating this culture in teams the obvious choice. They may not have an award for the leader who has the highest psychological safety at an institution. But the effort will speak for itself as the leader will be seen as someone worth trusting enough to follow. After all, what's a leader without followers?

REFERENCES

Edmondson, A. (1999). Psychological safety and learning behavior in work teams. *Administrative Science Quarterly, 44*(2), 350–383.

Gallo, A. (2023, February 15). What is psychological safety? *Harvard Business Review*. https://hbr.org/2023/02/what-is-psychological-safety

Jimenez, J (2022, October 17). *Why psychological safety at work matters and how to create it.* Better Up. https://www.betterup.com/blog/why-psychological-safety-at-work-matters#section4.

Schein, E. H., & Bennis, W. G. (1965). *Personal and organizational change through group methods.* Wiley.

Test Gorilla (2023). *Psychological safety: 10 ways to empower your employees.* https://www.testgorilla.com/blog/psychological-safety

What is Psychological Safety? Psychological Safety (n.d.). https://psychsafety.co.uk/about-psychological-safety

CHAPTER 19

ACADEMIC LEADERSHIP AT A SMALL LIBERAL ARTS COLLEGE

Bradley Fuster

ABSTRACT

Small Independent Liberal Arts Colleges occupy a special and challenging place within the higher education landscape. Confronted with decreasing traditional-aged student demographics with less ability and willingness to pay, and increasing expenses and competition, the leadership required to make such institutions viable is significant. By focusing on the right priorities and courageously doing certain things differently, some higher education leaders have managed to stabilize and right-size their institutions and situate them to thrive amidst an otherwise hostile environment. Key personal leadership attributes can be intentionally developed to help arm college leaders with the capacity and capital to be effective, impactful agents of positive and transformational change. While one might argue that some of these attributes are needed to lead any institution, the highly relational nature of small independent colleges requires an affiliative approach more so than at larger public or research-intensive institutions, which are more political in nature. Intentionally developing these qualitative characteristics gives leaders the needed tools to lead small independent liberal arts colleges through the many modern challenges they face.

My higher education career began in 1999, when, at the tender age of 26, I accepted a position as assistant professor of music at Montana State University. At that time, the department was heavily tenured and politically and socially divided. During my third year, the department chair went on sabbatical, and I was offered the interim department chair position. Having enjoyed and learned from the experience, I later took a one-year leave of absence to finish my doctorate at the University of Southern California. The curriculum afforded me the opportunity to take three graduate courses outside of music, so I elected to take courses in higher education administration and leadership. I returned to Montana State for one year before accepting a position as founding music department chair at Buffalo State University. I served in this role for nine years and further honed my leadership abilities. In 2013, I began a string of interim positions during a time of institutional transition at Buffalo State, which included positions as chief information officer, in enrollment management, and the provost's office. I completed an American Council on Education (ACE) Fellowship at Vassar College and, after returning to Buffalo State for one year, transitioned to my current position as provost and vice president for academic affairs at Keuka College. Keuka College is a small independent liberal arts institution that also offers professional programs focused on Health and Human Services. In 2020–2021, the president was diagnosed with breast cancer and stepped away from the institution to focus on her recovery. During this disruptive and unpredictable time, I served as acting president to help the institution responsibly navigate to the other side of the pandemic.

In this chapter, I draw freely upon the above-described professional experience and my own observations as further supported by literature to offer leadership advice specifically through the lens of leading the academic enterprise at a small liberal arts college (SLAC). For clarity, I have segmented my observations into four constituent groups to include students, staff, faculty, and peers. There are obviously additional stakeholders such as community members, trustees, donors, emeritus faculty, alumni, and so on; however, the vast percentage of my time and energy spent as an academic leader is devoted to interacting with these four constituencies.

STUDENTS: DEVELOPMENTAL BARRIERS

I have intentionally and symbolically placed students first in the sequence of constituents higher education leaders must serve. Serving students and ensuring their success must remain our prime directive. One of the main reasons students are attracted to SLACs is for the small population size, which affords them closely mentored learning opportunities and individualized attention. Generally located in a bucolic setting and tucked away from the pressures and hustle of the real world, SLACs aim to create a safe haven in which students can focus and learn (Abrams, 2022). As Provost, students and their parents feel comfortable emailing me directly when they encounter a problem or concern. I interact informally with students every day, and work hard to keep their intellectual and social development at the core of my decision-making. It is important for me to remain connected to students because so many of my decisions impact them directly, and without being connected to their names, faces, and challenges, I might too easily stop making student-centric decisions.

Placing students at the center of the decision-making appears in numerous ways. One salient example is course scheduling. Many institutions have a faculty-centric course scheduling process, in which courses are scheduled around the desires and convenience of the faculty first, without much regard for how students flow through their courses and day (Hunter, 2020). As I have closely listened to students' grievances and their student evaluations, and examined student exit survey data I have noticed bottleneck courses that prevent students from maintaining satisfactory academic progress or reaching their anticipated graduation date. Leading the academic enterprise at a SLAC allows leaders to proactively consider such data and rapidly make positive change to best serve students.

Another common example I have noticed can be found in the General Education curriculum commonly found at SLACs. As with course scheduling, the content of many general education curricula is faculty-centric in so far as faculty, especially those in the liberal arts which generally contain fewer numbers of majors, insist that their course be included within the general education requirements as a means to ensure robust enrollment, and hence increased security for their positions and programs (Aylesworth, et al., 2022). I have worked hard with my faculty to reframe the general education content into the practical considerations of what outcomes do students need in order to meet the institutional mission, and what skills, qualities, and habits of mind do we hope to instill in them through the general education curriculum? These questions enable leaders to unearth misalignments and gaps. Highlighting these shortfalls through meaningful and pointed programmatic assessment is the first step toward making student-centered curricular change.

STUDENTS: MENTAL HEALTH BARRIERS

Generation Z students, in particular, require extra consideration from academic leaders because that they are emotionally frail by comparison to previous generations of students (Elmore & McPeak, 2019). When examining the data and underlying causes, I find that students who fail out or withdraw from my institution, aside from financial reasons, are not exiting due to a lack of intellectual horsepower, but rather because of a lack of emotional and social maturity. Students are arriving at institutions after two years of remote learning in which they experienced arrested development. Many of the typical high school rites of passage, such as a senior prom or graduation, were canceled due to public health concerns. Nearly all of the social learning that occurs outside of the classroom was forgone for two years, so consequently, students are graduating high school with a deficit of social skills. One of my faculty stated quite eloquently that the post-pandemic student is arriving at college appearing to be 18 years old, but with the emotional maturity of a much younger student.

Even without the developmental barriers induced by forced remote learning in 2020–2021, the mental health of generation Z was and remains a real barrier to student success. Here are the sobering statistics as compiled by the JED Foundation:

- 1 in 3 (30.6%) young adults between the ages of 18 and 25 experienced a mental, behavioral, or emotional health issue in the past year (SAMHSA, 2021)
- 26.9% of teens ages 12–17 have one or more mental, emotional, developmental, or behavioral problems (NSCH, 2019).
- 36.7% of high school students reported feelings of sadness or hopelessness in the past year. This percentage is higher for females (46.6%), Hispanic students (40.0%), and lesbian, gay, or bisexual students (66.3%) (CDC, 2020).
- Among college students, 29.1% have been diagnosed with anxiety, and 23.6% have been diagnosed with depression (NCHA, 2021).

Being a modern student-centered leader demands one to possess a keen awareness of these challenges. By shining a light on these concerns across the entire organization, leaders can work to destigmatize mental illness for students and redirect resources, programming, and interventions that best support students.

STAFF

At SLACs, staff are often the front lines of defense to solve student problems. Whereas faculty often incorrectly see themselves in the role of primary problem-solver for students, the fact remains that a tremendous amount of unseen and often uncelebrated work occurs amongst the staff to support students. Every college has a small army of caring and empathetic individuals working in every division as administrative assistants and professionals in the offices of Admissions, Registrar, Financial Aid, Bursar, IT, Athletics, Library, Disability Services, Health and Counseling, Career Development, Chaplain, Inclusion, Security, Dining, Residence Life, etc. who are wrapping 24–7 support around the student.

From my experience, both at large and small institutions, there is an unfortunate disconnection between the work of the faculty and the work of the staff. This siloism is fueled by many factors. Often faculty and staff are represented by separate unions and have separate governance structures and handbooks. Faculty and student affairs staff are often represented by two different Vice Presidents, and those Vice Presidents often find themselves in the unenviable position of competing for the same scarce resources. This can create a conundrum for SLAC Presidents to untangle. For example, whereas the primacy of the academic mission is never in question, the overall institutional mission might be best served by adding mental health counselors rather than tenure-track faculty. In this forced binary choice for resource allocation, winners and losers are created, and neither side understands or takes time to appreciate the plight of the other. In the end, I always remind stakeholders in these conversations that we serve students, and we must ultimately default to their greatest needs. Eventually, after enough encounters with these types of decisions, a cultural shift occurs in which the stakeholders will default to making student-centric decisions.

In Tia Brown McNair's book, *Becoming a Student-Ready College: A New Culture of Leadership for Student Success* (McNair et al., 2022), the author flips the common institutional trope of bemoaning the lack of college-ready students and rather focuses on how colleges can become more student-ready ecosystems. In particular, she focuses on designing eco-systemic partnerships between faculty and staff. She also illuminates the deepening equity gap in outcomes for underrepresented, Pell-eligible, and first-generation students.

When we hired new VP of Student Development at my institution, we wanted to intentionally collaborate and align the work of our respective teams. We used this book as a common read jointly with our teams and held a roundtable debrief to capture and catalog changes we might make to better align with the high-impact practices described in the book. As a result, there are now streamlined committee structures on which academic and student affairs administrators are both represented. The President also recently reorganized the Vice Presidents' physical offices such that my office as Provost is collocated in the same suite with the Vice President of Student Development. This physical proximity facilitates ad hoc problem-solving and helps ensure alignment of our agendas and daily work.

Removing the common siloism between academic affairs and student affairs is a key consideration at all institutions. I am reminded of the famous story of when John F. Kennedy was touring NASA and happened upon a janitor. The president asked him what he does at NASA. The janitor replied, "I am putting a man on the moon." This is such a beautiful analogy of how everyone who works on a college campus is an educator, whether or not they teach in the classroom. Coaches, maintenance workers, librarians, financial aid—virtually everyone is in a position to educate and develop students. This type of tight mission alignment between faculty and staff is desperately needed to help ensure that the entirety of the institution's resources are working in harmony and lockstep to support student success.

FACULTY

As Provost, the vast majority of my time is spent on faculty matters. The leadership skill set required to be an effective provost or chief academic officer, especially at a SLAC, is varied and sizable. First and most importantly, one must be able to build trust. While there is no single proven method to effectively doing this, many simple leadership attributes and skills, such as deep listening, authenticity, emotional intelligence, a sense of humor, storytelling, change management, and the ability to reframe challenges, are essential. Below is a list of books I have read and debriefed together with my team of academic leaders over the past few years. While these are all incredible resources, I have listed them in the order I found them most impactful to my team.

> *Reframing Organizations, Artistry, Choice, and Leadership* (Bolman & Deal, 2021)
> *The Emotionally Strong Leader: An Inside-Out Journey to Transformational Leadership* (Stern, 2022)
> *The Leadership Challenge: How to Make Extraordinary Things Happen in Organizations* (Kouzes, 2017)
> *Change Intelligence: Use the Power of CQ to Lead Change That Sticks* (Trautlein, 2013)
> *Navigating Polarities: Using Both/And Thinking To Lead Transformation* (Emerson & Lewis, 2019)

Each of these resources has allowed my team to build common vocabulary. For example, the impact of reading these books together is immediately apparent to me when I hear someone on my team reference a "*structural problem,*" citing Bolman & Deal, "*self awareness,*" citing Stern, "*leading with heart,*" citing Kouzes, "*the visionary versus the executor versus the champion,*" citing Trautlein, or "*walking in the third way*," citing Emerson & Lewis. Once these concepts organically permeate throughout my enterprise, it is evidence that the team is functioning at a higher level and with more universal understanding of important leadership concepts.

We have also completed and debriefed the DISC assessment and Leadership Practices Inventory (LPI) and examined extensive case studies and peer interviewing techniques. All of this was done in an effort to build common vocabulary and a high-performing team of established and emerging academic leaders. These sessions usually occurred at day-long retreats in between semesters. I've made these professional development opportunities voluntary for my team, however virtually everyone chooses to participate. Whereas I was fortunate to receive excellent mentoring and world-class professional leadership development as an academic, I realize that many academics, especially those working in smaller, resource-constrained institutions, will often rise into leadership positions with little or no support to develop their leadership skills. This expansion of leadership knowledge and common vocabulary supports not only existing leaders in their ability to work effectively in their units but also promotes morale and good will among those not yet in leadership positions by showing them the institution is invested in their professional growth and supports them when they seek to move into leadership roles, whether on key committees or as candidates for divisional leadership roles. Spending the time and money to build this capacity in my team and throughout the enterprise has been the single most important investment I have made during my time as Provost, and I attribute the many administrative successes we have enjoyed to this decision.

It will likely come as no surprise that Faculty can be a difficult group to lead. Faculty pride themselves on being self-directed, have been entrusted with academic freedom that provides a great deal of autonomy in how they spend their time, and have governance mechanisms that allow for votes of no confidence in leadership if they are pushed too far, or otherwise unsatisfied with the direction of things. As a result, academic enterprises have a high degree of change-resistance, making it difficult to innovate or remain agile as the nature and future of work continues to rapidly evolve. Anecdotally, I ascribe to the 20–60–20 principle of faculty. In this paradigm, roughly 20% of the faculty are distrustful, anti-administrative, promulgate an "us vs. them" mentality, and are change-resistant (Fuster, 2020). In the middle of this model, we find the 60% of influenceable faculty that really do not get involved with college politics, simply want to teach great classes, do a good job, and go home. The remaining roughly 20% of faculty are your institutional cheerleaders. They are mission-driven, trusting, and go the extra mile to show up and lead from within.

Understanding the 20–60–20 principle has been enormously useful to me and my team as we craft messages to communicate complicated and emotionally charged topics in an effort to make transformational institutional change. I usually try to focus messaging toward the 60% of influenceable faculty, knowing that 20% are likely not to listen or trust the messaging, and 20% are already institutional champions for change. By developing a team of leaders that understands this dynamic within their own respective aggregate faculties and amongst the faculty as a whole, my team is better equipped to lead and steward institutional change.

ADVICE I WOULD GIVE MY YOUNGER SELF

Whereas there is a robust body of leadership literature on managing up (Abbajay, 2018) and managing down (Allison & Allison, 1986), there is a paucity of resources on lateral leadership. It is a given that institutional Presidents and Provosts must remain in strategic lockstep to have a highly functioning collegiate enterprise and that this relationship must be authentically trusting and genuine to maximize institutional performance. However, as I noted earlier in the chapter, institutional structure and dynamics often pit vice presidents against one another as they compete for the same scarce resources, or work to protect interests for projects that are not always student-centered.

As I think about relationship management with my other vice president colleagues around the table, there are two salient and authoritative sources that always come to my mind which have definitively shaped my leadership philosophy. First is the titanic work of Daniel Goleman in emotional intelligence (Goleman, 2020). Goleman states that emotional intelligence consists of four basic domains: Self Awareness, Self Regulation, Social Awareness, and, finally, Relationship Management. Goleman's view of relationship management demands that one places intention and awareness around each relationship. He also states that in order to effectively manage relationships with others, leaders must have a keen awareness of and ability to manage the effect people have on them and be aware of what they are feeling and what has led them to feel that way. Whether I am being attacked by a disgruntled faculty member for a decision with which they do not agree, or an angry parent who's student is being dismissed, maintaining self awareness, self regulation, social awareness, and relationship management skills has proven of paramount importance to my leadership. My personal experience confirms that leaders must be able to deftly manage the relationship with themselves before they are able to really effectively manage their relationships with others.

This is certainly easier said than done. While Goleman's work is psychosocially valuable in helping to manage one's own emotions, I always turn to Zen Master, peace activist, and Vietnamese Buddhist Monk Thích Nhất

Hạnh's work to get a better understanding of my own emotions and reactions to others. Thích Nhất Hạnh authored 75 books in his lifetime, and most of them have similar messages. In November 2022, I had the opportunity to travel to Hue, Vietnam and visit the pagoda where Thích Nhất Hạnh trained and was eventually laid to rest at the age of 95. It was a deeply spiritual experience which has further anchored my leadership and remains a source of emotional inspiration for me. Thích Nhất Hạnh posits that in order to be free of pain, fear, and anxiety people must practice treating others with compassion, empathy, and loving kindness. Even "enemies." This practice is grounded in mindfulness through which you appreciate every moment and breath with intentionality and joy (Hanh, 1987). Mindfulness can be practiced while walking, eating, meditating, or in a host of other applicable activities. Even during high-stakes meetings or debates in which tensions are running high, if someone has practiced mindfulness daily, they will likely show up with more leadership effectiveness and emotional intelligence, and ultimately be a more successful leader. More importantly, they will lead a happier life.

STRATEGIES TO ACHIEVE SUCCESS

Get an Accountability Partner or Coach

It is extremely difficult to improve self awareness, and, by extension, emotional intelligence if the only critical voice you hear is your own. Keeping someone close to you in your life, whether a spouse, family member, trusted friend, or trained professional who will call you on your bullshit and hold you accountable is invaluable for your leadership development.

Remain Thirsty and Humble

There is no replacement for the deep desire to keep improving. Academic leadership and leadership in general is part art and part science. Committing to the journey of self improvement is important. No one is perfect and everyone is a work-in-progress.

Everything is Impermanent

This is a Buddhist concept which posits that the way things are today is not the way they will always be. When things go wrong as they invariably do, it is important to remember that everything is temporary. Our jobs, titles, relationships, possessions, successes, and failures are all temporary. Live in the present moment, free of anxiety about the future and free of pain from the past. While this may sound simple, I have found it is extremely difficult to do. Meditation has helped me in this regard.

CONCLUSION

With shrinking student demographics, an unstable financial model, decreasing extramural support, and increasing skepticism with respect to the value of the liberal arts, leading a SLAC toward a more sustainable future requires leaders with multiple skill sets and abilities. An indefatigable determination to lead with authenticity, emotional intelligence, and commitment to develop these leadership attributes throughout the enterprise is required. Institutions that are stewarded by mindful, yet bold leaders will likely be able to make the best strategic moves to sustain themselves.

REFERENCES

Abbajay, M. (2018). *Managing up: How to move up, win at work, and succeed with any type of boss.* Wiley.

Abrams, S. J. (2022). *The liberal college bubble must burst.* Minding the Campus. Retrieved February 14, 2023, from https://www.mindingthecampus.org/2022/08/26/the-liberal-college-bubble-must-burst/

Advanced Solutions International, I. (n.d.). *Do you have a comprehensive picture of your students' health?* NCHA Home. Retrieved February 14, 2023, from https://www.acha.org/ncha

Allison, M. A., & Allison, E. W. (1986). *Managing up, managing down.* Simon & Schuster.

Aylesworth, A., Beneke, C., Betts, R. M., Carter, N. C., Dove, S., &; Moriarty, J. (2022). Advice: 7 hard-earned lessons from a curriculum makeover. *The Chronicle of Higher Education.* Retrieved February 14, 2023, from https://www.chronicle.com/article/7-hard-earned-lessons-from-a-curriculum-makeover?cid2=gen_login_refresh&cid=gen_sign_in

Bolman, L. G., & Deal, T. E. (2021). *Reframing organizations: Artistry, choice, and leadership.* Jossey-Bass.

Centers for Disease Control and Prevention. (2022). YRBSS. Retrieved February 14, 2023, from https://www.cdc.gov/healthyyouth/data/yrbs/index.htm

Elmore, T., & McPeak, A. (2019). *Generation Z unfiltered: Facing nine hidden challenges of the most anxious population.* Poet Gardener Publishing.

Emerson, B., & Lewis, K. (2019). *Navigating polarities: Using both/and thinking to lead transformation.* Paradoxical Press.

Fuster, B. J. (2020, August 20). Inside higher ed. A faculty member describes the lessons he's learned moving into an administrative position (opinion).

Retrieved February 14, 2023, from https://www.insidehighered.com/advice/2020/08/20/faculty-member-describes-lessons-hes-learned-moving-administrative-position

Goleman, D. (2020). *Emotional intelligence*. Bantam Books.

Hanh, T. N. (1987). *The miracle of mindfulness: A manual on meditation*. Beacon Press.

Hunter, L. (2020). *Your most powerful tool for improving outcomes may be hiding in plain sight: Student-centered course scheduling*. Higher Ed Connects. Retrieved February 14, 2023, from https://higheredconnects.com/course-scheduling/

Key Substance Use and Mental Health Indicators in the United States: Results from the 2020 National Survey on Drug Use and Health. SAMHSA.gov. (n.d.). Retrieved February 14, 2023, from https://www.samhsa.gov/data/taxonomy/term/110

Kouzes, J. M. (2017). *The leadership challenge*. Jossey-Bass.

McNair, T. B., Albertine, S. L., McDonald, N. L., Major, T., & Cooper, M. A. (2022). *Becoming a student-ready college: A new culture of leadership for student success*. Jossey-Bass.

Mental Health and Suicide Statistics. The Jed Foundation. (2022, September 30). Retrieved February 14, 2023, from https://jedfoundation.org/mental-health-and-suicide-statistics/

Stern, C. (2022). *The emotionally strong leader: An inside-out journey to transformational leadership*. Figure.1 Publishing.

Survey results. NSCH 2019: Children with mental, emotional, developmental or behavioral problems, Nationwide, Age groups, 3–17 years. (n.d.). Retrieved February 14, 2023, from https://www.childhealthdata.org/browse/survey/results?q=8183&r=1&g=828

Trautlein, B. A. (2013). *Change intelligence: use the power of Cq to lead change that sticks*. Greenleaf.

CHAPTER 20

CREATING A RIPPLE EFFECT THROUGH SMALL LEADERSHIP STRATEGIES

Lauren Harris

ABSTRACT

Lauren Harris shares her life-changing journey as an Assistant Director and Dean of Students at a military community college. She was tasked with launching a new state-of-the-art satellite campus enrolling 275 students in eight months. To achieve this goal, Lauren set a benchmark between growth and failure, requiring her to change her leadership philosophy. The moment she embraced the idea of failing her way to success, she created an unintentional ripple, accelerating her growth. As the ripple grew, it shifted Lauren's concept of leadership from transactional to transformational. The small leadership strategies she developed by leading authentically, with autonomy and creativity, created personal change and propelled community transformation. These strategies inspired trust and collaboration amongst a team in uncertainty, empowered members to lead at their level, and gave space for innovation.

OVERVIEW

I have been a practitioner in higher education for 15 years at various institutions including for-profit, community, public, and non-profit private schools. My experience working in a military community propelled my leadership to the next level as I launched a satellite campus from the ground up, hiring staff and personnel to maintain campus services, and overseeing student development. In less than two years, the campus grew from approximately 200 to over 700 students. I was essential in preparing the campus for SACSCOC accreditation and cultivating relationships with community members and stakeholders.

I held roles in admissions and student conduct, serving as Assistant Director/Dean of Students, Student Conduct Investigator, and Director of Student Integrity and Community Standards. I have professional training in restorative practices, mediation, Title IX, and conflict resolution, and is skilled in leading and developing large and small teams through organizational change and leadership development, including vision, mission, and goal attainment. I am able to develop strategic plans and initiatives that build and strengthen partnerships which has help establish my reputation as a bridge-builder amongst both internal and external stakeholders.

JOURNEY

Leadership, like sports, requires a balance between individual achievement and team collaboration. As a star player, you can garner enough confidence and skills through consistent practice to achieve winning results. Being a star player wasn't enough; when I was drafted as Assistant Director/Dean of Students at a military community college. The one-star retired army general who scouted me was tasked with overseeing the construction of a new state of the-art-satellite campus, recruiting personnel, and enrolling two hundred and seventy-five students within eight months. My role was to establish the operational service functions to support students. The game was unconventional, with no playbook or black-and-white rules; there was only gray. The conventional knowledge I had gained up until that point limited my ability to take risks. The gray was the unknown, and a benchmark between growth and failure—the necessary tipping point to elevate my leadership from most valuable player to coaching a championship team. My first day on the job was unreal. The college had leased a classroom in an elementary school that was transformed into a film hub to support the film production studio that was being built across the street. The same developers building the studio were overseeing the construction project of the satellite campus. As I walked down a corridor toward my first meeting with the developers,

I passed classrooms outfitted for film industry businesses such as a casting agency, film concierge, stunt animals, and camera crews. When I arrived at the college's leased space, it was clear the developers were waiting for me; they wanted my opinion on the layout of the building and desired interior styling. I was floored typical senior leadership in higher education defer construction to developers or project managers; I had no idea I could offer insight into construction designs considering both the educational curriculum and the service needs of staff and students. The energy from the first day was electric; I realized my role was more expansive than I had imagined, and that I was a strategic partner in the campus conception and development. I felt as if I had been launched into an ocean of possibilities.

KNOW YOUR WHY

Over the next few months I scouted and hired star players, and the team rapidly grew, plunging me deeper into the murky waters of leadership. Fear that I was not good enough started to paralyze me, even though I was achieving results. The anxiety of not knowing if my decisions were correct and being unable to predict the outcome was daunting. The tension in the water grew, and my arrogance of wanting to have all the answers and solve all the problems started to weigh me down further. Then a gust of wind came out of nowhere, and unintentional action happened—I surrendered to the uncertainty and unknowns of leadership. I humbled myself and embraced the idea that I would have to chart my own pathway to success, which granted me space to practice a renewed leadership style rooted in authenticity, autonomy, and creativity. This shift in mindset created a ripple.

As I practiced leading from this empowering space, the wind continued to blow, and more small ripples formed. These tiny ripples fostered team trust and collaboration, accelerating our growth and success. For example, the team wanted to generate mass prospective interest in the new campus to achieve the enrollment goal. We hosted promotional open houses in the cafeteria of the film hub and sent out movie ticket themed invitations. The team was inspired, and rallied to make the abstract concept a reality. We had two successful promotional open houses at the film hub with over 300 people in attendance. Knowing my why as a coach helped create clear, concise priorities that allowed others to co-create and contribute to the mission. The experience helped me renew my leadership approach from the thought that I had to manage people and a process to knowing that leading others forward is only necessary requirement in leadership.

Making space for others to lead on the court allowed me to stand on the sidelines cheering them, which gave me unspeakable joy. For years my reason for being in the field of education was participating in students' growth and development, seeing them grow and become more confident in their talents and skills. Their ability to dream big, challenge the status quo and desire massive change gave me hope for the future. My desire to participate in student transformation expanded, and now I want to participate in community transformation, where everyone works together to achieve a shared vision. The transformational leadership framework (Quinn, 2015) is key to making big dreams come true, changing the status quo, and creating massive change through inspiration.

Transformational leadership has been practiced by many successful educators of color throughout history. For example, Dr. Mary Mcleod Bethune, an American educator, activist, pioneer of the civil rights movement, and founder of a historically Black university Bethune-Cookman University, dedicated her life to transforming the African American community and lived by a threefold teaching method—head, hand, and heart. The way she wove together the connections of intellectual knowledge using your head, practical skills using your hand and emotional intellect using your heart to learn was genius. Dr. Bethune's simple teaching method influences my leadership reminding me leading with your head, hand and heart are the small approaches required in transformational leadership.

MULTIPLY YOUR WHY

Like Dr. Bethune, my approach to empowering others to lead at their level gave the team autonomy and the ability to contribute their gifts and talents to a shared vision. Shifting my mindset allowed me space to operate in autonomy and give others this same gift. It became clear that while challenging the team was necessary, giving them enough freedom to grow and challenge themselves would take us further than we could imagine. The more I led with my authentic self, the more I became attuned to my blind spots, adapting quickly to mistakes and pivoting to make adjustments needed for the team. These small leadership approaches enabled me to think ahead, delegate tasks and communicate clearly and concisely. Thinking ahead was something I had not previously done as a leader. In the past I would practice foresight, but then rely on my natural talents and stay in reactive mode when obstacles popped up. Now I had time to become more intentional with testing and developing my practice strategies in real time.

To be effective, I delegated and entrusted day-to-day operational tasks to the managers which gave me the autonomy to schedule time for proactive thinking about big-picture goals. I also recognized that building capacity with a small team required concise and clear communication while building influence and getting the team's buy-in on various initiatives. Instead of working through complex problems alone, I collaborated with team members and sought input from multiple stakeholders. I presented obstacles to the entire team so we could work together to leverage those obstacles into opportunities. As a result of honing in on these small leadership strategies, on August 3, 2015, the first day of the fall semester, we ushered in 285 students, exceeding the projected enrollment goal. Achieving this goal was significant for me on my leadership journey because it changed my understanding of leadership delegation and execution. By leading and not managing people the team gained ownership in the shared vision.

The ripples increased and waves grew when everyone realized that their success was interconnected and we were dependent on one another to achieve every milestone. Each victory was an accomplishment for the entire whole, not just an individual. In two years, the campus grew from 200 students to 700 students, and the waves continued to multiply. The inaugural class of students jumped into the waves, challenging us to dream bigger; they wanted an immersed two-year community college experience. They wanted to participate in the freedom of creating a college experience that they could imagine. Our team's diversity helped students feel comfortable to dream big, leading to better engagement and more successful student outcomes. For example, we formed a student government association, honor council, orientation ambassador club, honor society, intramural flag football and track teams, and two college ethics bowl teams. The rippling impact of change in such a short period was incredible, and I am still in awe of how much was accomplished when everyone worked together. It is so much fun when everyone has a chance to stand close to the wave and get wet!

INTEGRATE YOUR WHY

Integrating my creativity into my work helped me let go of perfectionism and allowed me to move forward on many unknown projects, initiatives, and goals. Letting go of trying to achieve success on the first go around helped me set realistic expectations for myself and my team. Also, I adopted another small leadership strategy that improved communication. Before scheduled meetings, I would send out an agenda with outlined materials to reference for the discussion and alert attendees to the function of the meeting. Our meetings had one of three focus areas: information only, decision-making, or brainstorming. The brainstorming meetings were my favorite to hold because, for an hour, we would think creatively about how to streamline processes, discuss new initiatives, or provide solutions to problems. Having members on the team practice developing skills reframing obstacles into opportunities, gives everyone chance to participate as thought partners in continuous improvement. The more the team is skilled in thinking creatively in solving obstacles the less day to day problems are dumped into your lap.

My good friend and colleague often says, "Good work should never be done in isolation." This is a constant reminder to me that individual achievements are excellent, but they are more meaningful and impactful when achieved as a part of a team effort, allowing everyone to recognize and celebrate community transformation.

CONCLUSION

Unknowingly, I used Dr. Bethune's threefold teaching method to create a ripple effect by getting out of my head, handing off opportunities to others, and changing hearts. Knowing my why and adopting unconventional knowledge helped me make transformative decisions that lead to positive outcomes for the team and myself. Integrating my why by using the small leadership strategies of authenticity, autonomy, and creativity has helped me navigate challenges. Lastly, understanding that success and failure are not black and white—what waits in the unknown is the very thing needed to challenge the status quo—allowed me to dream big and create the change I wanted to see. So, what is *your* purpose? How will you weave together your time, talent and treasures to multiply that purpose and create a ripple of change?

REFERENCE

Quinn, R. E. (2015). *The positive organization breaking free from conventional cultures, constraints, and beliefs.* Berrett-Koehler Publishers, Inc.

CHAPTER 21

LEADERSHIP IN STUDENT AFFAIRS

Merab Mushfiq

ABSTRACT

Student affairs professionals are those people who work in higher education and primarily support student experiences, success, transition, and retention. They are a vital part of the campus community as they innovate, design, and lead student programming on- and off-campus. As a student affairs professional working in the field from more than five years with so many ups and downs as an international student, woman of color, and an immigrant, I am providing some insights into student affairs field. In this chapter, I will be discussing student affairs professional's importance in higher education, leadership in student affairs, and providing some tips and strategies that were helpful for me along the way.

Student affairs professionals are usually working in higher education either directly with students and/or in the background designing and implementing programming which contributes to students' success and experiences on- and off-campus. Hence, student affairs professionals are the key resource to assist in making smooth transition, student success and retention, experiences, and overall student development (Jenkins & Owens, 2016). According to Guthrie and Jenkins (2018) student affairs professionals have a responsibility to help students identify the core knowledge and practices of leadership which aids students to make meaning of their own lives and the society that they live in (p. 157).

I started working in student affairs as an orientation leader and that is where I was exposed to this field. Since then, I have had the opportunity to wear multiple hats in various roles. I recently went back to school to earn a graduate degree in Education which was focused on student affairs and that helped me to learn theories in student success and retention, lived experiences, engagement, co-curricular environment, mental health, and so much more. I also learned about research methods, assessments, competencies in student affairs, frameworks, and current trends in student affairs. From this theoretical knowledge and experiences, I am fortunate to apply it in my professional and personal life. These experiences, knowledge, and research are shaping my identity, ideology, and overall, how I define life and experiences. I deal with students on everyday basis, and it is so crucial for me, as a student affair professional, to be able to provide support to students and be an advocate for them. I strongly believe that I need to make sure that I have the knowledge, adaptability, understanding, and most important of all, empathy in my role so that I can support students, colleagues, faculty members, and the community that I serve in. As a student affair professional, I am an active contributor to students' learning and continuously working to improve students' experiences and having these skills help me to get to know my students and campus community in a broader and deeper way Students are my main motivation and the very key reason that I am thriving in my career.

CHALLENGES AND LEADERSHIP IN STUDENT AFFAIRS

I have had a fair share of struggles as an aspiring student affairs professional getting into this field. Around a decade ago, when I first wanted to enter student affairs, it was challenging as an entry-level professional trying to get into it. First, I did not have educational background in student affairs which made me look that I had no knowledge and skills to contribute towards the entry-level roles that I was applying to. Secondly, I had no prior experience in student affairs as a professional even though I worked on-campus and wore multiple hats and had various roles. Third, at that time when I was in my early 20's, I had no knowledge about networking, informational interviews, and job market as such so I missed on a lot of opportunities such as volunteering, interview skills, presence of mentors to name a few. Even after applying for hundreds of jobs, I was not able to secure any role. After several months of not finding work in student affairs, I became stressed and depressed and before my mental health was severally impacted, I reflected on my experiences and knew that customer service, student-facing roles are my passion, and I will thrive in that career. However, since all my experience was based on student jobs and as a new immigrant, it was not easy to get into this field as a professional. . I started using multiple strategies that were helpful for me and gave me an opportunity to pursue my passion which I will be sharing in the next section.

I was introduced to student affairs when I first started working as an orientation leader as a student. Later, I worked with international students in the international department, writing center, career center, and the experiential learning department. Some of the skills that I acquired during the initial years consists of working with diverse students, group facilitation, event planning, problem-solving, time management, basic research, effective communication, self-reflection, critical thinking, and bringing innovative ideas to reality. It was a very rewarding experience for me for the first two years as an orientation leader, I learned quite a lot about all the work that goes behind the orientation such as planning, preparing, hiring, event management, development, coordination among staff members and other departments. This role started to build my career and equipped me with leadership skills. I, then, worked in the writing center and had multiple roles. Since I was dealing with diverse students every day, I recognized the missing links that were preventing them to succeed on-campus. I collaborated with the international department and introduced coffee hours for international students. It was more of a social get together and we had guest speakers, community members, and domestic students along with international students so that they would get comfortable and build friendships. That social integration helped international students to build connections with domestic students, learned about the history of campus and community from various different community members, and overall boosted their confidence to talk. I ran that program for about two years and the feedback was terrific. The positive feedback from my supervisors at that time really encouraged me to pursue my career in student affairs. I was given Student Employee of the Year award and a couple others as well throughout these three and a half years. That is how I started my student affairs career and even though I was studying science during undergraduate and graduated with honors degree, I started loving my role in student affairs

TIPS

Some of the strategies that helped me to get off the ground are mentioned in the section. I am still using some of these strategies because it gives me ways to connect with my peers and colleagues, helps me to stay grounded, supports me in my work and provide feedback.

MENTORING

Mentoring is the key in student affairs field. It is one of the utmost need to have a mentor when you are in this field. Having a mentor(s) helps so much as it gives you an opportunity not to build only a relationship but also to explore ideas, discuss innovative projects, ways to enhance students' experiences and overall, it can be a source of encouragement and guidance along the way. Throughout my career, I have had the privilege of amazing mentors which have shaped my career, understanding of student affairs, have uplifted me during my difficult times, and encouraged and supported me during my ups and downs in professional life. Very early in my career, a few mentors that I found were on-campus and it was just great to meet face-to-face and discuss day to day life.

PROFESSIONAL ORGANIZATIONS AND SOCIAL MEDIA

A few years ago, I came to know about social media presence, organizations that are geared towards student affairs. I joined various groups and organizations. In the first year or so of joining these groups and organizations, I was a spectator and then became a follower. I followed my peers. However, I started participating more in professional development opportunities, started volunteering, attended various sessions on orientation, advising, graduate student networking, leadership, and so much more. Through these groups and organizations, I have now mentors from across North America and have been learning and growing in my professional and personal life

Student affairs field is evolving due to economic, political, and cultural diversity along with students' needs such as heightened mental health challenges. I recently completed mental health training which equipped me with the tools to provide support and resources to students if they are dealing with mental health issues. I also attended several workshops as well to learn more about the resources that are available locally on- and off-campus so I can direct students towards the right resource(s). It is important to continually learn to acquire knowledge, understanding, and the evolving need of students on-campus. Professional development is an important tool in student affairs field because it helps you to connect with others, learn, and grow your network circle. There are a lot of associations and organizations that are geared towards student affairs and have various committees specialized in different sectors such as orientation, residence, student success, international department, cultural office etc. Few associations in the United States are National Association of Student Personnel Administrators (NASPA), American College Personnel Association (ACPA), and many others that are focused on student affairs specialized programming.

VOLUNTEER

While roles in student affairs are very exhaustive and challenging, it is important to volunteer in any way possible and be an active member of the community. Looking back, when I was looking for jobs and while in graduate school, I had no idea about associations that are focused on student affairs. Now when I am a part of various student affairs associations and on several committees, volunteering, mentoring, and participating in multiple events throughout the year has strengthened my skills, expanded my networking circle, and had multiple opportunities to collaborate with my colleagues nationally and internationally. Becoming a member at student affairs associations would help professionals from all levels. It is helpful for aspiring student affairs professionals to connect with those who are already in the field.

NETWORKING AND INFORMATIONAL INTERVIEWS

Another important tip that I would like to give to aspiring student affairs professional or to those who are trying to get from one role to another within student affairs is to not only build relationships and expand network circle but also conduct informational interviews. These interviews can be beneficial to get to know about student affairs professional field, organization, leadership, day-to-day work and culture. While this is not a job interview, it gives an opportunity to speak with an individual and get to know them and their career journey along with the student affairs insights (Doyle, 2022). Additionally, it is an effective way to understand this field in a detailed way and make decisions accordingly.

GRADUATE SCHOOL

Last but the not least, graduate school helped me advance in the field and there are endless opportunities to grow in the career. Since then, I have had the opportunity to serve in various roles and I have seen tremendous growth in my leadership skills such as learning from my own mistakes, adaptability, willingness to mentor and be mentored, empathy, patience, understanding and knowledge of student needs and institutional policies, critical thinking, and being resilient to name a few. These skills have shaped my thinking process and to make informed decisions. Because of lived experiences and interaction with students have made me more compassionate towards them. I now have more active listening skills than before.

One can explore multiple avenues and focus on either one functional unit within student affairs or look at even a broader spectrum of student affairs. I believe graduate degree in student affairs or related can provide multiple tools to practitioners, leaders, and aspiring professionals to learn and meet the evolving needs of the profession (Wright-Mair, 2022). While graduate school can be expensive, time-consuming, and may not be suitable for everyone, this is just another option to explore.

ADVICE I WOULD SHARE WITH MYSELF AS A NEW HIGHER EDUCATION LEADER

When I was trying to get into this field as a professional, I did not the know importance of affiliation with professional organizations and be an active member in those play an important role. Looking back, I wish I knew about associations. Some of the professional associations that I am a part of now could have helped me a lot to climb a ladder in this career sooner. I found amazing mentors, learned about conferences, professional development opportunities, and so much more after about a couple of years into this career. I would share this with myself as a new higher education leader the importance of professional associations are a key element to learn and evolve in this career.

CONCLUSION

A career in the student affairs field is very rewarding because it gives an opportunity to interact with students, faculty members, various departments, and other stakeholders. While there are some challenges in this field, it is also constantly evolving. One needs to stay updated accordingly and there are educational opportunities to collaborate and interact with so many members on- and off-campus. There are endless opportunities to switch from one role to another within the institution or take your leadership skills to another institution.

One of the key reminders that I give to myself every day is that I am making a difference in my students' lives and making sure that I am setting up my students for success. The leadership skills that I have acquired over the years are helping me to establish connections, programming, and structure in the unit. As an aspiring student affairs professional, I would encourage you to never give up. Keep continuing to learn, explore different avenues, make connections and networking, expand your networking circle, conduct informational interviews, and have mentors in your life who can support and guide you.

REFERENCES

Ciobanu, A. (2013). The role of student services in the improving of student education in higher education. *Procedia-Social and Behavioral Sciences, 92*, 169–173.

Doyle, A. (2022). *How an informational interview can boost your career?* https://www.thebalancemoney.com/how-an-informational-interview-can-help-your-career-2058564

Dunn. L. A., Moore, L. L., Odom, S. F., Briers, G. E., & Bailey, K. J. (2021). Necessary leadership educator competencies for entry-level student affairs leadership educators. *Journal of Leadership Education, 20*(2), 43–58.

Kezar, A., & Lester, J. (2009). *Organizing higher education for collaboration: A guide for campus leaders.* Josey-Bass.

Márquez, L. V., & Hernández, I. (2020). Midlevel leadership in student affairs. *New Directions for Community Colleges, 2020*(191), 81–87. https://doi.org/10.1002/cc.20408

National Association of Student Affairs Professionals Association. (2015). *Professional competency for student affairs educators.* www.naspa.org

Rocco, & Pelletier, J. (2019). A conversation among student affairs leadership educators. *New Directions for Student Leadership, 2019*(164), 39–53. https://doi.org/10.1002/yd.20357

Wright-Mair, R., Saadeddine, R., Peters, C., & Elmes, A. (2022). Higher education and student affairs master's students' perceptions of their preparation for scholarly practice and implications for program improvement: A mixed methods case study. *College Student Affairs Journal, 40*(2), 13–32.

CHAPTER 22

NAVIGATING TITLE IX OBLIGATIONS AND STUDENT SUPPORT

Lessons From Faculty Experiences in and out of the Classroom

Jaclyn Stone

ABSTRACT

As college students grapple with experiences of sexual assault and misconduct, they are forced to navigate complicated university response policies if they chose to disclose experiences to university staff and faculty members-many who are also confused or hold false beliefs about obligations as responsible employees. Students may disclose because they are seeking resources or processes, while others seek deadline extensions or accommodations. The student's desire and hope about what happens following the disclosure, specifically sharing information with others, is frequently obscured by their lack of understanding about institutional mandates, despite efforts to inform them. Through research with faculty at six institutions of higher education, (public, private, PWIs and HBCUs), I found that key to understanding faculty experiences of receiving disclosures were faculty members' perceptions of their role as mediators between the institution and students. I present progressive strategies for success that could improve care for students and engagement and for faculty and staff.

In 2011, the Obama Administration issued a Dear Colleague Letter (DCL, Ali, 2011) that reinvigorated a national conversation about institutional responsibility in providing equal access to education, regardless of sex and gender and paved the way for new sexual assault discourse in post-secondary education. Institutional prevention and response of sexual assault, often referred colloquially as "Title IX," became, and has continued to be, a focal point of higher education for the next several years. While the important work in higher education sexual assault prevention and response pre-dated the issuance of the DCL, this particular moment called upon institutions to further define roles and processes.

I found myself at a pivotal moment in my career and socio-political consciousness where the DCL had substantial impact. Despite not working directly with Title IX or gender violence spaces at the time, I felt a connection to social justice and equity work and knew there was an opportunity to contribute to fostering a safer campus community across social ecological domains. In this chapter, I begin by providing context that led to my interests in both navigating and wayfinding college and university efforts to mitigate and respond to sexual assault and misconduct. I then describe the findings from a study I conducted with university faculty about their experiences with students' disclosures of sexual assault, specifically focusing on how they view their roles as mediators between students and the institution, how they work deliberately in compliance with or in opposition to university policies, and their general understanding of those policies. I conclude the chapter with key strategies that all aspiring leaders can integrate into their practice, regardless of role, positionality, and expertise.

CONTEXT FOR NAVIGATING TITLE IX

I believe it was the combination of past experiences supporting students who had experienced harm from violence, my interests in well-being, and my career positionality combined with my identities that fostered a sense of connectedness to the subject matter; a connection that has continued to be sustained through research and practice for more than a decade. In this section, I briefly introduce my professional and theoretical standpoint and reflect on the ways that I see Title IX shaping social justice conversations and my professional landscape.

People come to student affairs work for many reasons and I am fortunate that my journey began and continued because of meaningful relationships. I had amazing peers, leaders, and supervisors in my college experience who encouraged me. At a large public institution, I could have become a statistic, but the simple gesture of a door decoration on my residence hall room and the warm greeting by my resident advisor were meaningful to me. I have studied and practiced professionally in higher education for two decades. I present explicitly as a White, cisgender, able-bodied woman and also hold less visible, marginalized identities pertaining to ethnicity, religion, and disabilities. Both dominant and subjugated aspects of my identities inform my work and privilege my access to many spaces.

I have served in four-year, predominantly White institutions, one with a Minority Serving Institution designation and one with Hispanic Serving Institution designation. My career started in residential life working with individuals and groups in an on-call capacity where students would make disclosures of sexual misconduct and the work also required response to mental health emergencies. As I moved throughout student affairs, I gained experience in several other functional areas such as conduct, Title IX, leadership development, and well-being although some positions have been adjacent to those functional areas rather than direct. For example, in one role I worked closely with senior leaders in conduct and Title IX to administer interim processes to address high-risk behaviors although I was not the designated Title IX or conduct administrator. I also supervised staff who design, implement and evaluate programming for healthy relationships and bystander intervention and who also confidentially support students who are looking for a supportive campus resource. Finally, I have presented locally and nationally on various topics related to sex and gender violence, consulted on projects, and delivered programming to students, faculty, and staff.

I deeply value the simultaneity of theory and practice, which have provided the scaffolding for the process by which I obtained my formal education in interdisciplinary, humanistic subjects, but also has continued to support the ways in which I critically examine and deepen my understanding of new constructs. Reflecting on my personal experiences as a student, student affairs professional, and scholar, I am drawn to Bronfenbrenner's (1979) ecological systems theory as a useful frame to conceptualize the complex and interdependent nature of individual and institutional relationships, as well as social and cultural values, particularly in the intricate ecosystem of higher education, contextualized by policy and undergirded by structural racism, sexism, and classism. The model presents nested spheres to demonstrate the influence and interconnection between the outer spheres (the exosystem and macrosystem) on the inner spheres (microsystem and mesosystems) with the individual at the foundation. Social ecological framing is particularly useful for policies, such as a those related to sexual assault. There are obvious individual impacts from those problematic behaviors, but there are also multiple layers of policies, and practices which impact multiple individuals and relationships, and thus the climate of an institution. In the next section, I will discuss a particular study with faculty and how those interactions across the social ecological framework can better help emerging leaders, regardless of role, navigate Title IX and Higher Education generally.

LEARNING FROM PEOPLE, PLACES, AND POLICY

I continue to learn from the people and systems with whom and which I interact just about every day. In higher education settings, the students are changing regularly and, particularly since the syndemics of 2020, the staff turnover has made it such that employee changes have been substantial as well. The settings in which we do our work are also important to consider. The shared setting that most readers will have in common is a college or university, but narrowing down further in the context of Title IX, you may consider residence halls, fraternity houses, or the setting of your "town and gown" relationships. Zooming out from your institution, you may consider the city or state and the socio-political climate that you are in and how that impacts the discourse around Title IX. Again, this is where systems theory can be a useful tool to critically consider the interactions.

Through in-depth interviews with faculty members, I found that key to understanding faculty experiences of receiving disclosures were faculty members' perceptions of their role as mediators between the institution and students. Faculty members' beliefs about the extent to which they should work in compliance with or in opposition to policies, combined with their understanding of the purpose of such policies and practices, informed beliefs and actions with students. Faculty demonstrated limited knowledge of policy and a disconnect between what they believed they were required to do as responsible employees and what they actually did when faced with disclosures. This presents a real challenge when they are presenting both their obligation to students and what they are going to do if confronted with a disclosure. In this section I briefly introduce the participants from the study I conducted and share some of the intersections and divergences of beliefs, knowledge and actions.

I interviewed 16 full-time faculty members from six institutions in the mid-Atlantic, five public institutions and one private. Three of the participants identified as Black and 13 identified as White. Among the three participants of color, all of them worked at Historically Black Colleges and Universities (HBCUs). Four participants identified as male and 12 as female and all participants identified as cisgender. Women represented 75% (n=12) of the participants in this study. Among those women, four had the rank of associate professor, three were assistant professors and each of the assistant professors were actively seeking promotion to tenure. Five participants had full-time non-tenure track lecturer appointments. Among the four men, representing 25% of the participants, three were associate professors and one full-time, non-tenured position. Of these men, all of them had more teaching and student engagement obligations, than research. They are also parents, grandparents, immigrants, first-generation students, and first-generation English speakers. They are artists and activists. Some of them also shared that they were survivors of sexual assault, relationship violence or stalking. The faculty bring these intersectional identities to their roles as instructors, advisors, and mentors.

Knowledge, Beliefs, and Action or Inaction

Students do not typically select faculty members for their first disclosure of sexual assault or intimate partner violence, nor are faculty members the recipients of the majority of disclosures of campus-based disclosures (Fisher et al., 2000; Newins et al., 2018), however they do receive disclosures through multiple mechanisms, and they should be prepared to respond to the student. Institutions are asking them to respond in a way that is compliant with policy despite lacking specific competencies and minimal training and students are collectively asking for trauma-informed responses at best and transparency at a minimum. Without training and what may be perceived as lack of support for employees from the institution, faculty and administrators do not often see a combination of care and compliance as compatible interests. As a result, the institution may be in out of compliance with the federal government, compromising aid for students and grants, while students are simultaneously not receiving the resources and supports they want and need. Higher education leaders should be seeking ways to be knowledgeable and resourceful while also knowing the boundaries of their roles. While students may ask us to be there for them, in times of great pain and vulnerability, boundaries are a skill leaders will teach employees and mentees. Compromising that for individual students will put the institution at risk. Some of you may read this and consider that the institution does not deserve our compassion. That is the choice you will need to make in service your career progression. I believe a balance can be done thoughtfully and with care and that has informed my approach and will continue to do so.

One of the key findings my from research was that faculty bring with them to their roles a set of values and beliefs about the institutional processes and those values and beliefs may obstruct the way faculty act in accordance with their duties as a responsible employee. This can play out in several different ways. If a faculty member has knowledge of a duty to respond to the student, how the faculty member generally chooses which response scenario they are going to enact is likely to be based on a combination of what the student asks the faculty member to do, how the faculty member believes the university is going to act with the information that is shared, and the potential consequences the faculty member might face for not complying with the compelled disclosure mandates. In the case of the faculty members I spoke to, only four of the 16 participants (25%) were able to accurately describe their institution's process for receiving a disclosure and then following it. For the remaining 75%, when reflecting on their disclosure experiences, they did not necessarily describe an experience where a student begged them not to tell anyone else. Instead, they simply did not ask the student what additional resources they might like a referral to and instead projected much of their own perceptions and beliefs onto the student. Each of these conversations could have shifted just slightly with a simple question at the end of the conversation where the leader asked the student what resources they might be interested in being connected to. This approach sets the boundary that the student and leader relationship is not one rooted as the therapeutic helper and it allows the student to identify the specific resources they are looking for. These are skills that I have used often, but they do require me to be knowledgeable about the available resources or I can learn alongside the student as we search together.

The language the faculty use to talk about the process is important. Specifically, their use of the word "report" was reflective of personal belief and policy language. In some cases, a report was referring to a form that the faculty member was asked to complete after receiving a disclosure. In another instance, "reporting" was a punitive act. Reporting is the compelled disclosure that the faculty must do after the student discloses. Both in interviews and in my professional interactions as a university administrator, I hear faculty talk about their obligation to "report students" and thus force them, without consent, to take part in a disciplinary process. I now take a much more mindful and intentional approach to my language in my own work. When I train faculty and staff or when I work with students, I try to avoid using the word report altogether. I use phrases like "elevate your concern" or "bring someone else into the conversation to make sure you are getting what you need" so that students do not feel like they are getting into trouble or that employees are getting students. Language matters and sexual assault and misconduct are no exception.

Relationships and Care Guide Faculty Response

Circumstances, such as the relationship between the faculty member and the student, that are present before, during, and after a disclosure of sexual violence will impact how the disclosure is received and responded to, although care will be the central principal despite it looking different for each person. Faculty receive disclosures in the many ways that they work with students as instructors, advisors, and mentors. Whether or not they teach a sensitive subject that touches upon aspects of interpersonal violence or have small classes where they build close relationships with students, each of them received a disclosure from students and reflected on a response that was rooted in what Nel Noddings (2002) identified as care as a caring encounter. I illustrate the caring encounter with the faculty member receiving and responding to a disclosure. The faculty member cares for the student and the care is characterized by attention and motivational displacement. In the college environment, this is when the faculty member turns their attention to the student to address the issue at hand, which may start off initially as accommodation-seeking, course content, or directly about emotional support. This displacement is where motivation shifts toward the student. The second dimension is that the faculty member performs an act in accordance with their attention and motivational displacement. According to their institutional policies, the faculty member would notify the Title IX coordinator. As demonstrated, there are a series of other acts that are in accordance with individual faculty members' values, despite being inconsistent with policy. The third and final dimension of a caring encounter is that it occurs when the student recognizes that the faculty member cared for them.

In the faculty members' reflections, they shared a variety of responses. In one instance as a student was about to share some experience about sexual abuse, the faculty member gestured to her mouth with her thumb and forefinger across her lips and said "Zip. I don't know what you're going to say, but I kind of have a feeling what you're going to say, and I have to tell you that if you tell me this, I have to report it." This professor is compliant with the policy. She knows that if she has information, she is required to elevate it to the Title IX coordinator, however, she is simultaneously diminishing the value of that process, regardless of the validity of that. The faculty member, however, is centering her care for the student in her response. Theoretically, she is presenting the choice for the student to consent to the report in the moment. However, she might also be framing the choice to "report" in a negative light and using her authority to influence the student's choice to not receive formal assistance or adjudication.

The student in this scenario wanted someone to know their story and maybe even wanted more help, but maybe they did not want university involvement. Perhaps they went to another leader to get what they needed and perhaps they never did, from this administrator's story, we do not know. There are some important lessons to be learned from this story, however. Interrupting a student to inform them of our roles is a good choice. It empowers students to move forward with consent. Setting up training employees to do that with tact is critical. Individual students need different things from their disclosures and students arrive at that experience different knowledge and skills, just as employees will receive those disclosure with varying knowledge and skills. As leaders, we must do our best to share as much knowledge about institutional process and resources so that if students choose to make a disclosure, everyone is as equipped to know what processes will follow.

STRATEGIES FOR NAVIGATING TITLE IX

If you have student contact as a faculty or staff member there is a good chance that you may receive a disclosure of sexual assault. As you step into progressive leadership positions, you may have less direct student contact, but more responsibility for other faculty and staff and potentially even more influence over policy and procedures that impact the sexual misconduct process. With this in mind, it is important to be equipped with the knowledge of institutional obligations and the resources for the students who disclose to faculty and staff. It is important to be aware that employee disclosures may also be included in the responsible employee roles and require Title IX reporting, although I only focus on student-centered language in these recommendations. There are a number of strategies that aspiring leaders could employ to have success in navigating Title IX, and I describe my top three in detail in this section. While I believe these strategies are timeless, leaders should always defer to their institution, state, and the most recent federal guidance for the most up to date laws and policies. I describe the strategies in progressive order such that they address what I believe to be a minimum standard and move toward being an institutional change agent.

Preparation

Be prepared to respond to a student who discloses to you. You should always defer to your institution's policies and procedures, which I discuss further in my next recommendation, but it is important to be familiar with your institutional reporting obligations and let the student who is disclosing to you know that you will be engaging the Title IX coordinator. Everyone will have varying boundaries and skills when it comes to a difficult topic such as sexual assault, particularly because the student presenting the issue may also disclose with a wide range of emotions. You can remind students about your role throughout the semester in course syllabi, when discussing sensitive course topics, or when personal issues arise in communication. If you are sensing that a student is going or might share something reportable with you and you want to remind them of your responsible employee status, you can use a short script similar to the following:

> I want to stop you for just a moment. I have a responsibility to share information related to things like sexual misconduct or threat of harm to self or others with the university, but that does not mean I don't want you to share those things with me. It just means I need to bring other folks into the conversation to get you the best resources.

This technique is often called "interrupt to inform." You can search for other example scripts to help you frame how you might respond to a student, so you feel the most prepared when a student makes the decision to disclose to you.

As demonstrated by the faculty experiences in my study (Stone, 2020), there are not always opportunities to remind students of your reporting obligations. They may disclose in research papers, emails, or share unexpectedly in a conversation or class discussion. In those circumstances it will be prudent to know where to quickly find the reporting documents for your institution. You may have learned about the Title IX reporting in your new employee orientation. You can either go back to those training sessions or search for Title IX on your institution's website. I strongly recommend saving that website as a bookmark. If your institution uses an online reporting tool, familiarize yourself with what information you will need to submit and also save that form as a bookmark. If your institution is using a paper form, it may be useful to print a couple copies to keep in your home and campus-based offices after familiarizing yourself with the fields on that form. Once you have completed the form, you will want to submit it in a timely fashion.

Common practice for many institutions is to provide or even require training for faculty and staff about sexual misconduct policies and procedures, which should include your responsible employee obligations; what your obligations are, how to fulfill them, and where to go with questions. When beginning a new role, employees are inundated with so much new information, akin to drinking water through a firehose. I, of course, recommend fulfilling those requirements in a timely fashion and suggest making a note to come back to the links and resources that those training modules refer to. Specifically, save the institutional Title IX website as favorite. Be confident in your "reporting" obligations and know how to submit the report so you can do it in a timely and compliant manner.

Awareness of Higher Education Title IX Changes

Even if this is not your passion area, if you choose to work in higher education, it is critical to stay on top of the ways political discourse and action impacts your work. Different political administrations and on federal, state and local levels can have substantial impacts on the climate of your work. Whether you make the decision to subscribe to the Chronicle of Higher Education, follow some key accounts on social media, or connect with colleagues around this topic on campus, your engagement in Title IX news will serve your own leadership development as well as your student and employee constituents.

Community Engagement and Change Agent

Institutions of higher education continue to grapple with the most effective ways to reduce the prevalence of sexual assault and sexual misconduct. Current and aspiring leaders who demonstrate an interest in being involved are an asset to the research and best practices. There are many ways to offer your skills to the movement at your institution, even if sexual assault is not your area of expertise. Faculty perspectives about relationships with students and peers, experiences with disclosures, or helping to promote the university's bi-annual climate survey to other faculty are of incredible assistance. The other benefit that comes from engaging in places where you are not the expert is that you get to know the people who are. Whether they are the mental health providers, victim/survivor advocates, well-being staff, Title IX case managers or even a community partner, there are specialized individuals equipped to do this work so you do not have to extend beyond your skills or boundaries. When you get to know who those offices and people are, you are even more likely to refer students who disclose their experiences of sexual violence to those helpful resources in caring and compassionate ways, which supports the preparation strategies that started this section.

CONCLUSION

Sexual assault, whether it occurs during a student's time of enrollment, or they bring experiences of pre-enrollment trauma with them to campus, presents many challenges to the university environment. Aspiring leaders in higher education must be able to identify and navigate the complex and often changing laws, institutional policies, campus culture(s) and interdisciplinary best practices associated with the sexual assault and misconduct. The analyses and strategies that I have presented here are applicable to faculty and staff at any level and there is a clear necessity for interventions that reach across contexts including policy, training, and relational dynamics, in order to provide students with a caring response, while maintaining compliance within a challenging regulatory climate. I believe everyone can be involved and there may be times when you don't have a choice because a student will disclose to you and then the only choice will be to help them or not. What that help looks like will be up to the student, you, and your interests and knowledge in fulfilling your obligations to the institution.

REFERENCES

Ali, R. (2011, April 4). *Dear colleague letter.* U.S. Department of Education, Office for Civil Rights.

Baker, M. R., Frazier, P. A., Greer, C., Paulsen, J. A., Howard, K., Meredith, L. N. Anders, S. L & Shallcross, S. L (2016). Sexual victimization history predicts academic performance in college women. *Journal of Counseling Psychology, 63*(6), 685–692.

Campbell, R. (2002). *Emotionally involved: The impact of researching rape.* Routledge.

Chuang, C. H., Cattoi, A. L., McCall-Hosenfel, J. d., Camacho, F., Dyer, A., & Weisman, C. S. (2012). Longitudinal association of intimate partner violence and depressive symptoms. *Mental Health in Family Medicine, 9*(2), 107–114.

Fisher, B. S., Cullen, F. T., & Turner, M. G. (2000). *The sexual victimization of college women.* U.S. Department of Justice, Office of Justice Programs.

Jordan, C. E., Combs, J. L., & Smith, G. T. (2014). An exploration of sexual victimization and academic performance among college women. *Trauma, Violence & Abuse 15*(3), 191–200.

Lhamon, C. (2014, April 29). *Questions and answers on Title IX and sexual violence.* United States Department of Education. Retrieved from http://www2.ed.gov/about/offices/list/ocr/docs/qa201404-title-ix.pdf

Newins, A., Bernstein, E., Peterson, R., Waldron, J., & White, S. (2018). Title IX mandated reporting: The views of university employees and students. *Behavioral Sciences, 8*(11), 106–124.

Noddings, N. (2002). *Educating moral people: A caring alternative to character education.* Teachers College Press.

Office for Civil Rights. (2015). Title IX resource guide. U.S. Department of Education, Office for Civil Rights.

Smith, C. P., & Freyd, J. J. (2013). Dangerous safe havens: Institutional betrayal exacerbates sexual trauma. *Journal of Traumatic Stress, 26,* 119–124. doi:10.1002/jts.21778

Stone, J. (2020). *Receive, respond, report: Faculty experiences with students' disclosures of sexual assault* (Doctoral dissertation, University of Maryland, Baltimore County).

CHAPTER 23

BETWEEN ACADEMIC AND STUDENT AFFAIRS

Advice for New Student Services Leaders in Academic Units

Zayd Abukar

ABSTRACT

Dr. Zayd Abukar (he/him/his) is a student services director at a large public institution in the Midwest. In this chapter, he provides an overview of his background and career trajectory, including a couple of the most defining moments in his career. Next, he shares what he wishes he would have known as a new higher education leader. Finally, he provides readers with three tips for being successful as a new student services or student affairs leader within an academic unit setting.

AUTHOR OVERVIEW

My name is Dr. Zayd Abukar (he/him/his), and I serve as a student services administrator at a large, four-year, public land-grant institution in the Midwest. I have over 15 years of experience working in higher education in various roles including, but not limited to: intramural sports work-study student employee; graduate administrative associate in residence life; academic counselor and advisor for multiple academic majors; program manager for tutoring and supplemental instruction services; assistant director for academic and scholarship services; and currently, director of the student services office within an academic department. While each of these experiences is unique, the throughline, especially in my work over the last decade, is that of practicing, planning, and leading student services and student affairs work within academic affairs contexts.

As an administrator and scholar, I am interested in how institutions and practitioners can rethink or leverage existing resources to better support their students, particularly those from underserved populations. I have authored and presented on topics related to this theme in local, state, and national outlets, including the Ohio College Personnel Association (OCPA), the American College Personnel Association (ACPA), and the National Association of Student Personnel Administrators (NASPA). My educational background is that of having a bachelor of arts in communication with a sociology minor from the University of Louisville, a master of arts in Educational Studies (Higher Education and Student Affairs specialization) from The Ohio State University, and a doctorate of education in Educational Studies (Higher Education and Student Affairs specialization) with a Public Policy and Management graduate minor from The Ohio State University.

On a personal level, I identify as a Black male, first-generation college student, who grew up in a working-class, single-parent household. More than my professional and educational exposures, it is my lived experience that most informs my belief in higher education's potential to mitigate social inequities and create opportunities for those from marginalized populations.

MY PROFESSIONAL JOURNEY

My introduction to higher education and student affairs as a career path stemmed from my undergraduate employment with the Department of Intramural Sports and Recreation at the University of Louisville (UofL), as well as my involvement with the institution's Cultural Center. I had always considered something related to education as a career path, but it was not until my time at UofL that I learned about the provision of collegiate student services as a pursuable niche. As a full-time student working two jobs and upwards of 25 hours/week to support myself and finance my education, it was the guidance and encouragement of student affairs practitioners that truly helped me to complete my degree. After much research and reflection, I decided to take a gap year after earning my bachelor's to study for the GRE, build my finances, and apply to higher education and student affairs master's programs.

Eventually, I was admitted and enrolled in a higher education and student affairs master's program, where I was offered a residence life graduate associate position as an assistant hall director. I supervised resident advisors, conducted student conduct meetings, and planned and executed community-building programs and events. This training period as a master's student allowed me to narrow down the kinds of professional activities that most and least resonated with my strengths, interests, and temperament. This led me to explore academic advising.

After I graduated, I secured an academic advising role and would remain doing this kind of work for almost five years. I then transitioned to a program manager role, overseeing tutoring and supplemental instruction, eventually was promoted to an assistant director role, and now, I am a director.

Experiences That Shaped Me a As a Leader

Two experiences come to mind when I think about what has shaped me the most as a leader: my time as an academic advisor, and my promotion to assistant director.

Looking back, serving as an academic advisor early in my career was a potent professional development experience. Academic advisors are "on the ground" practitioners. They regularly interact with a wide variety of students and student cases, and therefore, at any given time, have a pulse on the major issues and opportunities affecting those within their unit. As an advisor, I was fortunate enough to work closely with faculty and senior leadership on the creation of new programs and curricular change processes as well. To be effective in my role, I also had to stay in tune with campus-wide policies, processes, and resources so that I could educate students and colleagues who could benefit from this information. Being an academic advisor taught me how students navigate institutional systems and resources, how they interface with faculty and academic plans of study, and even how they view themselves and each other. Academic advising steered my decision to pursue student services leadership roles because I experienced firsthand the wide-ranging impacts of the decision-making that takes place at those levels and believed strongly that I could make a difference. As a director today, this foundation was extremely valuable because now I quickly identify numerous factors at play with any given student affairs-related dilemma with implications for the academic unit at large.

The other transformative experience I had was being promoted from program manager to assistant director. The unit I oversaw as a manager was expanded to include new functional areas: scholarship and financial aid counseling. With this unit expansion came four additional full-time staff members that would report to me. This provided the challenge (and opportunity) of learning to lead and oversee services I was not as familiar with, while at the same time, building credibility amongst those with more experience in those areas. In a very short period, I realized I had to shift my mindset from leading others through direct instruction to leading through delegation. No longer was I able to independently manage all aspects of the unit. The new circumstance I was in compelled me to figure out, through trial and error, how to craft a shared vision, define objectives, and then empower my staff to independently make decisions within the framework of what we were trying to do.

Reflecting on These Experiences

In my current role, I oversee and work closely with various functional areas: recruitment, admissions, orientation, advising, course scheduling, curriculum change processes, departmental student funding processes (fellowships, assistantships, and scholarships), graduation, and other initiatives that support students, faculty, and leadership in our department. The nature of my role requires me to be an effective bridge between the worlds of fostering student success and belonging, staff leadership, stewarding university processes—and—the politics and idiosyncrasies of academia, working closely with tenured faculty, and aligning office activities with the vision of senior leaders.

Reflecting on my trajectory, it was incredibly developmental to have been able to work in student-facing roles, managerial roles, and leadership roles before being in the one that I am in today. Everything I learned, endured, and accomplished over the years have instilled in me the confidence, clarity, familiarity, and resolve that I regularly rely on to both lead a student services office while managing faculty and senior leadership relationships. Experiences such as advocating for academically at-risk students to departmental senior leadership, or supervising undergraduate students, graduate associate, and full-time staff members, to leading the reorganization of a new unit. All in all, I have become a believer that you cannot master the big things without mastering the little things. Leadership development is an iterative process, and does not only begin when you have earned a formal title. The journey is on-going, and the extent to which you can recognize it as such and learn from these moments will prepare you for when the stakes are elevated.

ADVICE FOR MY PAST SELF

One of the most important pieces of advice I would give my past self is that there is no one-size-fits-all approach to leadership. When I first started supervising as a graduate associate, I subscribed to this idea that I had to behave and present myself in a very specific way in order to be taken seriously or garner my team's confidence. I came to this belief because all my student affairs leadership examples up to that point in time were charismatic, take-charge extrovert types. Even though I care deeply about people and helping others succeed, I am a natural introvert, and so I thought acting more like those I looked up to could be in my best interest as a new leader. Instead of following a prescribed set of actions or behaviors, I eventually found it more productive to operate from a set of leadership principles while being my true, authentic self. Furthermore, the fact of the matter is that different circumstances require different kinds of leadership. Shifting my mental conception of what it means to be a leader allowed me to think less about the minutiae of appearing like a "legitimate" leader, and more on my values, the needs of my team and students, and the direction we were trying to go.

There are several ways one can begin to cultivate a leadership philosophy. The first and most important step is to reflect on what your most important core values are as a leader. For example, if recognizing your staff members as holistic people is valuable to you, then this can guide what reaction to have when one of them misses an important deadline due to a family matter. Another option is one can explore others' leadership philosophies. My own leadership philosophy is an iteration of Kouzes and Posner's (2019) Five Practices of Exemplary Leadership, as their emphasis on modeling the way (setting an example and not requiring of others what you are not willing to do or believe in), challenging the process (being open to change if it benefits those we are tasked with serving), and enabling others to act (trusting my team and giving them the tools to be their best professional selves) all resonate deeply with what I believe in. A leadership philosophy can serve as a North Star when you are faced with unique dilemmas, challenges, or even scrutiny. Instead of internalizing outside noise as if it were objective truth, your philosophy can be your barometer. If I could advise my younger self based on what I know today, it is that leadership takes many forms, and drawing from principles rather than limiting yourself to prescribed characteristics is a more fruitful approach.

TIPS FOR BEING SUCCESSFUL AS A NEW STUDENT SERVICES LEADER IN AN ACADEMIC UNIT

I introduced my background, my journey into the field, experiences that have shaped me as a leader, and advice I would share with my past self. Lastly, I am going to provide three tips for new or aspiring student services leaders, particularly those who work within an academic unit or college.

1. Get Clear on Your Objectives

It is important for you to be clear on the type of leader your organization wants you to be. Ideally, you would begin this exploration the moment you read the job description and continue it as you progress through the interview process and learn more about the demands of the role. These are certainly not hard and fast descriptions, but I argue that in essence, organizations look for one of three types of leaders: a game manager, a foundation builder, or a driver.

Game Manager: is here to preserve the status quo. You are not here to enact deep-rooted systemic change, but rather, to focus your efforts on maintaining consistency in the kinds of outcomes your position has been producing.

Foundation Builder: Perhaps the unit absorbed a brand new function and needs someone who is comfortable managing change. Perhaps the unit was awarded a multi-year grant to create a new programmatic initiative. Or, perhaps, the previous leader eroded key relationships with staff and other stakeholders, and the hope is that the new leader can start to rebuild those relationships. Some leaders are sought after to build a foundation either in the absence of one, or when what is currently there is suboptimal.

Driver: a driver is hired to take a good thing and make it better, bigger, or broader. For example, an impending surge in enrollment is on the horizon, and to prepare, this student services unit will need to double its staff and broaden its portfolio.

Whether the type of leader your organization wants you to be fits into these criteria or not, the point is to identify early on what you were called to do. Sometimes this information is clearly deducible, sometimes it is not. In the latter instance, you should initiate these conversations with your senior leader(s) so that what is expected of you is made explicit at the outset of your tenure. It is impossible for a leader to satisfy all constituents and solve all problems. However, once you know what you are fundamentally there to do, then it becomes much easier to curate a vision for the future, establish priorities, and perform the work of leading your team and unit towards those ends.

2. Be Amongst the People

Prioritize learning about and building relationships with key stakeholders, especially the staff you supervise, the students you serve, the faculty you will collaborate with the most, and senior leadership. Regarding your staff, remember: you only go as far as your team goes. Dive deep into studying their roles and how they fit into the larger organizational picture. More importantly, get to know your supervisees as individuals; their likes, dislikes, career goals, hobbies, loved one(s), and fun facts. This can be in the form of introductory meetings, a request to complete a questionnaire, or a combination of both, which is what I like to do. The more you know your team, the better equipped you will be to put them in position to succeed. Inevitably, there will come a time when you must deliver professional criticism or enforce expectations. Difficult conversations are much easier when a genuine relationship has already been established.

Outside of your team, take time to hear from students. This can be structured meetings, shadowing student appointments, or even initiating informal interactions with students who come to your unit for services. As higher education professionals, there are theories, frameworks, and other constructs we take for granted as guides. As the student services leader within your academic unit, it is your job to take the extra step of considering how those constructs may or may not apply to your specific student population. Get to know who your students are, the challenges and opportunities they face, and how you and your team can help them maximize the collegiate experience.

Lastly, connect with your faculty colleagues. Get to know them as people, but also get curious about their area(s) of expertise. Acquainting yourself with the academic discipline(s) of your department can lend further insight into your students' journeys and how your services can be a support. Connecting with faculty can also help you understand how they interact with your unit, and how both parties can mutually support each other moving forward.

This tip extends to other stakeholders as well, from senior leadership to colleagues in other offices across campus who you regularly interface with. The main idea is to uncover the key players in your network, and take time early on to build relationships.

3. Balance Achieving Short-Term Wins with Not Changing Things Too Quickly

New leaders often feel like they must prove themselves. This is understandable. After all, you were chosen after a lengthy, competitive search process because of your strengths, abilities, and accomplishments. Naturally, you want to hit the ground running and show everyone that they made the right choice. Before you charge ahead, however, be cautious: you just got there. There is a long-established culture and many networks of relationships and between people that all predate your first day on the job. "Hit the ground listening," as they say, before you start communicating grandiose visions of change and transition. It is not that your ideas and expertise should be sidelined or disregarded. Rather, get to know your terrain first so that you are in the best position to implement those initiatives without offending cultural norms or prematurely damaging important relationships.

At the same time, it is okay—if not encouraged—to seek out and act on short-term win opportunities early on. As a new leader, you will start to notice (and likely, people will make you aware of) persistent annoyances that plague your staff or students. Some of these problems might even have simple and achievable solutions, from your fresh, outsider's perspective. This can look like moving a paper-based process online, updating confusing information on the website, or removing an arbitrary procedure that has outlived its necessity. Easily implementable solutions to legitimate issues will build your momentum as a leader, and demonstrate to stakeholders that you are here, you care, and you are getting things done. Once you establish yourself more and master the policies, procedures, practices, and levers, you will be in a much better position to enact bigger changes without being needlessly disruptive.

REFERENCE

Kouzes, J., & Posner, B. (2019). *Leadership in higher education: Practices that make a difference.* Berrett-Koehler Publishers.

CHAPTER 24

MY JOURNEY INTO HIGHER EDUCATION LEADERSHIP AS A BLACK IMMIGRANT

Neijma Celestine-Donnor

ABSTRACT

When people think about immigrants in the United States, the Black immigrant experience is often ignored and this is also true within institutions of higher education. The erasure of the Black immigrant experience on college campuses often results in conflating all Black identities as the same. This chapter will explore my experience a Black immigrant woman working in leadership on a college campus. It offers strategies to aspiring leaders on successfully navigating higher education leadership, and discusses what universities can do to better support Black immigrant faculty and staff as they matriculate into leadership. This chapter will also discuss how creating community for one's self and having the support from campus leaders to navigate the complexities of these intersecting identities, is essential for Black immigrants to be successful leaders.

WHO AM I?

I exist at the intersectional identities of Black, immigrant and woman. This identity is deeply connected to how I perform my current role as a Clinical Assistant Professor and the Associate Dean of Diversity, Equity, and Inclusion at the predominantly White public university in the MidAtlantic region where I work. In my current role, I lead our university's diversity and anti-oppression efforts and help to guide the achievement of a new standard for inclusive excellence. As a member of the Dean's leadership team, I have a strategic position responsible for promoting and enabling an inclusive environment for faculty, students, and staff while championing organizational change. The work is heavy and challenging, but I love my job on most days! Prior to my current role, I served as a director in the Division of Diversity and Inclusion at our flagship state university.

HOW DID I GET HERE? MY JOURNEY INTO HIGHER EDUCATION AND TRAJECTORY TO LEADERSHIP

Although I have worked in higher education for the last decade, I never saw myself being a Dean on a college campus. When I left the Caribbean and came to the United States for college, I was advised to major in something that "made money." I ended up majoring in computer science but struggled deeply to find my place in that department-not because I was not smart enough, but because this was not a space where I could thrive and be my true self. I felt isolated and disconnected from others in the department because I did not see myself represented in the student body, faculty, or staff. Additionally, I faced ongoing stereotypes in which professors made assumptions that I was less academically prepared. I also did not receive the same level of academic, social, or emotional support from my peers which made it harder for me to succeed and feel like I belonged. Being my authentic self and having a strong sense of belonging has always been important to me. Further, my professional success is not and has never been rooted in how much money I make. Rather, my success is defined by my ability to effect change while staying true to my values and the core of who I am. After about a month of being a computer science major, I switched to Sociology and after graduating with my bachelors, went on to get my Masters in Social Work. Upon graduating with my MSW in 2009, I began working for a child welfare agency.

I would not be the leader I am today had it not been for my experience working with families in the child welfare system. That experience taught me to lead with empathy and gave me the skills to lead through crisis and conflict. While working in the child welfare system, I began noticing some troubling trends. Children of color were more likely to be removed from their families and placed in foster care and there was bias in the decision-making by child welfare workers, judges, and other professionals involved in the system. Despite these dynamics, everyone came to work and went home business as usual. I, however, knew something had to be done. I started facilitating a series of courageous conversations with our child welfare staff about cultivating equity and inclusion in our work. I was often asked by local colleges and universities to facilitate similar discussions on cultivating equity for their staff. While doing this, I developed relationships with some of the university employees. Facilitating these courageous conversations at my agency and local colleges, opened up doors that eventually led me to work in higher education.

In 2013, I began my first role in higher education working as a facilitator within a training academy at a large Mid Atlantic public university. I assumed the transition from child welfare to higher education would be really difficult, and although it was challenging at times, the trauma-informed and conflict management skills I gained working in the child welfare system proved quite valuable on a college campus. To this day, I continue to engage in trauma informed leadership. The training academy focused on preparing individuals to work in the child welfare system and I played a large role in integrating antiracist practices into the training curriculum. After doing this work for several years, I was ready to take on more responsibility and challenges so I created a strategic plan that aligned with my personal values.

I set a goal to attain a leadership role within 3–5 years and I included the objectives I needed to meet in order to achieve this goal. Some of the objectives included leadership training, chairing committees and leading projects. I established metrics for my success, and regularly reviewed my progress towards achieving my goal. As I worked on my personal strategic plan, I applied for jobs and eventually got hired at our state's flagship university (a predominantly White institution) working as a director in the Diversity, Equity and Inclusion (DEI) Unit. Part of my portfolio included helping the university develop effectives policies and protocols to respond to bias incidents. Although I had worked in higher education prior to starting this position, this was the first time I was in a leadership role where I had such significant and impactful responsibilities. It was also the first time that I reckoned with what it meant to be in higher education leadership as a Black immigrant woman. As I matriculated through this director role, I faced many struggles and experiences that helped shape me as a leader.

For one, despite having a sizable Black immigrant population on campus, there was a lack of representation among the campus leadership. When I shared my observations with other leaders, they responded by saying there were many African Americans leaders on campus. In this moment, I realized campus leadership were conflating Black immigrant identities with

Black/African American identities. And while there are certainly similarities between the two, my distinct struggles and experiences as a Black immigrant including dealing with the immigration system and facing cultural barriers and assimilation, were being erased. The lack of understanding displayed by campus leaders about my identity put me in a position where I was constantly explaining my identity to others. Not only was this exhausting, but it made me frequently question my sense of belonging.

I often fought the perception of myself as an "outsider." I was an outsider to White leadership because I was not White, and I was an outsider to Black/African American leadership because I was not American. This would manifest itself in subtle ways, such as assumptions about my cultural background or language proficiency, or more overtly, excluding me from decision-making processes involving key stakeholders because as some put it, "You just would not understand." As a leader, being denied the opportunity to have input into key decisions was especially demoralizing. As an example, during the time period when major immigration reform was being discussed in this country, there was a meeting with university leaders to discuss our immigrant, undocumented, and DACA students. I was not invited to the meeting and when I approached leadership about being excluded, they noted that they had forgotten about my "immigrant experience." The truth is that often when people think about immigrants in the United States, the Black immigrant experience is often ignored or erased and this is also true in institutions of higher education. While these experiences made me question my sense of belonging, they also shaped how I approached leadership. I began to lead with intention and strategy, especially when it came to leveraging the strengths that were rooted in my lived experience as a Black immigrant woman. In both my former and current leadership role, I have learned many lessons and tips along the way that have helped me attain continued success.

WHAT WERE MY STRATEGIES? RECOMMENDATIONS FOR NEW AND POTENTIAL HIGHER EDUCATION LEADERS

First, I learned in order to be an effective leader, one must fully understand one's self as a cultural being which means getting to know the parts of yourself that experience oppression and the parts of yourself that experience privilege. A critical analysis of one's self is necessary to deconstruct and dismantle the systems of oppression that exist within higher education. This requires one to continuously engage in the process of learning, unlearning, and self-interrogation. It also means holding space for yourself to be yourself to just be. As I engaged in self-interrogation, I realized that I had never truly processed my experiences of migrating from the Caribbean to the United States. I came from a place where I was in the racial majority and had to adjust to become a person that was minoritized. Transitioning from seeing my reflection in so many different angles, positively portrayed in the media and in positions of authority and power, and then moving to the United States where it was rare to see my reflection in more than one or two angles and underrepresented in almost every domain, was a huge and at times traumatizing adjustment. I also experienced on-going anti-immigrant sentiment rooted in anti-Blackness. If I was going to lead with intention and strategy, then I had to deal with the confusion, hurt, and pain I felt by these experiences. Self-work can vary depending on your situation. My work entailed going to therapy, reading, journaling, seeking feedback from others in my personal and professional life, attending workshops, and most recently—getting an equity coach. Doing all of these things allowed me to get clear about who I was and to stand in my power as a Black immigrant woman leader. Most importantly, doing my work allowed me to reclaim my joy, my belonging, and to resource myself with the courage, awareness and skills to lead and inspire others.

Another lesson I learned is the importance of intentionally building a network of support. I was, and still am, purposeful about connecting with leaders and mentors who understand and support my unique experience as a Black immigrant, and who can share valuable institutional knowledge. It is also important to expand your network beyond your home institution. I have met many people in my support network at out-of-state conferences, and some I have met from literally searching the internet, reading bios, and reaching out to folks whose values or lived experiences seem to align with mine. Cultivating these relationships has given me a strong sense of community and belonging which allows me to lead from a place of connectedness.

One final tip to share with new and potential higher education leaders; leverage the strengths rooted in your lived experiences. This means thinking about what strengths you've gained from your life experiences (both positive and negative) then demonstrating to others the positive impact that your strengths have on individuals, groups and the institution you work for. While lived experiences alone are not enough to be an effective leader, the skills you develop from them can come in handy when navigating leadership dynamics. I have come to realize that as a Black immigrant, I bring a distinct perspective and set of strengths to the leadership table. This includes having an understanding of different cultures, the ability to create bridges across differences, and one of my greatest strengths—adaptability. Since migrating to the United States, I have always had to adapt to new environments, which makes me effective in navigating the complex situations that often arise in higher education. I have leveraged this strength in almost every leadership position I have held. I started my current position as an Associate Dean during the height of the COVID-19 pandemic and it was my adaptability that allowed me to be successful in this role. Being adaptable enabled me to navigate the changing circumstances and uncertainties at the onset of the pandemic with confidence, resilience, and creativity. It also helped me to see things from different perspectives, find innovative solutions and allowed me to be flexible in my approach to problem-solving and decision-making.

WHAT WOULD I DO DIFFERENTLY?

While these strategies have helped me achieve success as a leader, looking back, there are many things I could have done differently along my career path. If I could travel back in time, I would be more visible and accessible to other staff, students, and faculty. I would have made more time for office hours, attended more campus events, and been more present in the campus community. I try to be more visible in my current role because I understand now more than ever, the importance of other Black immigrant persons on campus seeing someone they can relate to and someone who can be a potential resource. In my last role, I was often overwhelmed with trying to fulfill the demanding duties of my job while also trying to navigate the leadership space as a Black immigrant woman. As a result, I was not as visible and accessible as I would have liked. I am now more intentional with my visibility and accessibility in my current role, but I am also investing in my own well-being and self-care including spending more time with my wonderful spouse and my amazing two sons. Likewise, institutions must also be invested in their Black immigrant campus members. One concrete step that colleges and universities can take is to make a concerted effort to recruit and retain Black immigrants into leadership positions; while also ensuring that they have access to resources and support systems tailored to their specific needs. This for example, can involve creating a Black immigrant affinity group or network. Colleges and universities can also incorporate more of the Black immigrant experience into their diversity and antiracist initiatives and programming. This ensures that Black immigrant voices are represented and promotes a greater understanding and appreciation of the entire Black diaspora. As colleges and universities make more concerted efforts to support Black immigrants, my hope is that we will see more Black immigrants like myself stepping into leadership.

While my story recounts my journey into higher education leadership as a Black immigrant woman, I hope what I have shared can help any new and aspiring higher education leader on their own journey to achieving success in the field.

ABOUT THE EDITOR

Antione D. Tomlin, PhD, PCC: Rooted in core values like Autonomy, Flexibility, Learning, Respect, Transparency, Honesty, and Fun, I live and breathe principles that not only shape my life but also guide my interactions with others. As a proud native of Baltimore City, these values have been my compass in navigating life's journey. Being a first-generation undergrad and grad student, I recognize the transformative power of education, a value intricately tied to my passion for continuous learning. This passion steered me into a fulfilling career in higher education, where I've been teaching English since 2013. The classroom, for me, is an ever-inspiring space filled with dedicated students who continually fuel my curiosity and growth. Beyond teaching, I wear the hat of a trained and certified Life and Engagement Coach, proudly holding the Professional Certified Coach (PCC) credential from the International Coach Federation (ICF). Feel free to explore more about my coaching venture, Best AT Coaching!, LLC. As a Baltimore native, I earned my academic stripes from local institutions: a BS in psychology from Stevenson University, an MA in higher education administration and student affairs from Morgan State University, and a PhD in language, literacy, and culture from the University of Maryland, Baltimore County. My current research focuses on the experiences of Black and Brown faculty, staff, and students in higher education.

ABOUT THE CONTRIBUTORS

Zayd Abukar has worked in higher education for 15+ years in roles ranging from work-study employee to administrator. A first-generation college student, he believes strongly in the role education can play in mitigating social inequities. As a scholar and professional, Dr. Abukar is interested in how institutions and practitioners can rethink or leverage existing resources to better support their students, particularly those from underserved populations. He has authored and presented on topics related to this theme in local, statewide, and national outlets, i.e., Columbus African American News Journal, the Ohio College Personnel Association, the American College Personnel Association, and the National Association of Student Personnel Administrators. He holds a BA in communication from the University of Louisville, an MA in higher education and student affairs from The Ohio State University, and an EdD in higher education and student affairs from The Ohio State University with a graduate minor in public policy.

Jennifer Alanis, EdD (she/her/Ella) is a first-generation Mexican American and a justice, equity, diversity, and inclusion (JEDI) leader; she seeks to improve the campus climate of any institution she is a part of. She does this by creating shared learning experiences, equitable policies, and building collaborative relationships that challenge barriers, bring forth diverse dialogue, and provide educational opportunities. By exploring all dimensions of diversity, she hopes to develop positive and inclusive leaders who have a global understanding and can be accountable for creating a more equitable community. Dr. Alanis is the Executive Director of the Taylor Family Center for Student Success at Washington University in St. Louis. Her teaching areas have included foundations of student affairs in higher education, leadership at minority-serving institutions, and practicum experiences for students.

Jacob Ashby serves as the executive director, University System of Maryland Hagerstown (USMH). In this position he runs one of three regional centers in the state of Maryland. Prior to his appointment at USMH, he served as an assistant dean, academic assessment and articulation and demonstrated leadership at two community colleges in the state of Maryland. Dr. Ashby has higher education leadership experience in assessment, accreditation, articulation, planning, guided pathways, open educational resources, multiple measures, academic support services, faculty professional development, and institutional effectiveness. He has also worked at the state level on multiple committees in the state of Maryland. Dr. Ashby is a transparent leader who focuses on relationships to lead his team to success. He has leveraged his even-keeled demeanor, passion for higher education, and his desire to create socioeconomic mobility in western Maryland to continue to provide students with opportunities to achieve their academic goals.

James R. Calvin, PhD, New York University, is currently a professor of management and organization practice with international expertise and experience in areas of leadership development, minority leadership, organization development, and community economic development and nonprofit organizations. James is a professor in the Center for Africana Studies in the Krieger School of Arts and Sciences at Johns Hopkins. Dr. Calvin is co-editor of *Innovative Community Responses to Disaster* published by Routledge/Taylor & Francis Group (2015). James has authored book chapters and refereed journal articles. James is the 2019 recipient of the Ted K. Bradshaw Outstanding Research Award from the Community Development Society. He is the recipient of the 2021 Inaugural James Calvin Award for Excellence in Diversity, Equity, and Inclusion, Johns Hopkins University. James is a member of the International Board of PYXERA Global an organization that works globally with business, governments, and communities in 100 countries.

Alea Cross is the advising manager at Milwaukee Area Technical College where she supports central advisors within niche groups of last dollar scholarships, GED; Adult High School; ELL/ESL. Alea has a Master of Science in student personnel administration in higher education from Concordia University Wisconsin and Bachelor of Arts in corporate communications from Marquette University. Ms. Cross is known within her academic community for conversations around race, class, gender, and ableism. As a public speaker, her latest discussion within higher education, Trading Places:

Creating Inclusion and Understanding at PWI, takes a critical perspective on the success of black professionals and institutional responsibility of predominately White institutions to support professionals of color. Alea is also the self-published author of *Scabs and Scars*. Her most recent work *Hope is What I Wrestle* with is a short write published through the Wisconsin Historical Society (Fall 2021).

Bradley Fuster, DMA has served as provost and vice president for academic affairs at Keuka College since 2018. At Keuka College, Fuster founded the School for Health & Human Services and Center for Experiential Learning, as well as worked with faculty to revise the general education curriculum and create new programs. Prior to Keuka College, Fuster served as associate vice president of academic affairs and full professor of music at Buffalo State University. Fuster was an ACE Fellow, serves the Middle States Commission as a peer evaluator, and has published numerous articles for *U.S. News. & World Report, Inside Higher Ed*, and *eCampus News*.

Mark C. Gillen, PhD, is a professor in the counseling program at the University of Wisconsin-River Falls. He served as program director, department chair and associate dean over eighteen years. He has published more than fifty articles and presented hundreds of times.

Amir Gilmore is an assistant professor in cultural studies and social thought in education at Washington State University. He is also the associate dean of equity and inclusion for student success and retention in the College of Education. His interdisciplinary background in cultural studies, Africana studies, and education allows him to traverse the boundaries across the social sciences, the arts, and the humanities. Amir's broad research interests are Black aesthetics, Black masculinities, Afrofuturism, Afro-pessimism, and the political economy of schooling.

Juan R. Guardia is a scholar/practitioner with 25 years in various higher education and student affairs administrative roles. He currently serves as the Vice President for Student Affairs at Texas A&M University–San Antonio. Previously he was Assistant Vice President for Student Affairs and Dean of Students at the University of Cincinnati (UC) and Adjunct Faculty in the College of Education, Criminal Justice, and Human Services at UC. He was also adjunct faculty at Loyola University Chicago and Florida State University.

He earned a graduate certificate in Leadership and Management from the Linder College of Business at the University of Cincinnati, a PhD in Educational Leadership and Policy Studies–Higher Education and a graduate certificate in community college teaching from Iowa State University, a master's degree in Higher Education and a bachelor's degree in Communication from Florida State University, and an associate in arts degree from Miami-Dade College.

Lauren Harris is a student affairs professional with fifteen years of experience at public and private colleges and universities across the Atlanta Metropolitan area. These diverse experiences have contributed to her well-rounded background in several areas of higher education, including roles as an admissions manager, assistant director and dean of students, conduct investigator, and conduct coordinator/Title IX investigator. She also enjoyed serving on various college-wide committees focused on academic integrity, students' well-being, and strategic planning, implementing the quality enhancement plan (QEP). In addition, she has worked closely with faculty and staff in conducting Title IX investigations and advising student organizations and clubs. Over the last seven years, Mrs. Harris has been actively engaged in student advocacy work. She is professionally trained in restorative practices, mediation, and other forms of alternative dispute resolutions. She is well-versed in students' educational rights and advocates for the conduct process to be fair, impartial, and educational for all students. Mrs. Harris earned a bachelor's degree from Johnson C. Smith University and a master's degree in business administration from the University of Phoenix. She is married to her college sweetheart and has two beautiful daughters.

Juan M. Hernandez (he/him/his) is the vice president for diversity, equity, and belonging at Curry College. In this role, Hernandez provides vision, strategic leadership and direction to guide all diversity, equity, inclusion, and belonging (DEIB) programming and initiatives. He received the prestigious PosseFoundation Leadership Scholarship to attend Trinity College in Hartford, Connecticut, where he graduated with a BA in political science and history and an MA in public policy with a concentration in education policy. Hernandez also graduated from the University of Hartford where he received his EdD in educational leadership after conducting research on the experiences of cabinet-level administrators of color, their journey to the president's cabinet, and an examination of the role that mentoring played throughout their journey.

Nadia Ibrahim-Taney, MEd, MA, MS, is an assistant professor of career education and professional studies, teaching and coaching students majoring in STEM fields. She identifies as an LGBTQ+ woman and neurodivergent professional which influences her research and interest in how personal and professional identity intertwine in the workplace.

Tony Jimenez is the dean of students in the Office of Chicano Latino Student Affairs at the Claremont Colleges. With over twenty years of experience in higher education, he has become an expert in creating pathways to graduate and professional schools. In the past, Dr. Jimenez has directed and coordinated NSF STEM diversity programs for the University of California and also coordinated an MD/PhD program at a large research-intensive Midwestern University. He currently is a steering committee member of the Mellon Mays Undergraduate Fellowship Program at the Claremont Colleges. Dr. Jimenez received his doctorate from the University of Illinois, his master's degree at Harvard University, and his bachelor's degree from the University of California at Santa Cruz.

LaToya Jordan, PhD is the founder of Lead by Design Lab, a consulting firm that provides coaching and consulting services in leadership development, team effectiveness, and strategic planning to university and business leaders, employees, and community-based organizations. With a PhD in social-organizational psychology from Columbia University, LaToya supports clients as they step into leadership roles—ensuring they manage teams from a place of purpose, inclusivity, and respect. She specializes in supporting women of color leaders in higher education by providing them with the foundational tools to lead effectively and authentically. Prior to launching her consulting practice in 2019, she was the director of talent management and diversity at JetBlue Airways and spent nine years as a director in student affairs for several universities across the country. LaToya continues her passion for higher education as an adjunct professor at Columbia University and Stanford University's dSchool.

Heather D. Maldonado, PhD, serves Keuka College as the vice president for student leadership. In this role, she provides leadership for college-wide retention strategy and diversity, equity, & inclusion efforts, as well as providing oversight of athletics & recreation, student life, higher education opportunity program, campus safety, client & conference services functional areas and Title III grant activities. Dr. Maldonado previously held the role of assistant provost for academic success—which followed her positions of assistant dean of University College and assistant director of residence life—at Buffalo State University where she was deeply involved in shared governance with the State University of New York's University Faculty Senate. Dr. Maldonado teaches undergraduate and graduate courses, pursues her scholarly interests related to college attainment and leadership, and regularly volunteers as a peer reviewer for the Middle States Commission on Higher Education.

Merab Mushfiq has a master of education from Wilfrid Laurier University and has been working with students from the last 10 years. She is currently pursuing PhD of Education at York University. She serves as a Director of Cross-Border Initiatives Team at STAR Scholars Network, Production Assistant at the Journal of Comparative International and Higher Education, and a Research Coordinator at Leadership Council at CACUSS.

Felix O. Quayson has earned degrees in educational sciences and health management, professional teacher certification in teaching English as a second/foreign language and completed a professional education credential certificate program in media and technology for education at the Harvard Graduate School of Education. Felix's research interests are in educational sciences focusing on workforce education, postsecondary career and technical education, educational technologies, STEM education, and higher education. Currently, Felix is at the Department of Educational Studies, College of Education and Human Ecology at The Ohio State University in Columbus, Ohio. He can be reached via email at Quayson.1@osu.edu or dr.felixoquayson@gmail.com

Shauntisha A. Pilgrim, EdD, MSW, is a native of Paterson, NJ. She is currently the director of student affairs and admissions and adjunct professor in the School of Social Work at Morgan State University. She earned her BSW and MSW degrees from Morgan State University School of Social Work. While practicing as a social worker, she returned to school to earn her doctorate in higher education from the Community College Leadership Doctoral Program at Morgan State University. Dr. Pilgrim has extensive experience working with teen parents and young adults as they enter college and prepare for independence after being in the foster care system. In her current role, she focuses on the engagement and retention of graduate students. Her interests are in supporting students in higher education, particularly marginalized populations, and how institutions can meet their needs. Dr. Pilgrim is also an active member of Delta Sigma Theta Sorority, Incorporated.

Darian Senn-Carter is director and professor of the Homeland Security and Criminal Justice Institute at Anne Arundel Community College (AACC). He is a nationally recognized leader, facilitating student engagement and success. Dr. Senn-Carter serves as a member of the board of directors for the Maryland Book Bank, Civic Works Inc., Reach Partnership School, Leaders of Tomorrow Youth Center, and CollegeBound Foundation Alumni Association. He is the founder and coordinator of the Aspiring Leaders Academy mentoring program, co-founder of the University of Maryland College Park Incentive Awards Visionary Scholarship Award, co-founder of the CollegeBound Foundation Alumni Scholarship Award, and co-founder of the Dunbar High School Alumni Scholarship Award. Dr. Senn-Carter has served in key leadership roles including serving as a member of the American Association of Community Colleges's National Faculty Council, city councilmember in the city of Bowie, instructor at the National Institutes of Health, and chair of AACC's Middle States Accreditation—Design and Delivery of the Student Learning Experience. Notably, he is a recent recipient of the Daily Record's Top 40 VIP Award, League for Innovations Excellence Award, CollegeBound Foundation Distinguished Alumni Award, AACC Transfer Champion Award, Dr. Martin Luther King Zeitgeist Award, Towson University Philanthropic Alumni Award, Edgewood College Promise Award. Dr. Senn-Carter earned a bachelor's degree from the University of Maryland in criminology and criminal justice, master's degree in homeland security and post-baccalaureate certificate in security assessment and management from Towson University and a doctorate degree in education from Edgewood College. He is a certified life coach (International Coach Federation), licensed emergency medical technician, obtained a teaching certificate in special education, and has completed numerous courses and trainings in leadership and education. Dr. Senn-Carter has participated in conferences, workshops, presentations, and panel discussions both regionally and nationally.

Dawn Shafer, PhD, LCSW-C, is the associate dean for student affairs at the University of Maryland School of Social Work. She earned her PhD in language, literacy, and culture from the University of Maryland Baltimore County and her MSW from San Diego State University. Dr. Shafer is a proud first-generation student whose academic work centers the experiences and strengths of first-generation graduate students.

Jaclyn Stone, PhD has been fortunate to serve and lead in student affairs for nearly 20 years. She earned her PhD in language, literacy and culture from the University of Maryland, Baltimore County, her MS in clinical community counseling from Johns Hopkins University, her MS in college student personnel from Western Illinois University, and BS in human development from The Ohio State University. Jaclyn lives with her beloved husband Andre and their dogs in Baltimore, Maryland.

Susan Swayze is an associate professor in the Department of Educational Leadership at The George Washington University. She teaches qualitative research methods, quantitative research methods, case study methodology, mixed methods research, and statistics courses to masters and doctoral students and has served on 100 dissertation committees. Her research interests and speaking topics focus on diversity, equity, and inclusion, creating safe spaces for critical conversations, psychological capital, and psychological safety.

D'Shaun Vance, EdD, has been working in higher education for the last 6 years. With an interest in building relationships with students, faculty, and staff, Dr. Vance places an emphasis on leading with empathy to connect with each person the way they need to be seen. As a higher education professional with experience working in and research academic advising, he finds ways to present his research on improving the quality of advising, with empathy as one of the main traits. He has presented at regional and national conferences and intends to continue to do so, recently being selected to present at the National Academic Advising Association's annual conference in Orlando, FL. D'Shaun loves working with and helping HBCUs, wanting to be a leader of one of the historic institutions in the future.

Wagner-Clarke is the senior research specialist and lead content writer at Kaizen Human Capital and an adjunct faculty member at Wilmington University–College of Business. Over her tenure, she has facilitated courses in four disciplines: organizational management, business management, human resource management, and economics. Dr. Wagner-Clarke holds exemplary level instructor status at WilmU, demonstrating her engagement as a higher-education instructor and one that cares deeply about student success. She is skilled in writing and editing and regularly writes articles for Kaizen Human Capital and QuestionPro's *Experience Journal*. Dr. Wagner-Clarke received a Doctor of Education in organizational leadership, learning, and innovation from Wilmington University (EdD), a Masters in Professional Human Resources (MPHR) from Georgetown University, a Masters in Organizational Leadership w/track in human resource management (MSOL) from Quinnipiac University, and a Bachelors of Science in Business Administration from Post University. Additionally, Dr. Wagner-Clarke is a SHRM senior certified professional (SHRM-SCP).

Tasha Wilson is a Maryland native who values the transformative power of education. She is an innovative change agent with expertise spanning in policy implementation, educational equity, stewardship, and compliance. She is a subject matter expert in student success support, leadership development, scholarship, and awards. Currently, Tasha sits on the Board of Directors for Kids' Chance of Maryland, Inc. Outside of student affairs, Tasha is the dynamic force propelling transformative change in Maryland through the supercharged trio of diversity, equity, and inclusion (DEI). An innovative change agent, she excels in policy implementation, employee relations, and compliance. Tasha thrives on strategic problem-solving, relationship-building, and contributing to organizational growth. A powerhouse in succession planning, crisis intervention, leadership development, and project management, she wears many hats with finesse. Currently serving on the Board of Directors for Kids Chance of Maryland, Inc., Tasha champions scholarships for children affected by catastrophic workplace injuries. A trailblazer for millennial women, she's not just a leader—she's an international bestselling author and speaker, using her experiences to inspire others to break glass ceilings and transform pain into power. Tasha's influence extends to academia, with one of her books serving as a discussion guide at Johnson C.

Smith University for undergraduate students and emerging leaders. In 2015, she founded the Royalty Refined Movement, fostering sisterhood around self-discovery, personal development, and autonomy. Acknowledged for her community activism, Tasha received the Governor's Volunteer Service Certificate in 2016. Joining Grammy Award-winner Michelle Williams' launch team for "Checking In" in 2021 showcased her diverse impact. In 2022, Maryland recognized her as a Christian Woman in Leadership and honored her with the Marketplace Forerunner Award.

Printed in the United States
by Baker & Taylor Publisher Services